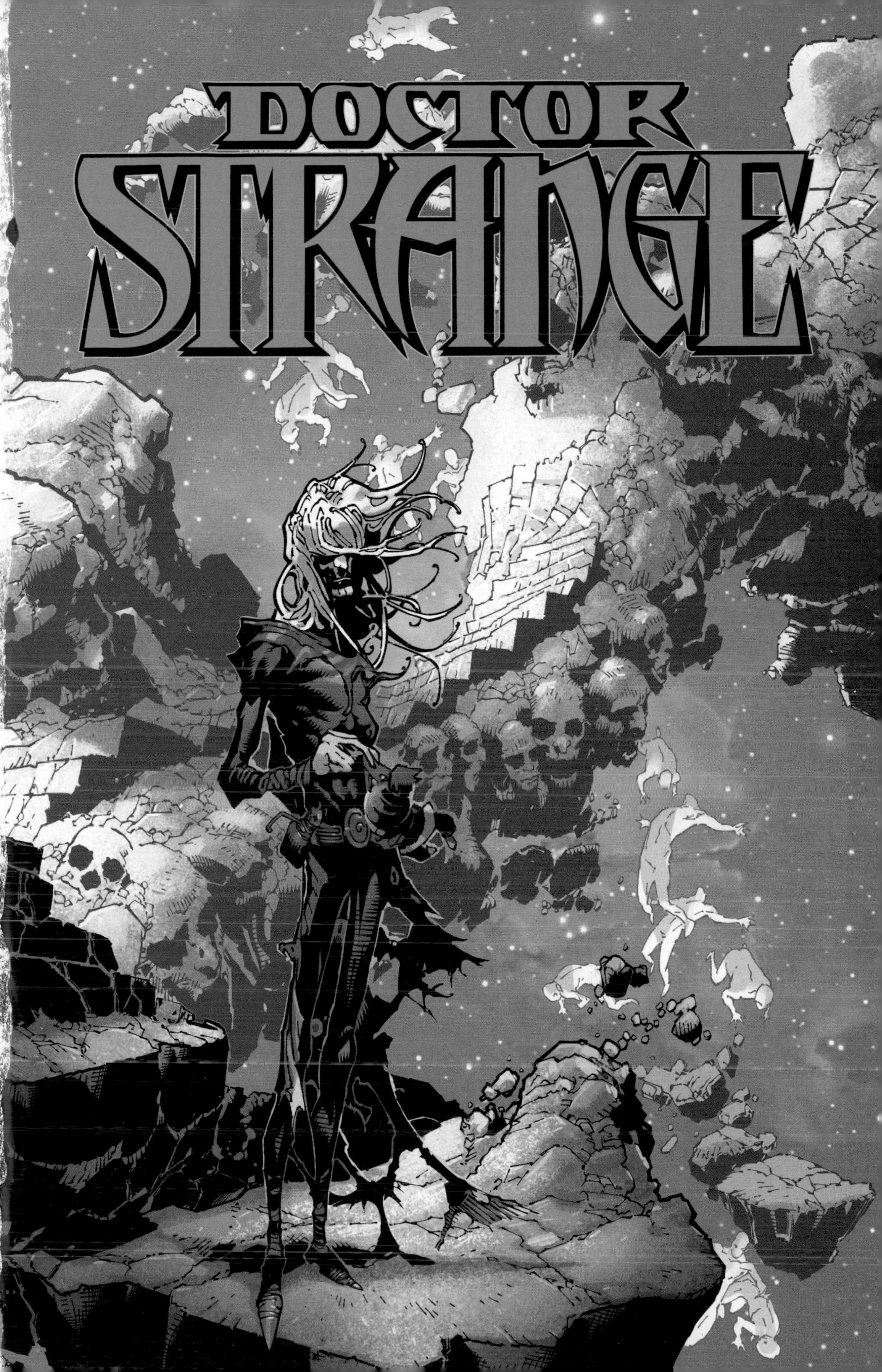
DOCTOR
STRANGE

DOCTOR STRANGE VOL. 3: BLOOD IN THE AETHER. Contains material originally published in magazine form as DOCTOR STRANGE #11-16. First printing 2017. ISBN# 978-1-302-90299-5. Published by MARVEL WORLDWIDE, INC., a subsidiary of MARVEL ENTERTAINMENT, LLC. OFFICE OF PUBLICATION: 135 West 50th Street, New York, NY 10020. Copyright © 2017 MARVEL No similarity between any of the names, characters, persons, and/or institutions in this magazine with those of any living or dead person or institution is intended, and any such similarity which may exist is purely coincidental. **Printed in the U.S.A.** ALAN FINE, President, Marvel Entertainment; DAN BUCKLEY, President, TV, Publishing & Brand Management; JOE QUESADA, Chief Creative Officer; TOM BREVOORT, SVP of Publishing; DAVID BOGART, SVP of Business Affairs & Operations, Publishing & Partnership; C.B. CEBULSKI, VP of Brand Management & Development, Asia; DAVID GABRIEL, SVP of Sales & Marketing, Publishing; JEFF YOUNGQUIST, VP of Production & Special Projects; DAN CARR, Executive Director of Publishing Technology; ALEX MORALES, Director of Publishing Operations; SUSAN CRESPI, Production Manager; STAN LEE, Chairman Emeritus. For information regarding advertising in Marvel Comics or on Marvel.com, please contact Vit DeBellis, Integrated Sales Manager, at vdebellis@marvel.com. For Marvel subscription inquiries, please call 888-511-5480. **Manufactured between 12/16/2016 and 1/30/2017 by LSC COMMUNICATIONS INC., SALEM, VA, USA.**

10 9 8 7 6 5 4 3 2 1

DOCTOR STRANGE

Blood in the Aether

Jason Aaron
WRITER

ISSUE #11

Kevin Nowlan &
Leonardo Romero
ARTISTS

Kevin Nowlan
& Jordie Bellaire
COLOR ARTISTS

KEVIN NOWLAN COVER ART

ISSUES #12-16

Chris Bachalo
WITH Jorge Fornés (#15)
& Cory Smith (#16)
PENCILERS

Tim Townsend, Richard Friend,
Al Vey, Victor Olazaba &
John Livesay
WITH Wayne Faucher (#13-14),
Jorge Fornés (#15) & Cory Smith (#16)
INKERS

Antonio Fabela
WITH Java Tartaglia (#13-14, #16) & Chris Bachalo (#13, #16)
COLOR ARTISTS

CHRIS BACHALO & TIM TOWNSEND (#13, #14) AND KEVIN NOWLAN (#13, #15-16) COVER ART

VC's CORY PETIT
LETTERER

ALLISON STOCK
ASSISTANT EDITOR

DARREN SHAN
ASSOCIATE EDITOR

NICK LOWE
EDITOR

DOCTOR STRANGE CREATED BY STAN LEE & STEVE DITKO

COLLECTION EDITOR: JENNIFER GRÜNWALD
ASSISTANT EDITOR: CAITLIN O'CONNELL
ASSOCIATE MANAGING EDITOR: KATERI WOODY
EDITOR, SPECIAL PROJECTS: MARK D. BEAZLEY
VP PRODUCTION & SPECIAL PROJECTS: JEFF YOUNGQUIST
SVP PRINT, SALES & MARKETING: DAVID GABRIEL
BOOK DESIGNER: JAY BOWEN

EDITOR IN CHIEF: AXEL ALONSO
CHIEF CREATIVE OFFICER: JOE QUESADA
PUBLISHER: DAN BUCKLEY
EXECUTIVE PRODUCER: ALAN FINE

STEPHEN STRANGE WAS A PREEMINENT SURGEON UNTIL A CAR ACCIDENT DAMAGED THE NERVES IN HIS HANDS. HIS EGO DROVE HIM TO SCOUR THE GLOBE FOR A MIRACLE CURE, BUT INSTEAD HE FOUND A MYSTERIOUS WIZARD CALLED THE ANCIENT ONE WHO TAUGHT HIM MAGIC AND THAT THERE ARE THINGS IN THIS WORLD BIGGER THAN HIMSELF. THESE LESSONS LED STEPHEN TO BECOME THE SORCERER SUPREME, EARTH'S FIRST DEFENSE AGAINST ALL MANNER OF MAGICAL THREATS. HIS PATIENTS CALL HIM...

DOCTOR STRANGE

The EMPIRIKUL, an interdimensional army, has destroyed almost all magic on Earth. Stephen and Earth's mages managed to defeat them, but the state of magic will never be the same again.

Now left to rebuild from the remains of the Sanctum Sanctorum, Doctor Strange finds himself at a crossroads.

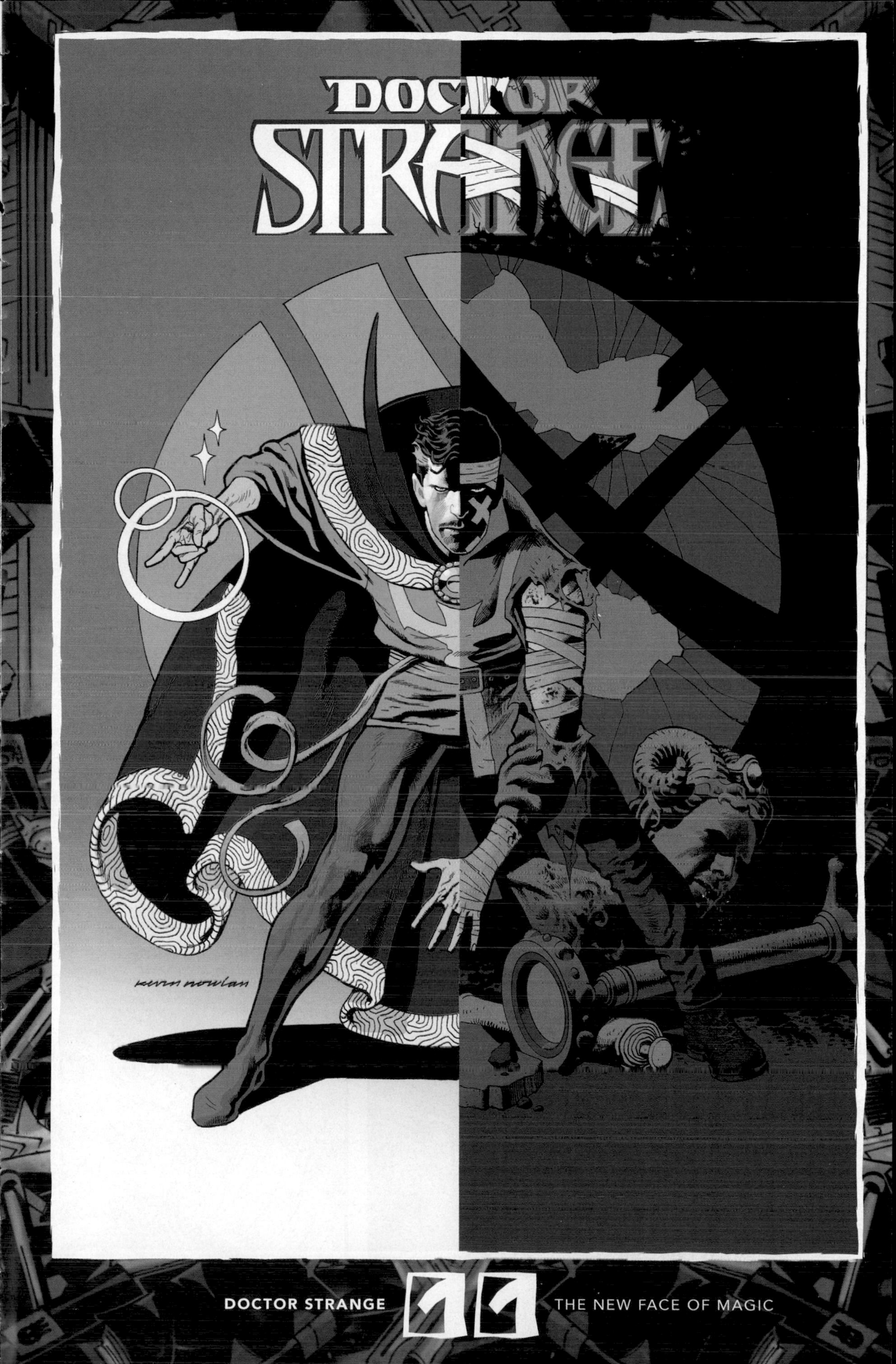
DOCTOR STRANGE
kevin nowlan
DOCTOR STRANGE
THE NEW FACE OF MAGIC

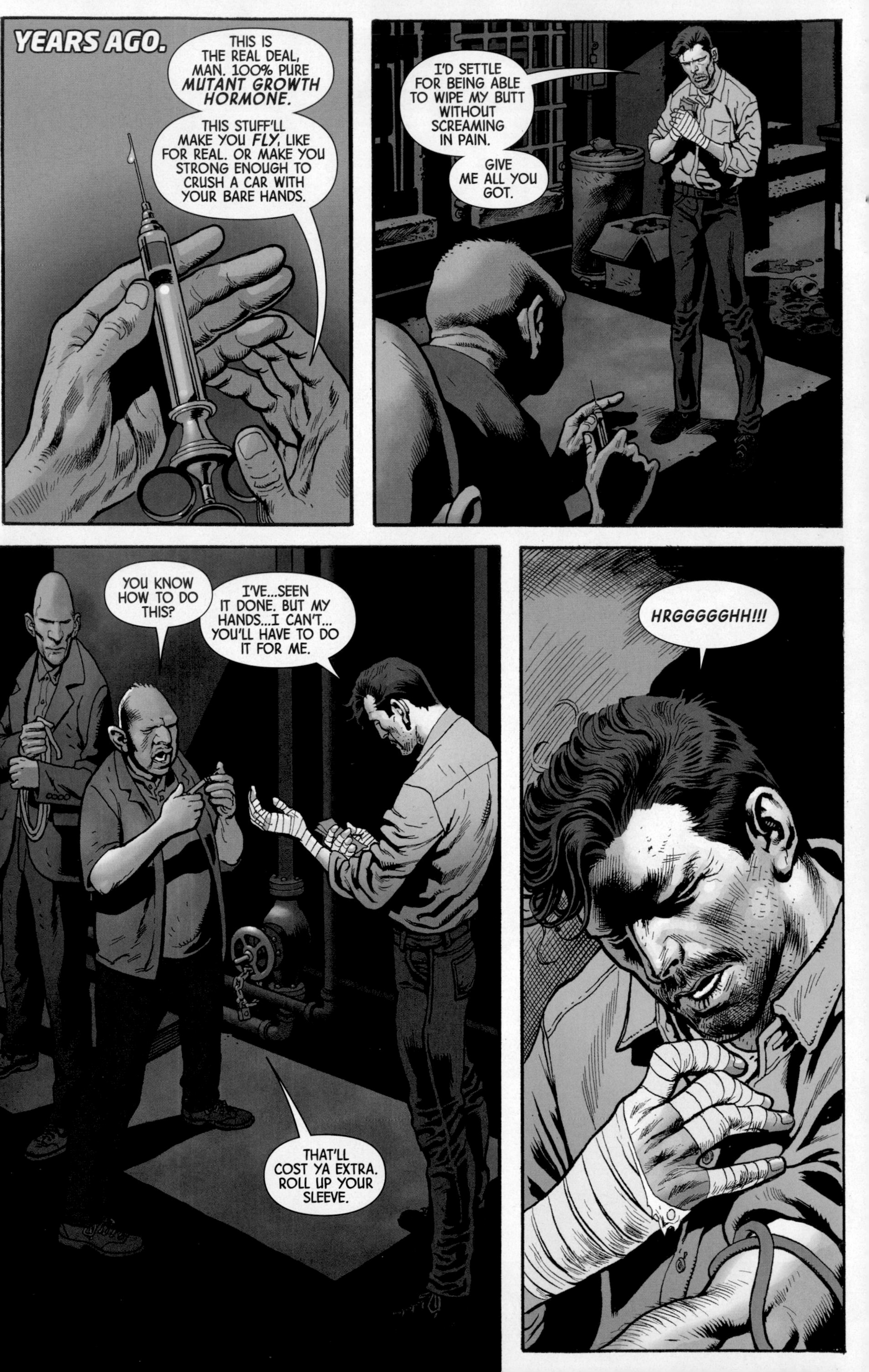
YEARS AGO.
THIS IS THE REAL DEAL, MAN. 100% PURE MUTANT GROWTH HORMONE.
THIS STUFF'LL MAKE YOU FLY, LIKE FOR REAL. OR MAKE YOU STRONG ENOUGH TO CRUSH A CAR WITH YOUR BARE HANDS.
I'D SETTLE FOR BEING ABLE TO WIPE MY BUTT WITHOUT SCREAMING IN PAIN.
GIVE ME ALL YOU GOT.
YOU KNOW HOW TO DO THIS?
I'VE...SEEN IT DONE. BUT MY HANDS...I CAN'T... YOU'LL HAVE TO DO IT FOR ME.
THAT'LL COST YA EXTRA. ROLL UP YOUR SLEEVE.
HRGGGGGHH!!!

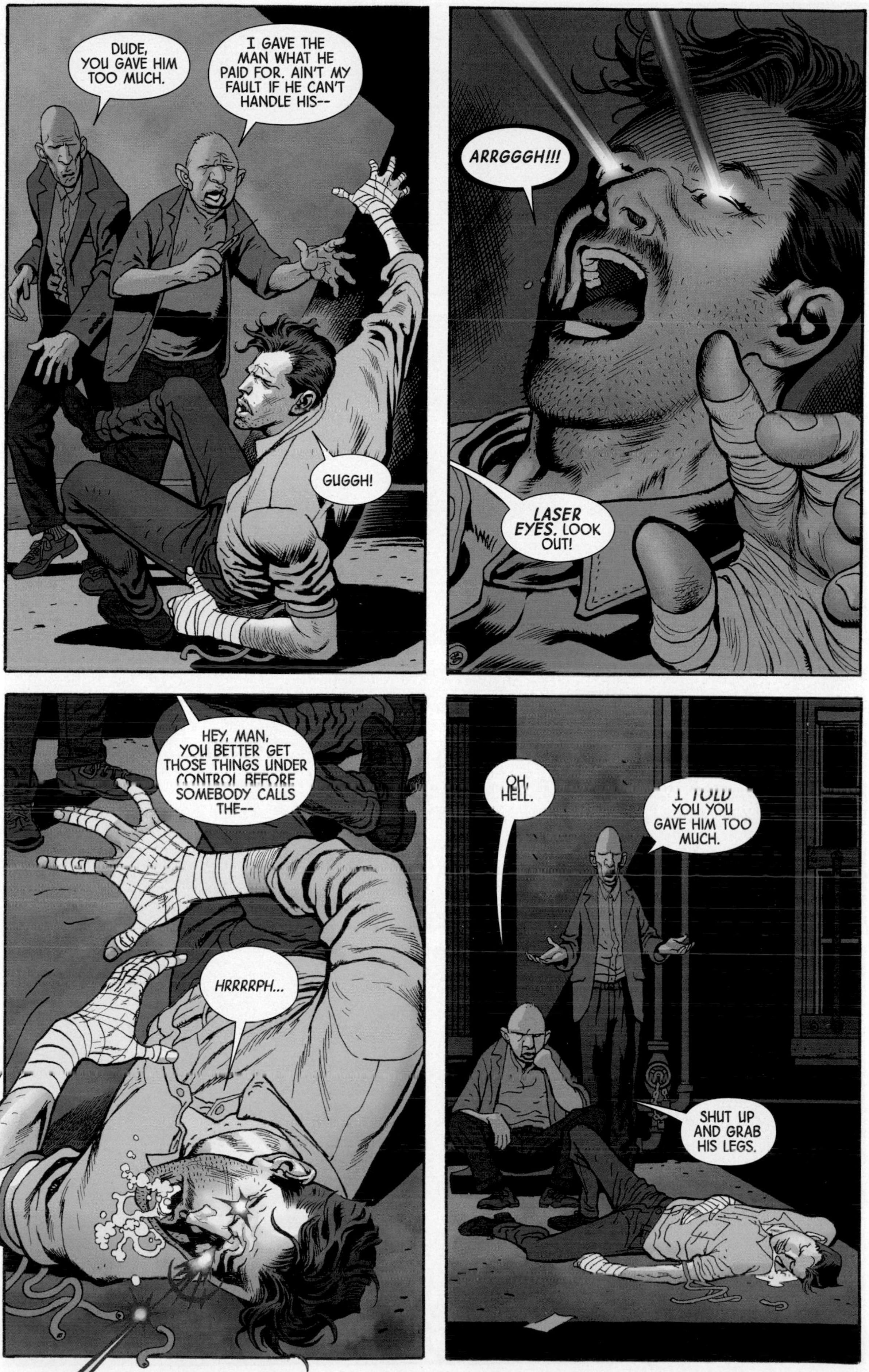
DUDE, YOU GAVE HIM TOO MUCH.
I GAVE THE MAN WHAT HE PAID FOR. AIN'T MY FAULT IF HE CAN'T HANDLE HIS--
GUGGH!
ARRGGGH!!!
LASER EYES. LOOK OUT!
HEY, MAN, YOU BETTER GET THOSE THINGS UNDER CONTROL BEFORE SOMEBODY CALLS THE--
HRRRRPH...
OH, HELL.
I TOLD YOU YOU GAVE HIM TOO MUCH.
SHUT UP AND GRAB HIS LEGS.

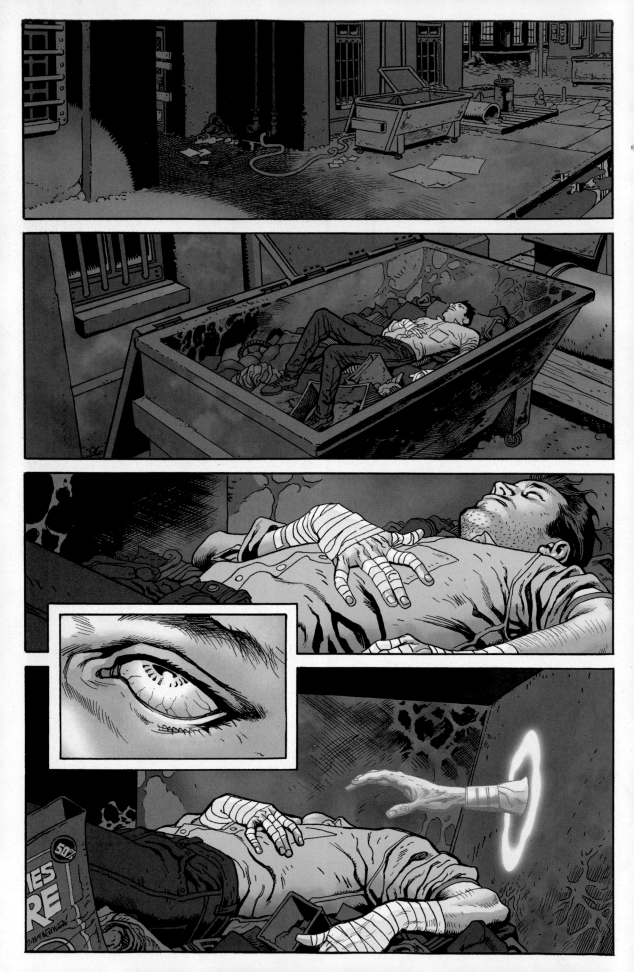

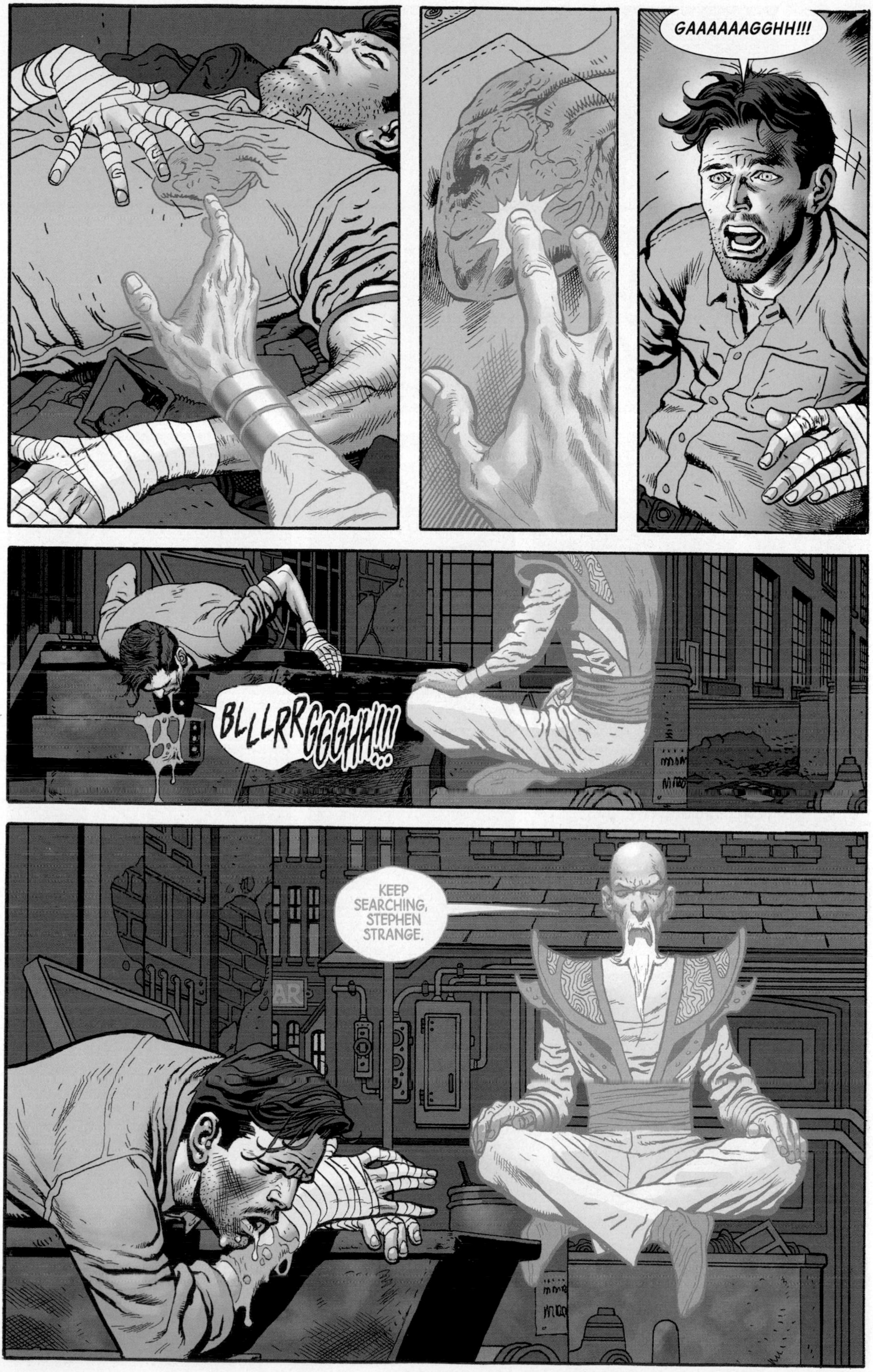
GAAAAAAGGHH!!!
BLLLRRGGGHH!!!..
KEEP SEARCHING, STEPHEN STRANGE.

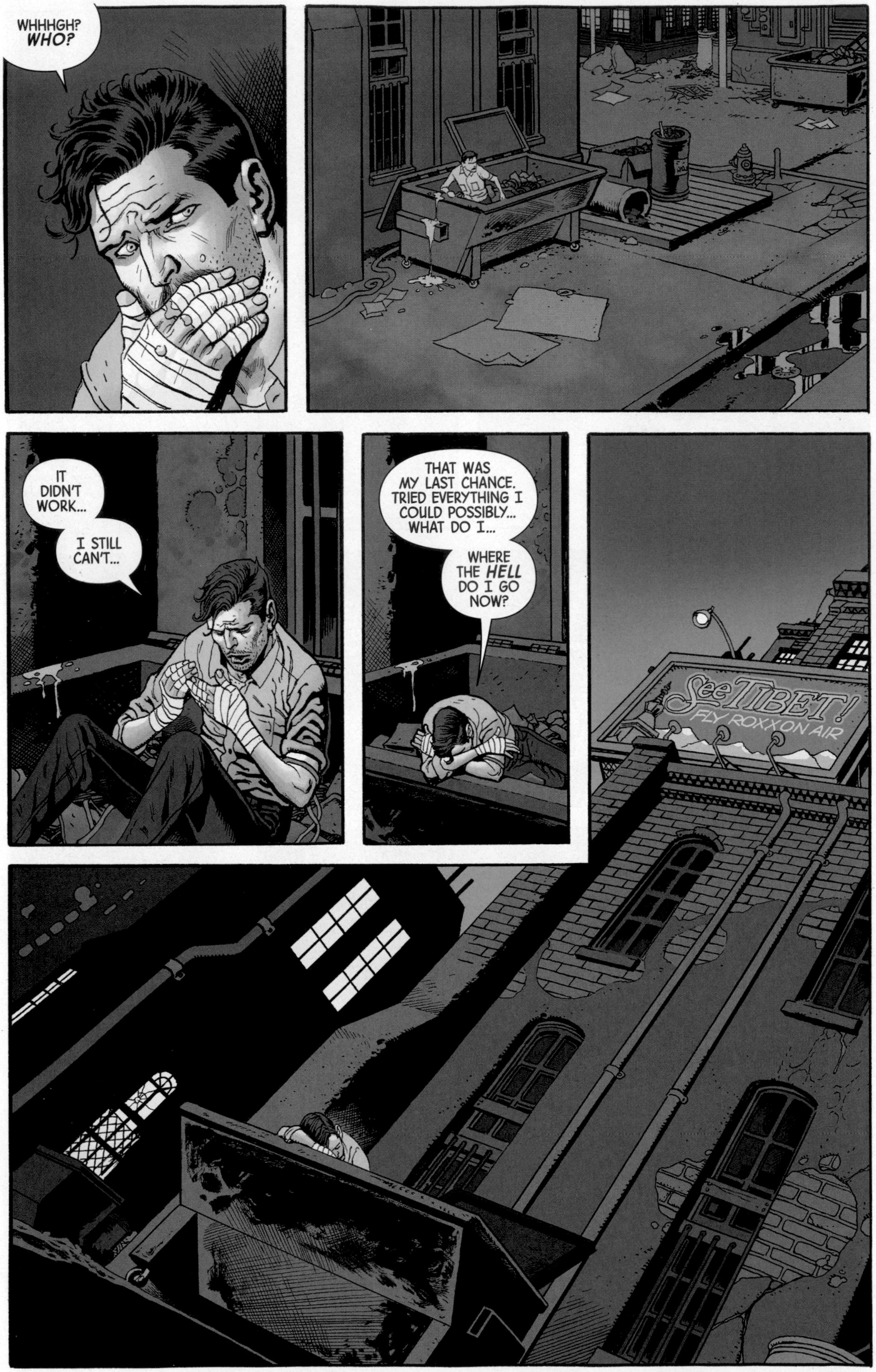
WHHHGH? WHO?
IT DIDN'T WORK...
I STILL CAN'T...
THAT WAS MY LAST CHANCE. TRIED EVERYTHING I COULD POSSIBLY... WHAT DO I...
WHERE THE HELL DO I GO NOW?
See TIBET! FLY ROXXON AIR

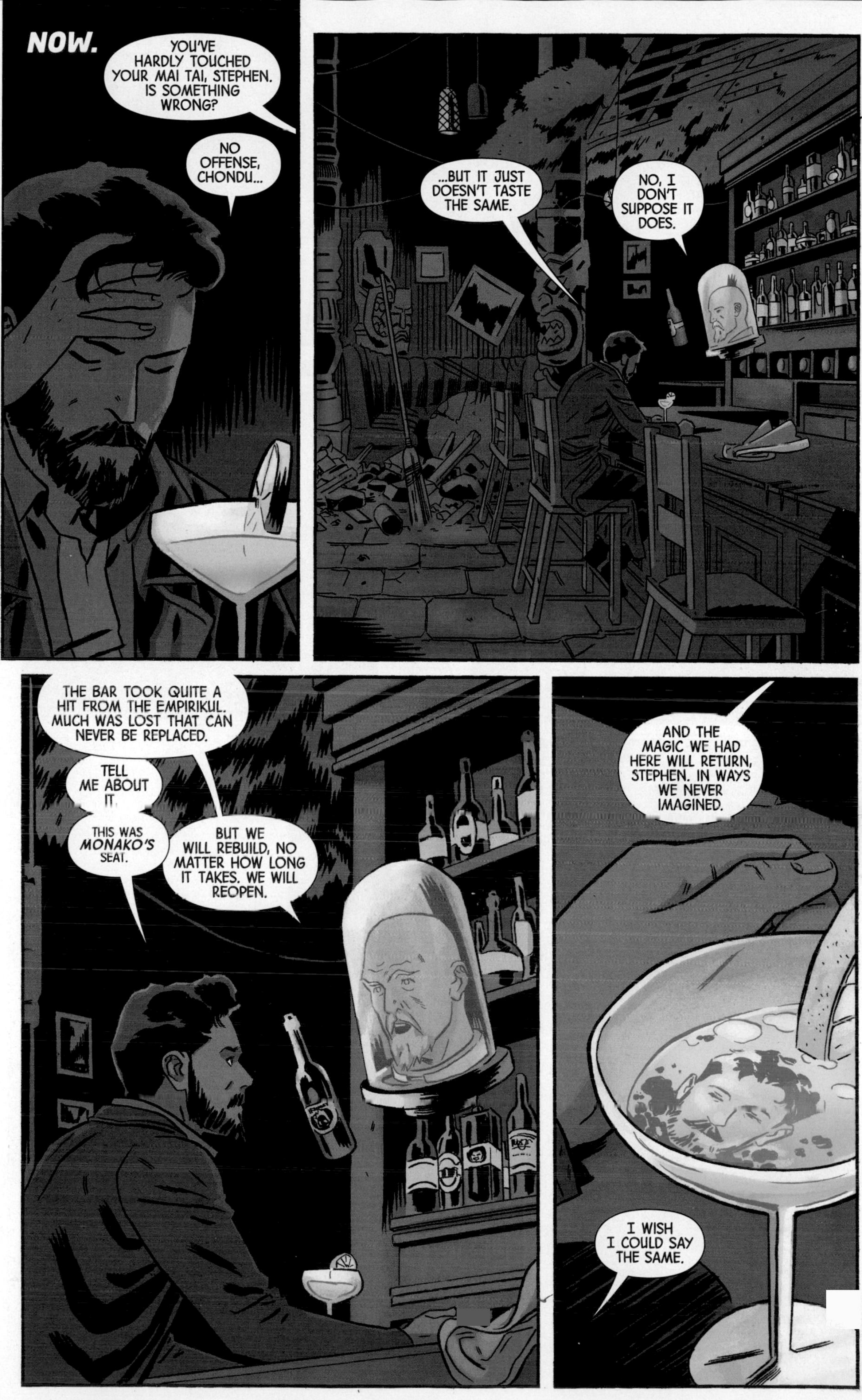
NOW.
YOU'VE HARDLY TOUCHED YOUR MAI TAI, STEPHEN. IS SOMETHING WRONG?
NO OFFENSE, CHONDU...
...BUT IT JUST DOESN'T TASTE THE SAME.
NO, I DON'T SUPPOSE IT DOES.
THE BAR TOOK QUITE A HIT FROM THE EMPIRIKUL. MUCH WAS LOST THAT CAN NEVER BE REPLACED.
TELL ME ABOUT IT.
THIS WAS MONAKO'S SEAT.
BUT WE WILL REBUILD, NO MATTER HOW LONG IT TAKES. WE WILL REOPEN.
AND THE MAGIC WE HAD HERE WILL RETURN, STEPHEN. IN WAYS WE NEVER IMAGINED.
I WISH I COULD SAY THE SAME.

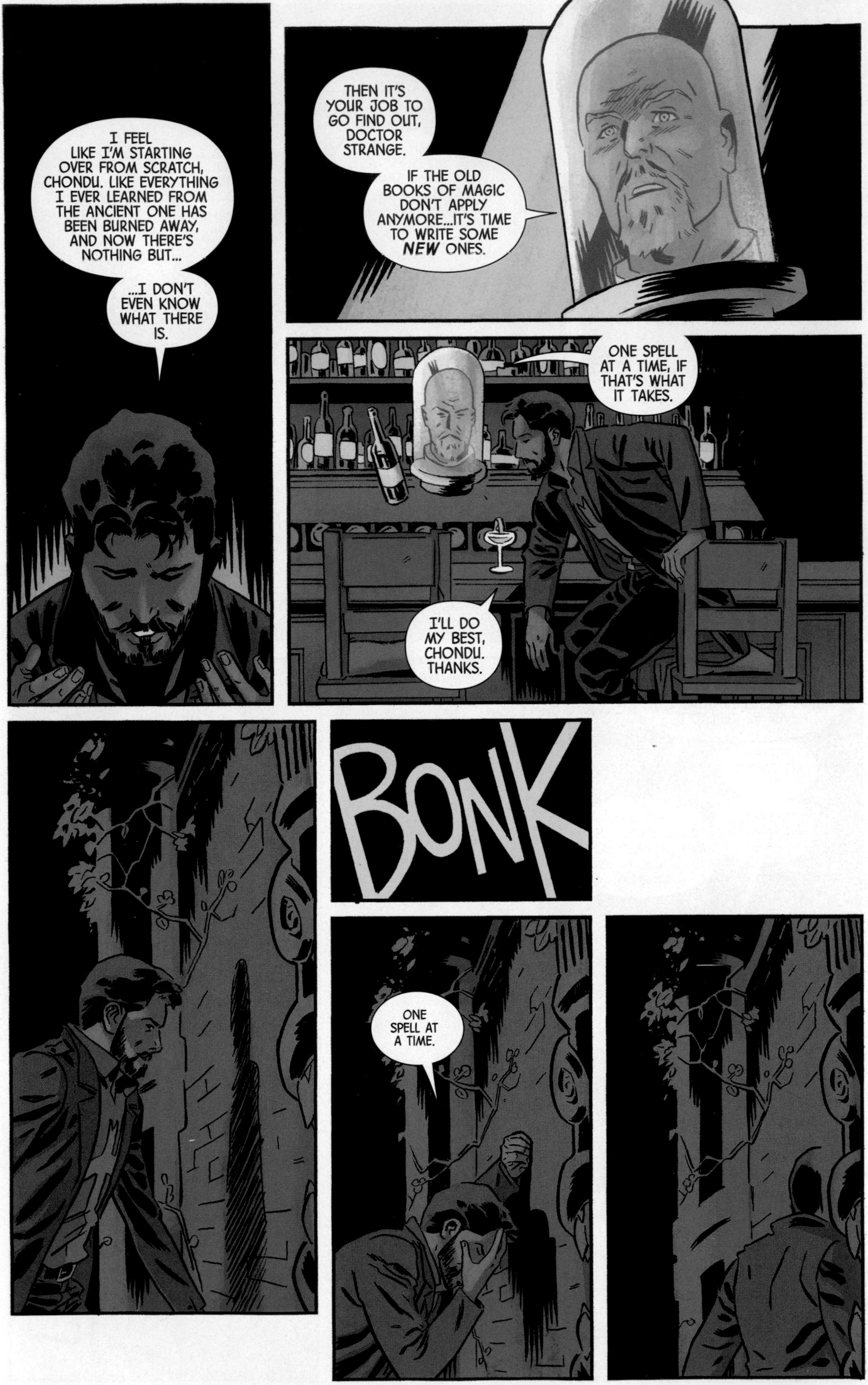
I FEEL LIKE I'M STARTING OVER FROM SCRATCH, CHONDU. LIKE EVERYTHING I EVER LEARNED FROM THE ANCIENT ONE HAS BEEN BURNED AWAY, AND NOW THERE'S NOTHING BUT...
...I DON'T EVEN KNOW WHAT THERE IS.
THEN IT'S YOUR JOB TO GO FIND OUT, DOCTOR STRANGE.
IF THE OLD BOOKS OF MAGIC DON'T APPLY ANYMORE...IT'S TIME TO WRITE SOME NEW ONES.
ONE SPELL AT A TIME, IF THAT'S WHAT IT TAKES.
I'LL DO MY BEST, CHONDU. THANKS.
BONK
ONE SPELL AT A TIME.

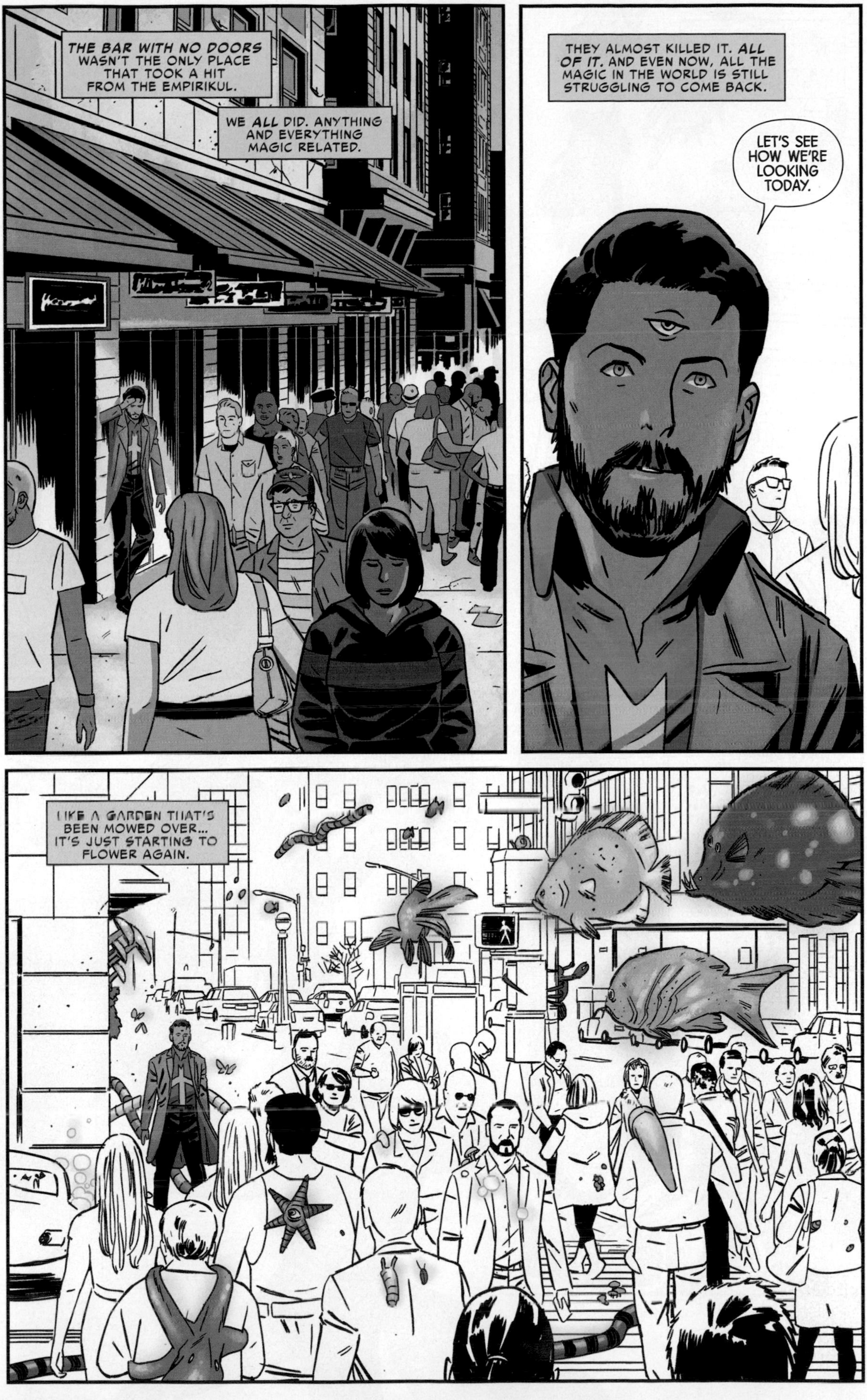
THE BAR WITH NO DOORS WASN'T THE ONLY PLACE THAT TOOK A HIT FROM THE EMPIRIKUL.
WE ALL DID. ANYTHING AND EVERYTHING MAGIC RELATED.
THEY ALMOST KILLED IT. ALL OF IT. AND EVEN NOW, ALL THE MAGIC IN THE WORLD IS STILL STRUGGLING TO COME BACK.
LET'S SEE HOW WE'RE LOOKING TODAY.
LIKE A GARDEN THAT'S BEEN MOWED OVER... IT'S JUST STARTING TO FLOWER AGAIN.

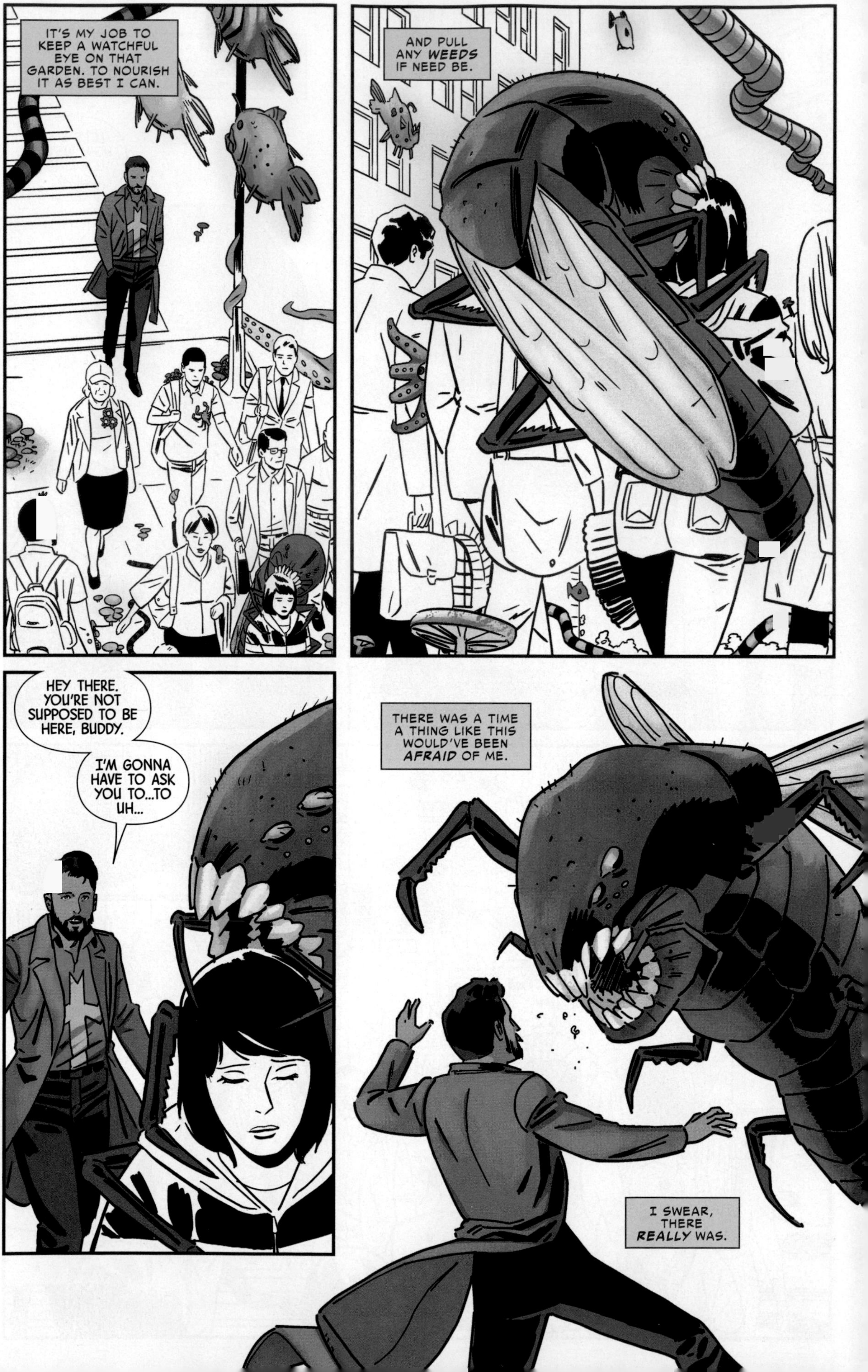
IT'S MY JOB TO KEEP A WATCHFUL EYE ON THAT GARDEN. TO NOURISH IT AS BEST I CAN.
AND PULL ANY WEEDS IF NEED BE.
HEY THERE. YOU'RE NOT SUPPOSED TO BE HERE, BUDDY.
I'M GONNA HAVE TO ASK YOU TO...TO UH...
THERE WAS A TIME A THING LIKE THIS WOULD'VE BEEN AFRAID OF ME.
I SWEAR, THERE REALLY WAS.

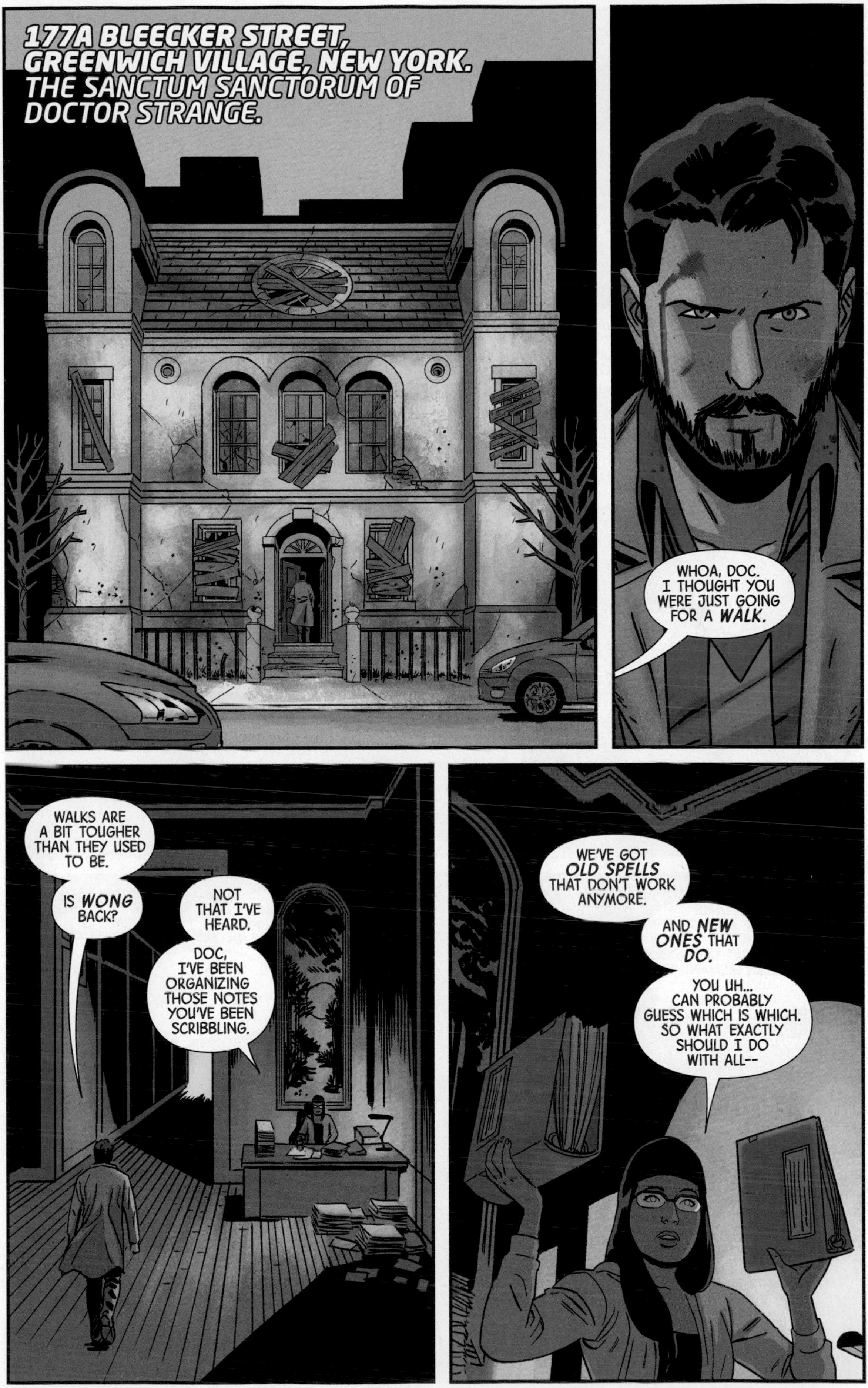
177A BLEECKER STREET, GREENWICH VILLAGE, NEW YORK. THE SANCTUM SANCTORUM OF DOCTOR STRANGE.
WHOA, DOC. I THOUGHT YOU WERE JUST GOING FOR A *WALK.*
WALKS ARE A BIT TOUGHER THAN THEY USED TO BE.
IS *WONG* BACK?
NOT THAT I'VE HEARD.
DOC, I'VE BEEN ORGANIZING THOSE NOTES YOU'VE BEEN SCRIBBLING.
WE'VE GOT *OLD SPELLS* THAT DON'T WORK ANYMORE.
AND *NEW ONES* THAT *DO.*
YOU UH... CAN PROBABLY GUESS WHICH IS WHICH. SO WHAT EXACTLY SHOULD I DO WITH ALL--

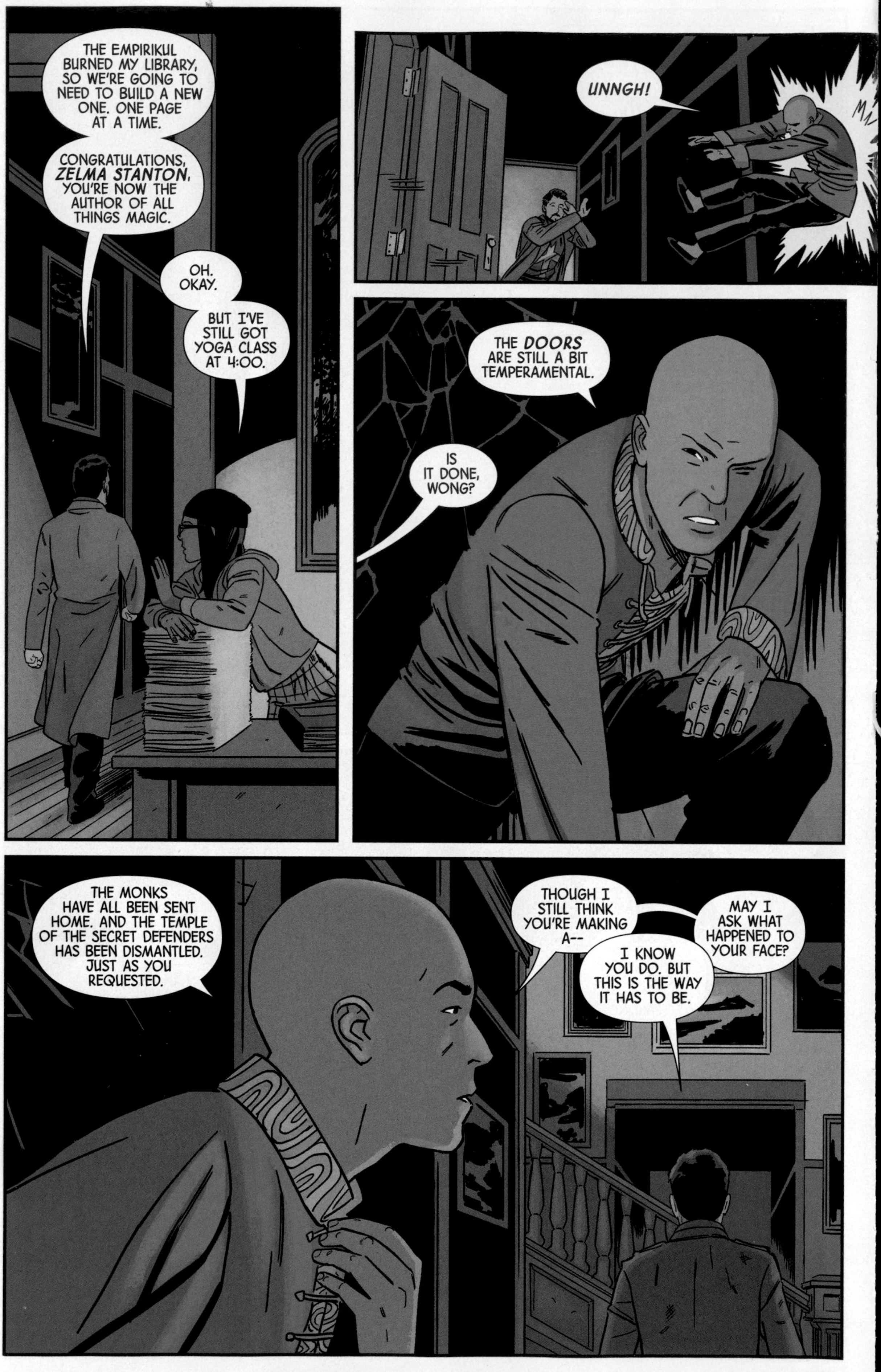
THE EMPIRIKUL BURNED MY LIBRARY, SO WE'RE GOING TO NEED TO BUILD A NEW ONE. ONE PAGE AT A TIME.
CONGRATULATIONS, ZELMA STANTON, YOU'RE NOW THE AUTHOR OF ALL THINGS MAGIC.
OH. OKAY.
BUT I'VE STILL GOT YOGA CLASS AT 4:00.
UNNGH!
THE DOORS ARE STILL A BIT TEMPERAMENTAL.
IS IT DONE, WONG?
THE MONKS HAVE ALL BEEN SENT HOME. AND THE TEMPLE OF THE SECRET DEFENDERS HAS BEEN DISMANTLED. JUST AS YOU REQUESTED.
THOUGH I STILL THINK YOU'RE MAKING A--
I KNOW YOU DO. BUT THIS IS THE WAY IT HAS TO BE.
MAY I ASK WHAT HAPPENED TO YOUR FACE?

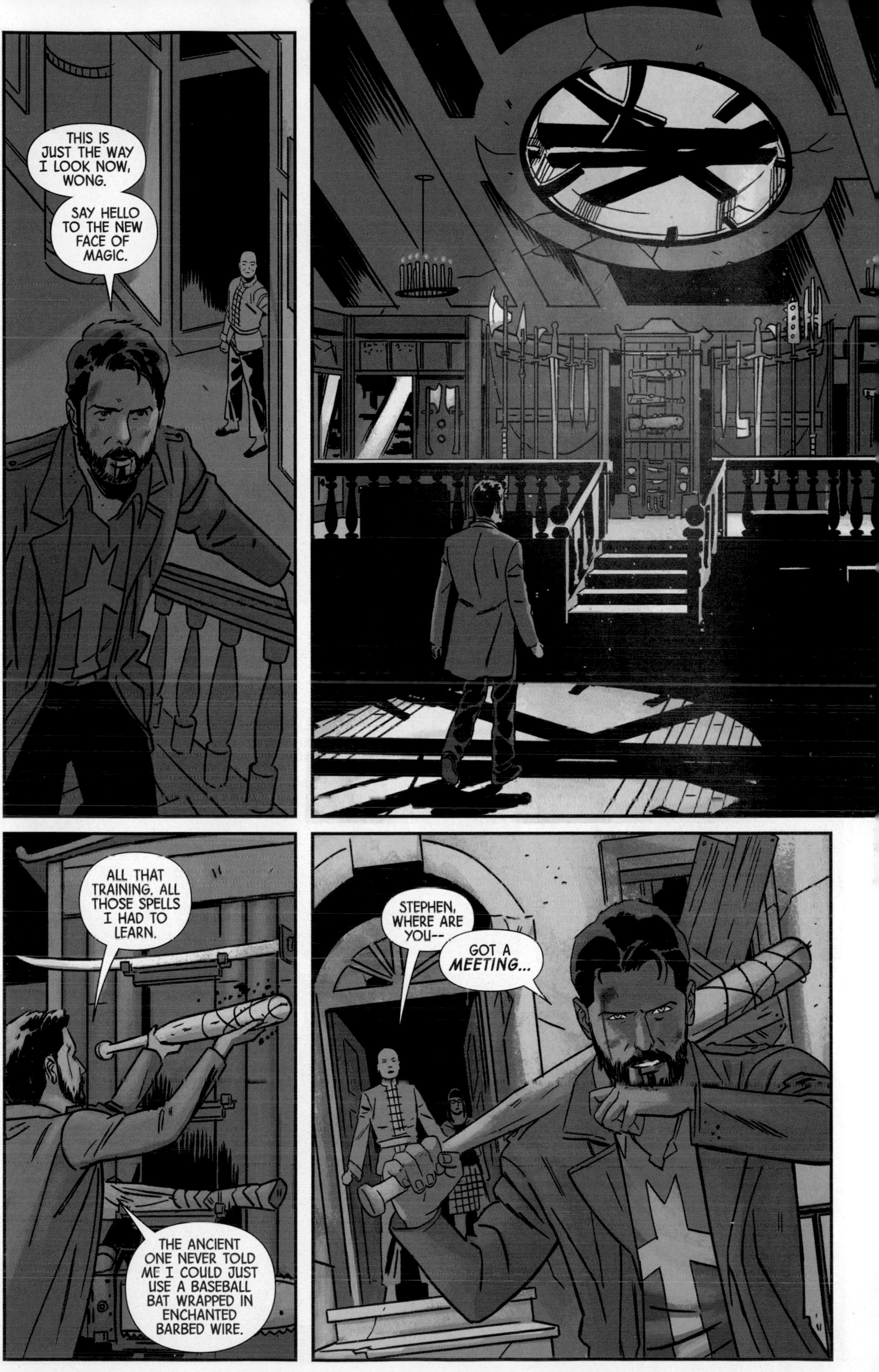
THIS IS JUST THE WAY I LOOK NOW, WONG.
SAY HELLO TO THE NEW FACE OF MAGIC.
ALL THAT TRAINING. ALL THOSE SPELLS I HAD TO LEARN.
THE ANCIENT ONE NEVER TOLD ME I COULD JUST USE A BASEBALL BAT WRAPPED IN ENCHANTED BARBED WIRE.
STEPHEN, WHERE ARE YOU--
GOT A *MEETING*...

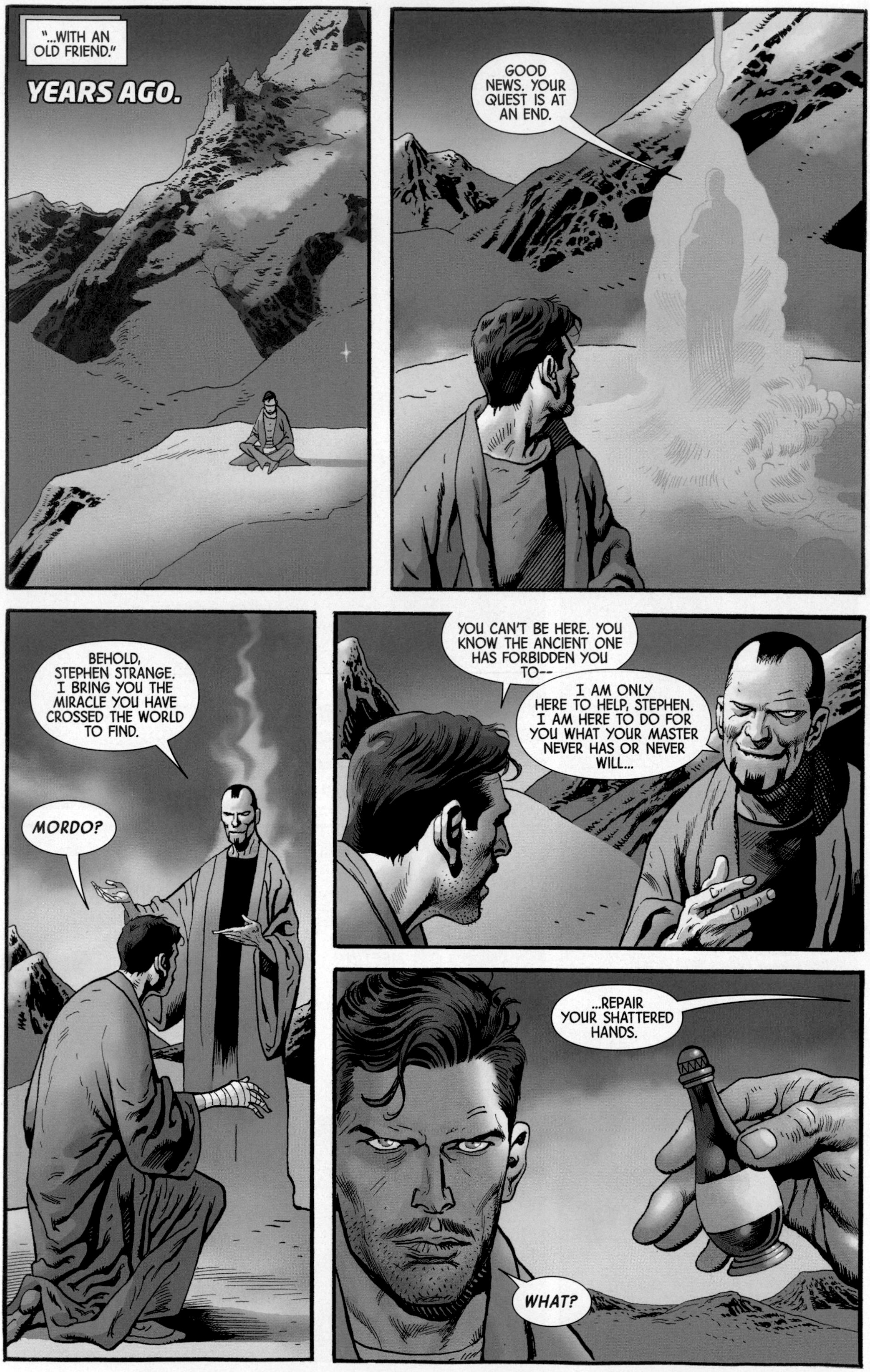
"...WITH AN OLD FRIEND."
YEARS AGO.
GOOD NEWS. YOUR QUEST IS AT AN END.
BEHOLD, STEPHEN STRANGE. I BRING YOU THE MIRACLE YOU HAVE CROSSED THE WORLD TO FIND.
MORDO?
YOU CAN'T BE HERE. YOU KNOW THE ANCIENT ONE HAS FORBIDDEN YOU TO--
I AM ONLY HERE TO HELP, STEPHEN. I AM HERE TO DO FOR YOU WHAT YOUR MASTER NEVER HAS OR NEVER WILL...
...REPAIR YOUR SHATTERED HANDS.
WHAT?

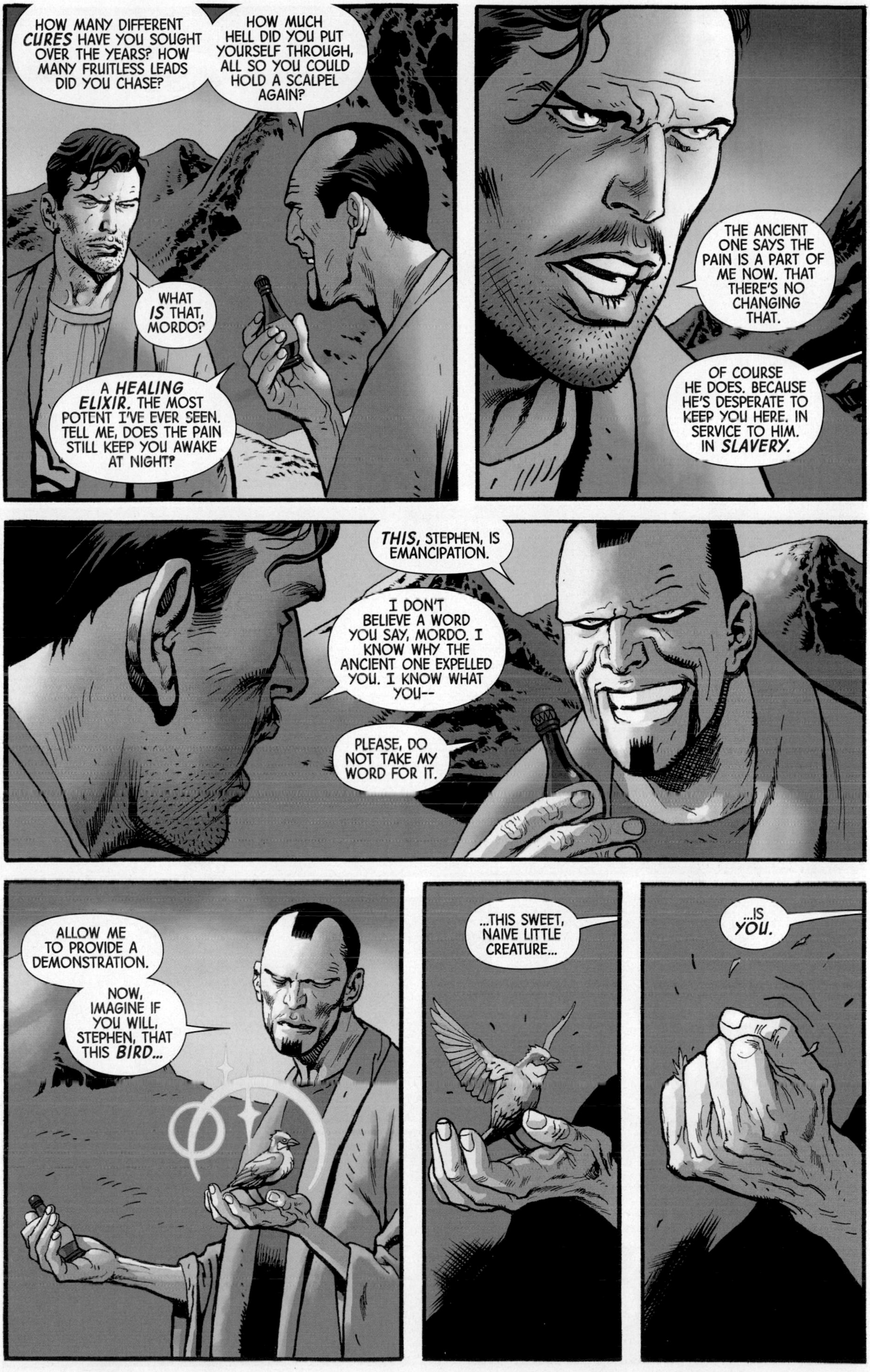
HOW MANY DIFFERENT CURES HAVE YOU SOUGHT OVER THE YEARS? HOW MANY FRUITLESS LEADS DID YOU CHASE?
HOW MUCH HELL DID YOU PUT YOURSELF THROUGH, ALL SO YOU COULD HOLD A SCALPEL AGAIN?
WHAT IS THAT, MORDO?
A HEALING ELIXIR. THE MOST POTENT I'VE EVER SEEN. TELL ME, DOES THE PAIN STILL KEEP YOU AWAKE AT NIGHT?
THE ANCIENT ONE SAYS THE PAIN IS A PART OF ME NOW. THAT THERE'S NO CHANGING THAT.
OF COURSE HE DOES. BECAUSE HE'S DESPERATE TO KEEP YOU HERE. IN SERVICE TO HIM. IN SLAVERY.
THIS, STEPHEN, IS EMANCIPATION.
I DON'T BELIEVE A WORD YOU SAY, MORDO. I KNOW WHY THE ANCIENT ONE EXPELLED YOU. I KNOW WHAT YOU--
PLEASE, DO NOT TAKE MY WORD FOR IT.
ALLOW ME TO PROVIDE A DEMONSTRATION.
NOW, IMAGINE IF YOU WILL, STEPHEN, THAT THIS BIRD...
...THIS SWEET, NAIVE LITTLE CREATURE...
...IS YOU.

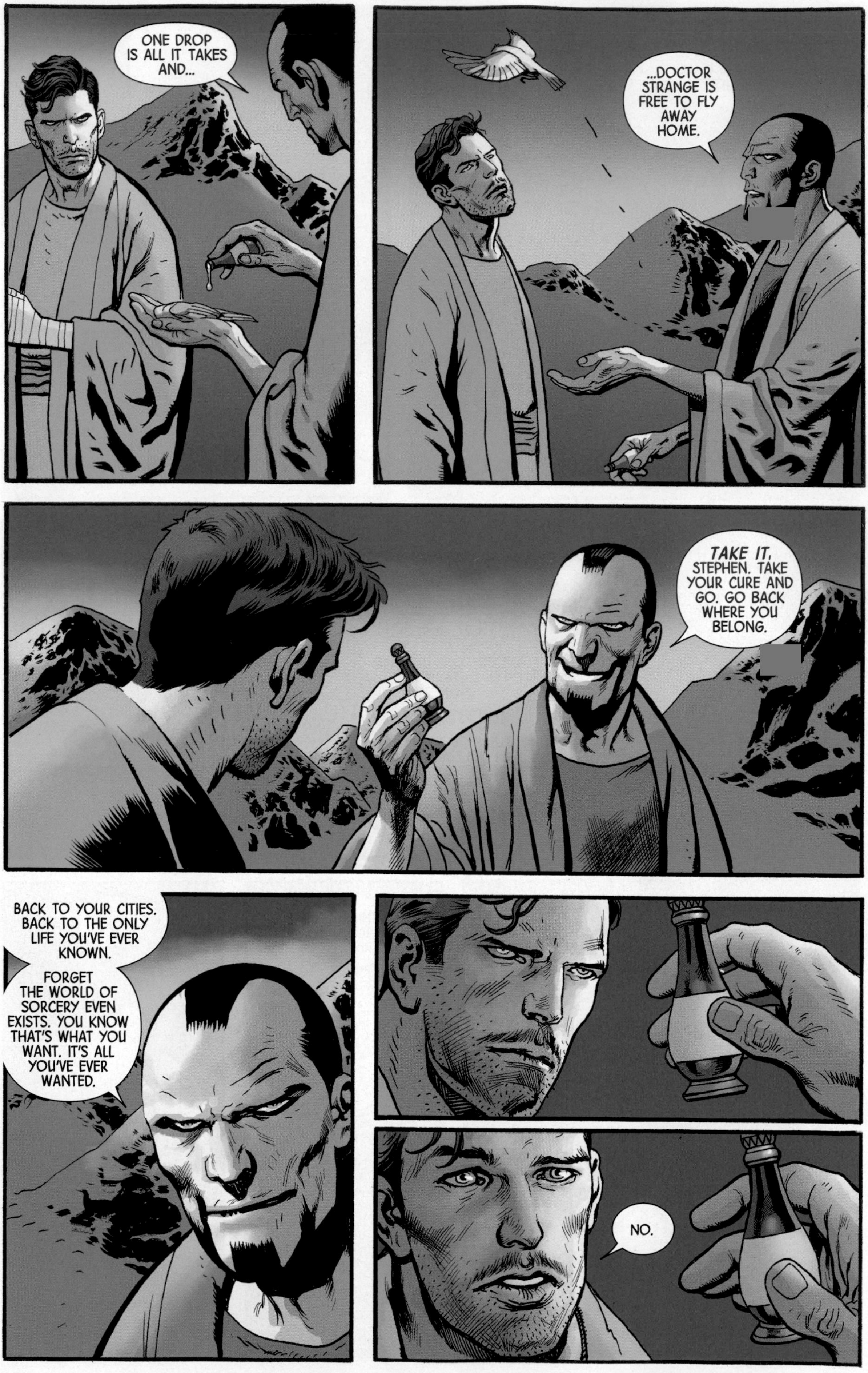
ONE DROP IS ALL IT TAKES AND...
...DOCTOR STRANGE IS FREE TO FLY AWAY HOME.
TAKE IT, STEPHEN. TAKE YOUR CURE AND GO. GO BACK WHERE YOU BELONG.
BACK TO YOUR CITIES. BACK TO THE ONLY LIFE YOU'VE EVER KNOWN.
FORGET THE WORLD OF SORCERY EVEN EXISTS. YOU KNOW THAT'S WHAT YOU WANT. IT'S ALL YOU'VE EVER WANTED.
NO.

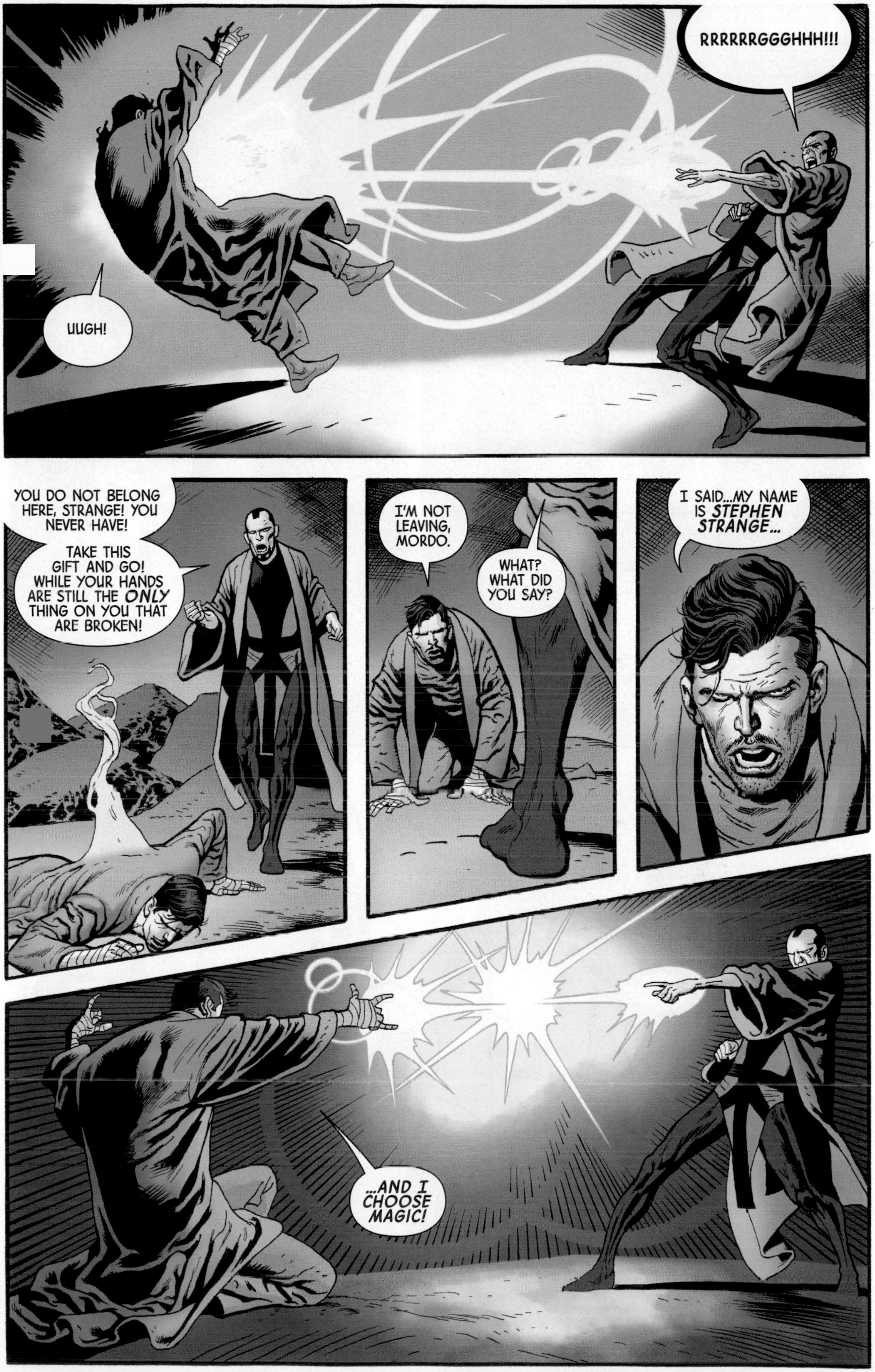
RRRRRRGGGHHH!!!
UUGH!
YOU DO NOT BELONG HERE, STRANGE! YOU NEVER HAVE!
TAKE THIS GIFT AND GO! WHILE YOUR HANDS ARE STILL THE ONLY THING ON YOU THAT ARE BROKEN!
I'M NOT LEAVING, MORDO.
WHAT? WHAT DID YOU SAY?
I SAID...MY NAME IS STEPHEN STRANGE...
...AND I CHOOSE MAGIC!

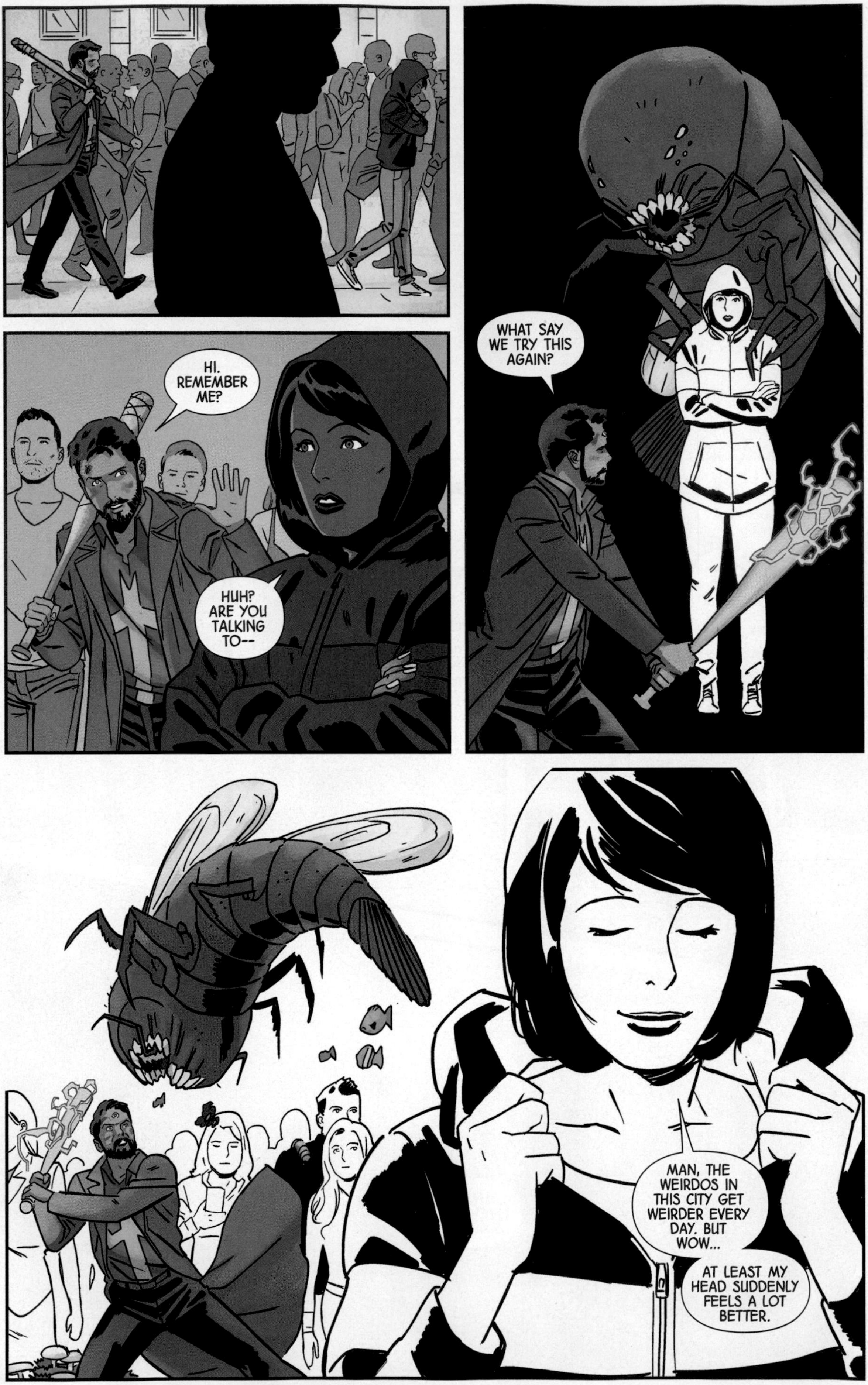

HI. REMEMBER ME?
HUH? ARE YOU TALKING TO--
WHAT SAY WE TRY THIS AGAIN?
MAN, THE WEIRDOS IN THIS CITY GET WEIRDER EVERY DAY. BUT WOW...
AT LEAST MY HEAD SUDDENLY FEELS A LOT BETTER.

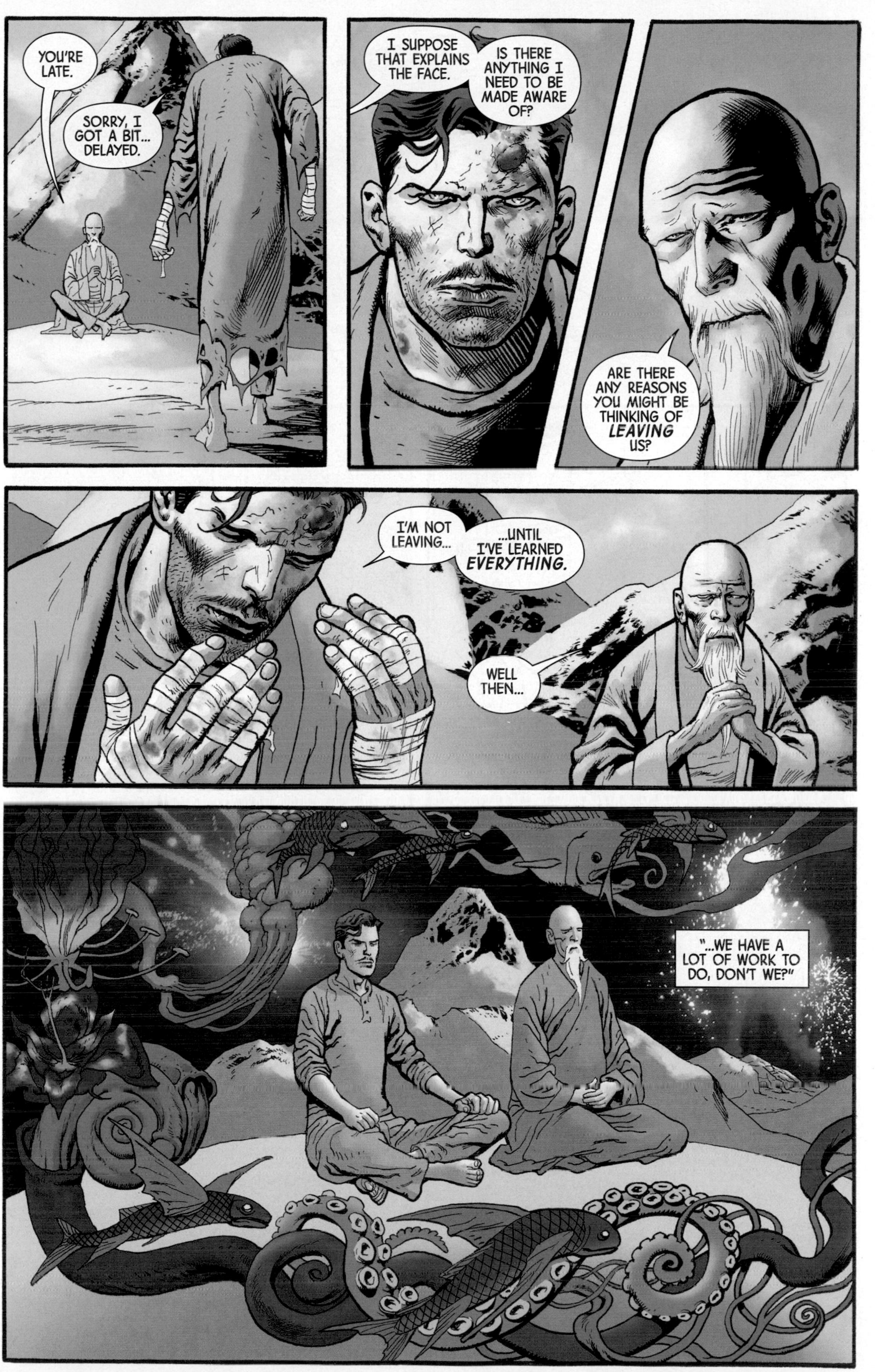
YOU'RE LATE.
SORRY, I GOT A BIT... DELAYED.
I SUPPOSE THAT EXPLAINS THE FACE.
IS THERE ANYTHING I NEED TO BE MADE AWARE OF?
ARE THERE ANY REASONS YOU MIGHT BE THINKING OF *LEAVING* US?
I'M NOT LEAVING...
...UNTIL I'VE LEARNED *EVERYTHING.*
WELL THEN...
"...WE HAVE A LOT OF WORK TO DO, DON'T WE?"

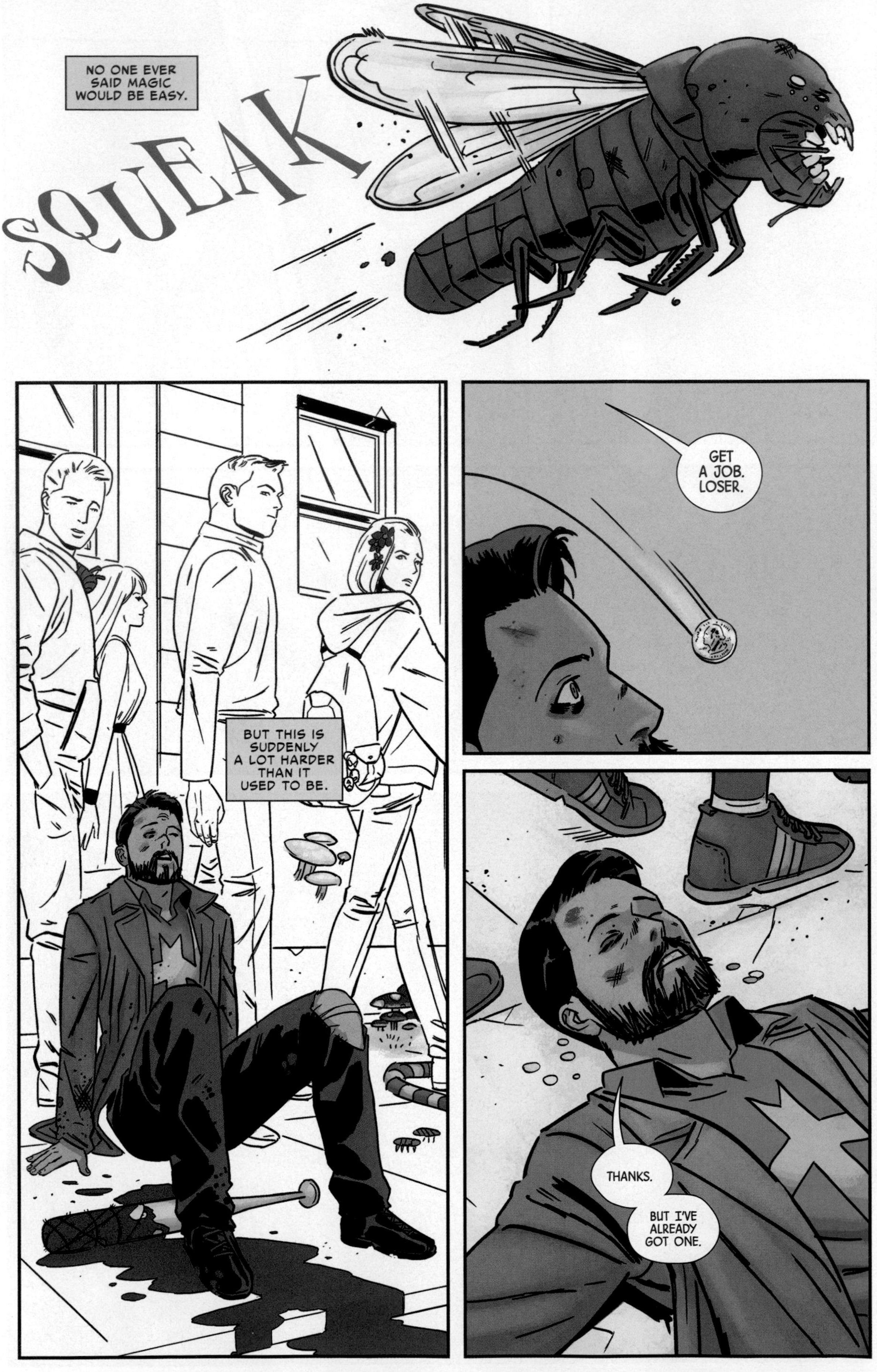
NO ONE EVER SAID MAGIC WOULD BE EASY.
SQUEAK
BUT THIS IS SUDDENLY A LOT HARDER THAN IT USED TO BE.
GET A JOB. LOSER.
THANKS.
BUT I'VE ALREADY GOT ONE.

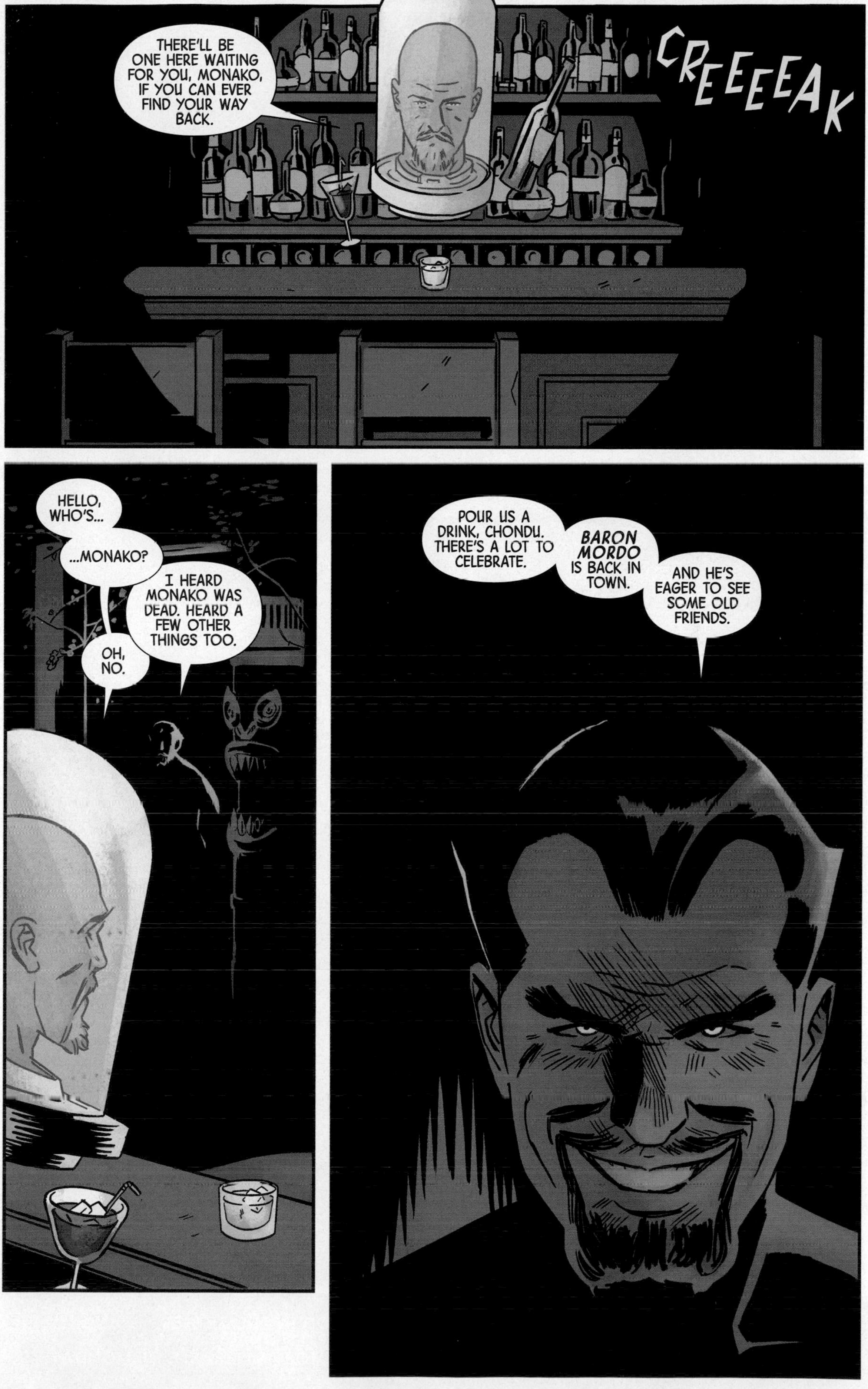
THERE'LL BE ONE HERE WAITING FOR YOU, MONAKO, IF YOU CAN EVER FIND YOUR WAY BACK.
CREEEEAK
HELLO, WHO'S...
...MONAKO?
I HEARD MONAKO WAS DEAD. HEARD A FEW OTHER THINGS TOO.
OH, NO.
POUR US A DRINK, CHONDU. THERE'S A LOT TO CELEBRATE.
BARON MORDO IS BACK IN TOWN.
AND HE'S EAGER TO SEE SOME OLD FRIENDS.

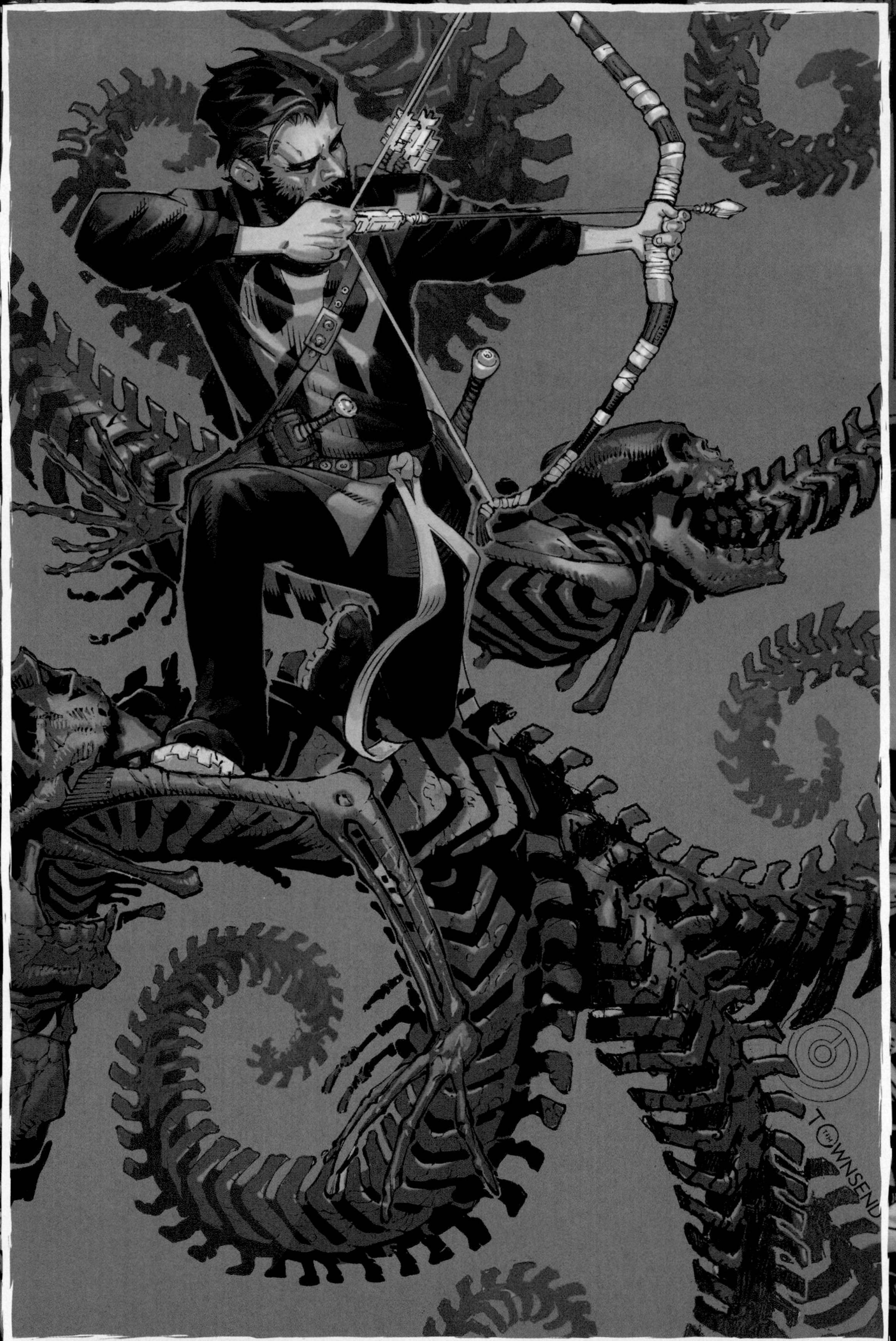
TOWNSEND

DOCTOR STRANGE 12

BLOOD IN THE AETHER
CHAPTER ONE:
THE MOST MISERABLE OF MONDAYS

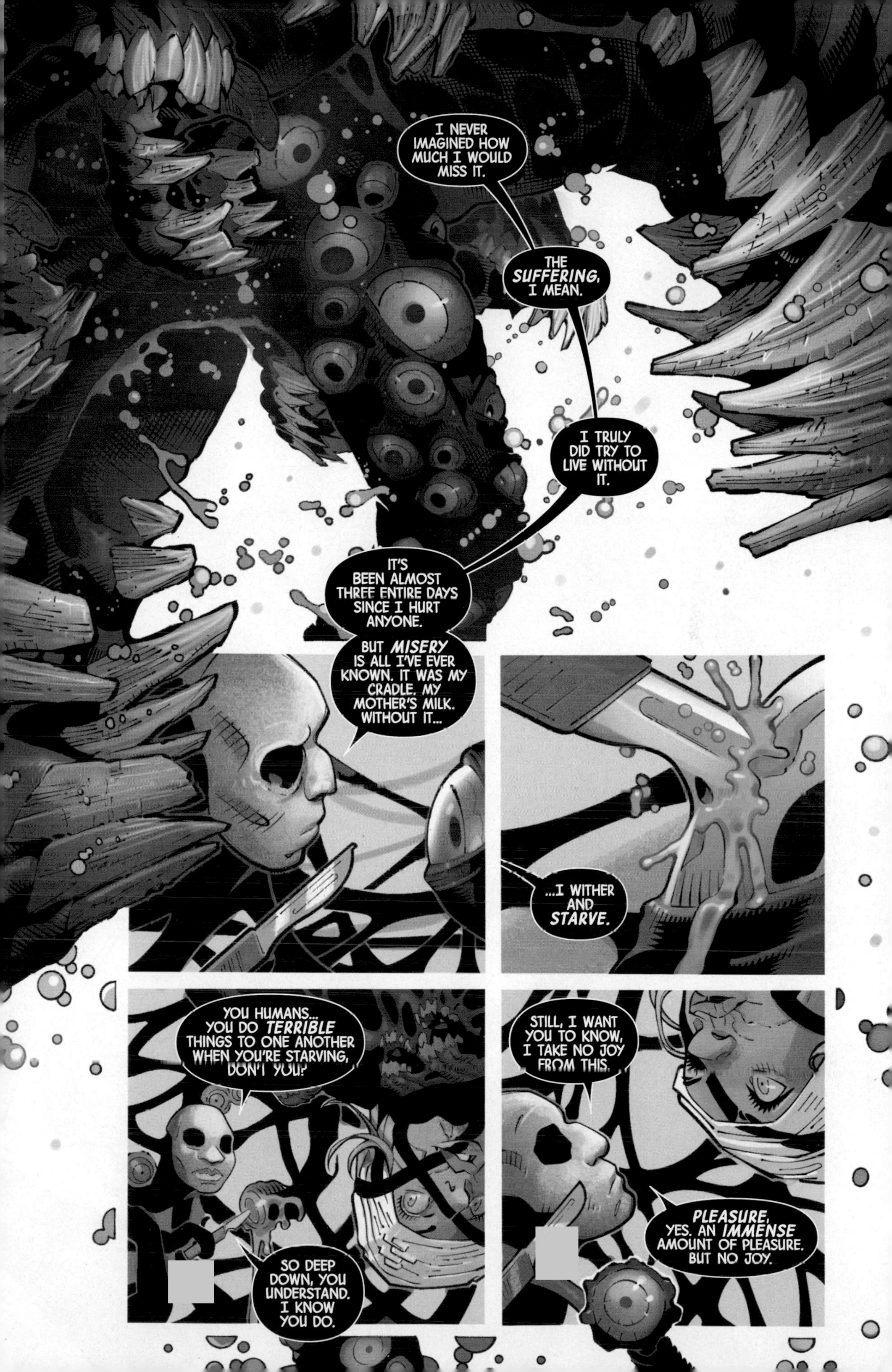
I NEVER IMAGINED HOW MUCH I WOULD MISS IT.
THE SUFFERING, I MEAN.
I TRULY DID TRY TO LIVE WITHOUT IT.
IT'S BEEN ALMOST THREE ENTIRE DAYS SINCE I HURT ANYONE.
BUT MISERY IS ALL I'VE EVER KNOWN. IT WAS MY CRADLE. MY MOTHER'S MILK. WITHOUT IT...
...I WITHER AND STARVE.
YOU HUMANS... YOU DO TERRIBLE THINGS TO ONE ANOTHER WHEN YOU'RE STARVING, DON'T YOU?
SO DEEP DOWN, YOU UNDERSTAND. I KNOW YOU DO.
STILL, I WANT YOU TO KNOW, I TAKE NO JOY FROM THIS.
PLEASURE, YES. AN IMMENSE AMOUNT OF PLEASURE. BUT NO JOY.

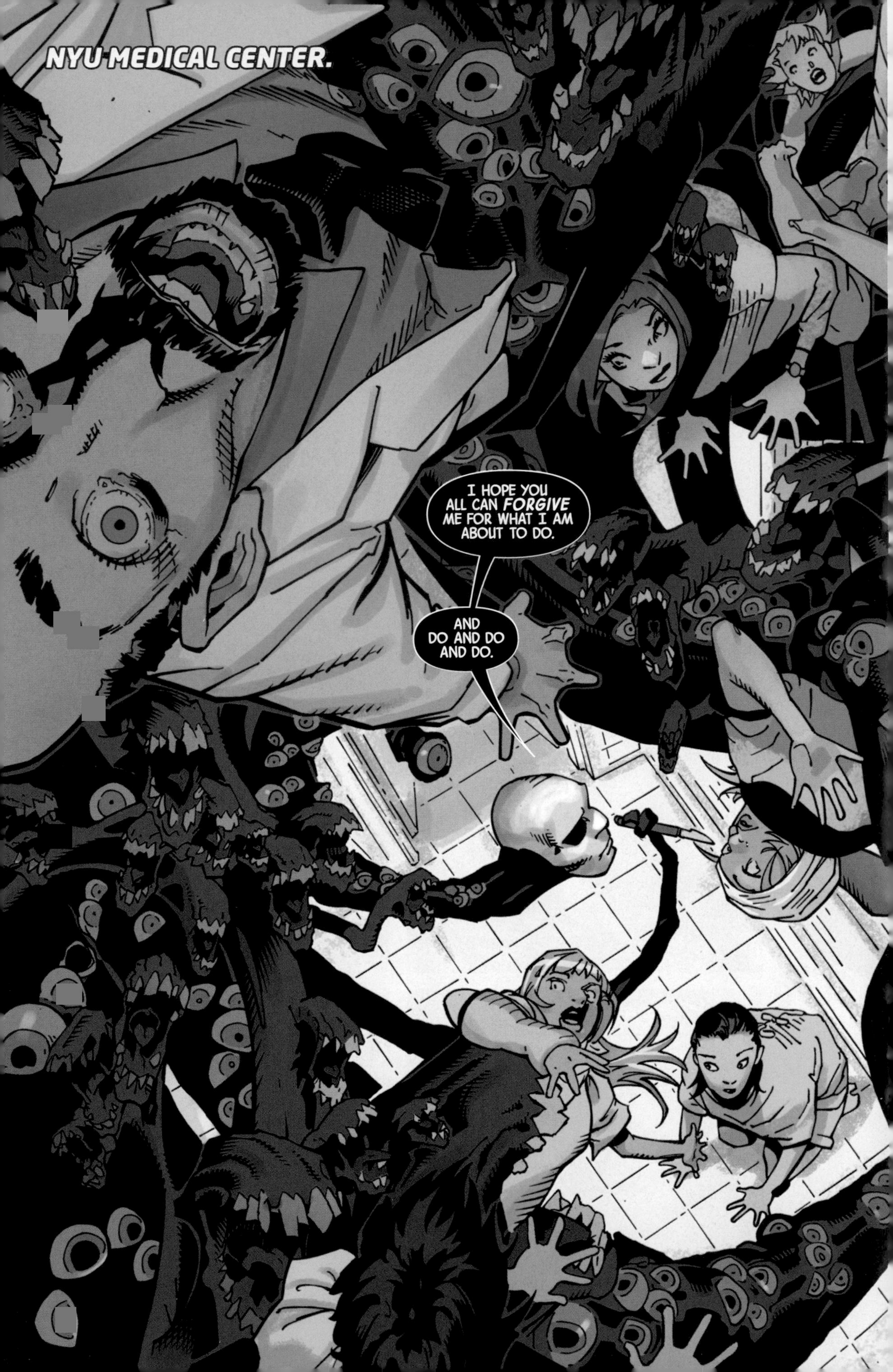
NYU MEDICAL CENTER.
I HOPE YOU ALL CAN FORGIVE ME FOR WHAT I AM ABOUT TO DO.
AND DO AND DO AND DO.

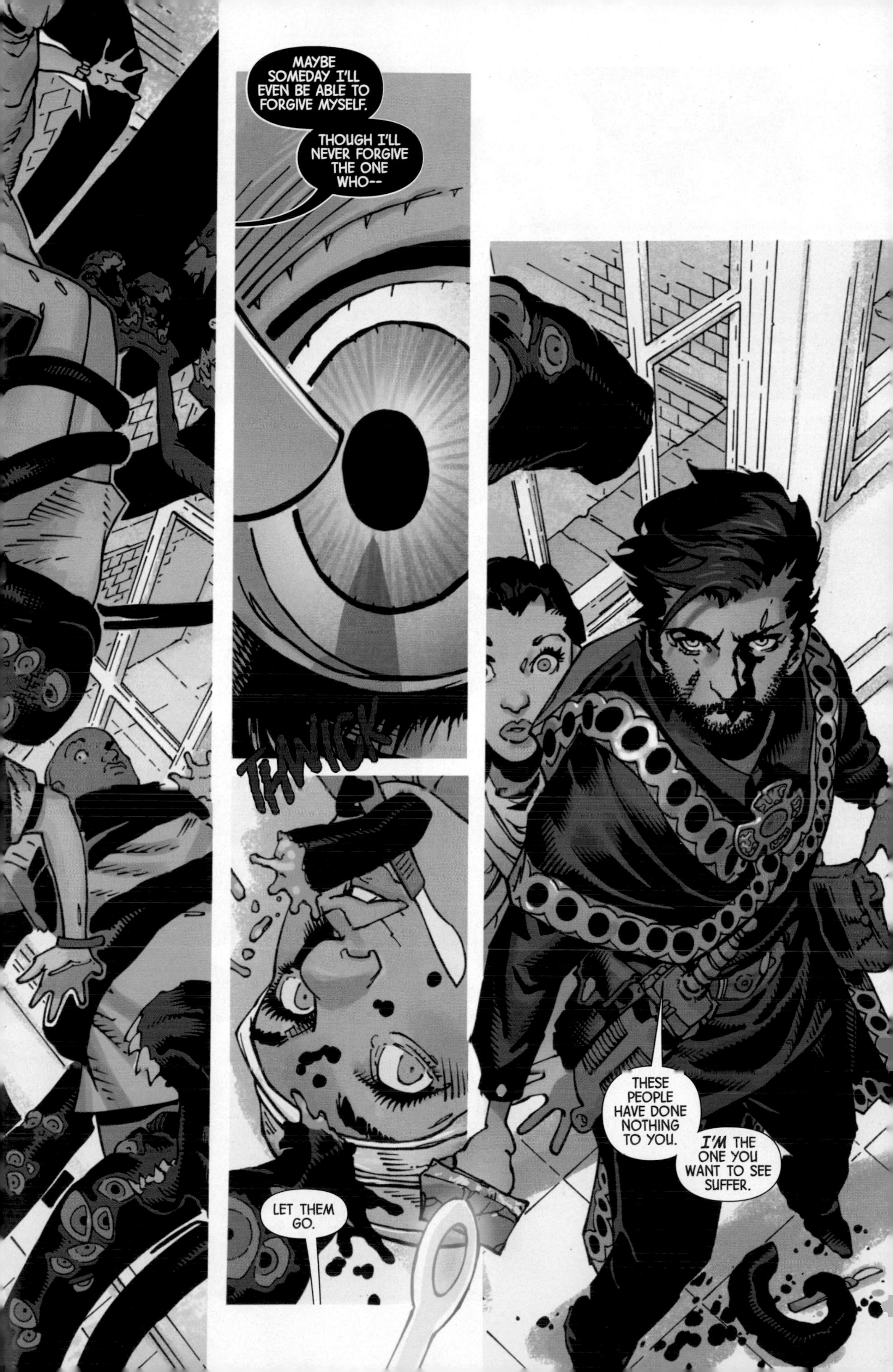
MAYBE SOMEDAY I'LL EVEN BE ABLE TO FORGIVE MYSELF.
THOUGH I'LL NEVER FORGIVE THE ONE WHO--
THWICK
LET THEM GO.
THESE PEOPLE HAVE DONE NOTHING TO YOU.
I'M THE ONE YOU WANT TO SEE SUFFER.

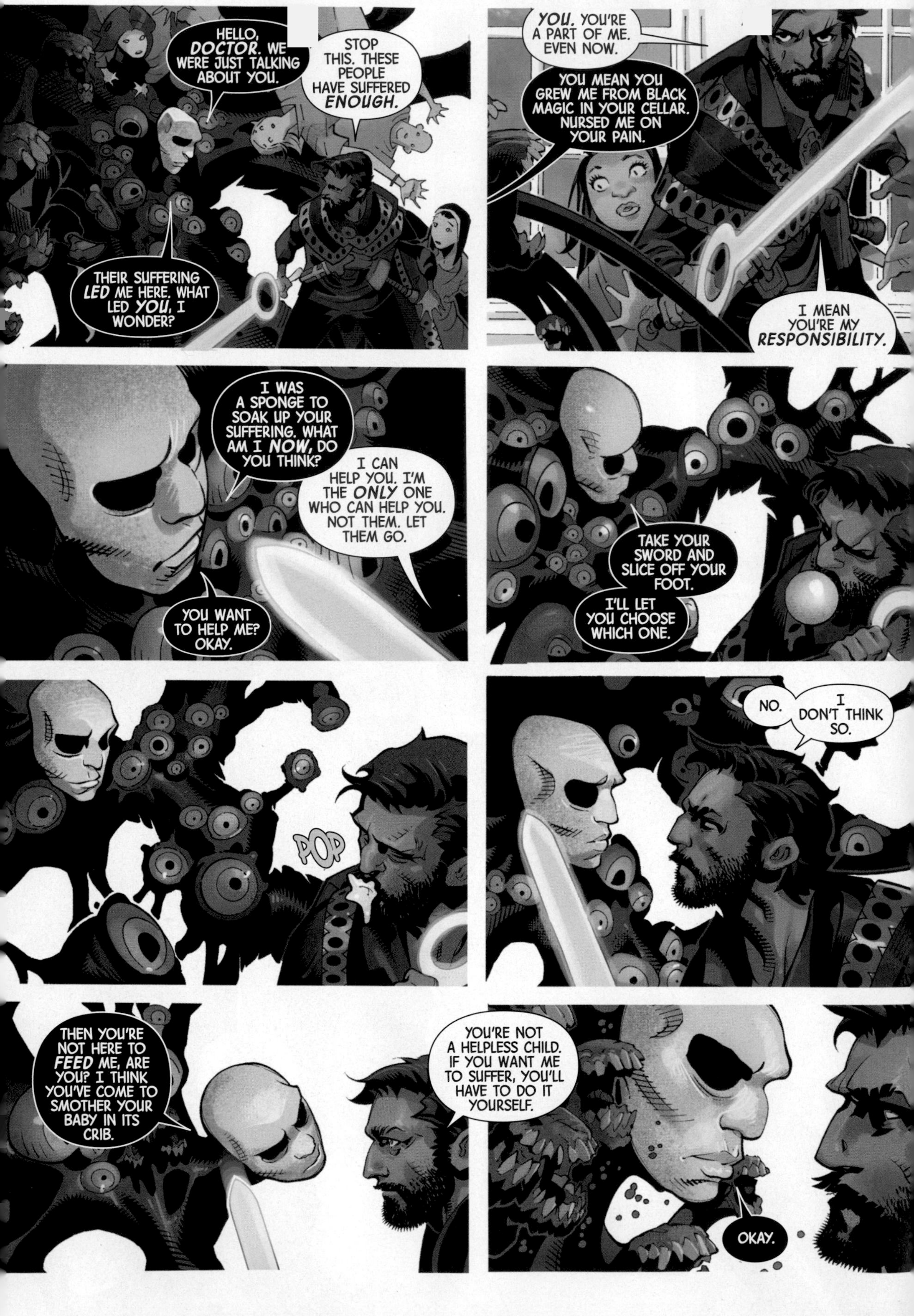
HELLO, DOCTOR. WE WERE JUST TALKING ABOUT YOU.
STOP THIS. THESE PEOPLE HAVE SUFFERED ENOUGH.
THEIR SUFFERING LED ME HERE. WHAT LED YOU, I WONDER?
YOU. YOU'RE A PART OF ME. EVEN NOW.
YOU MEAN YOU GREW ME FROM BLACK MAGIC IN YOUR CELLAR. NURSED ME ON YOUR PAIN.
I MEAN YOU'RE MY RESPONSIBILITY.
I WAS A SPONGE TO SOAK UP YOUR SUFFERING. WHAT AM I NOW, DO YOU THINK?
I CAN HELP YOU. I'M THE ONLY ONE WHO CAN HELP YOU. NOT THEM. LET THEM GO.
YOU WANT TO HELP ME? OKAY.
TAKE YOUR SWORD AND SLICE OFF YOUR FOOT.
I'LL LET YOU CHOOSE WHICH ONE.
POP
NO.
I DON'T THINK SO.
THEN YOU'RE NOT HERE TO FEED ME, ARE YOU? I THINK YOU'VE COME TO SMOTHER YOUR BABY IN ITS CRIB.
YOU'RE NOT A HELPLESS CHILD. IF YOU WANT ME TO SUFFER, YOU'LL HAVE TO DO IT YOURSELF.
OKAY.

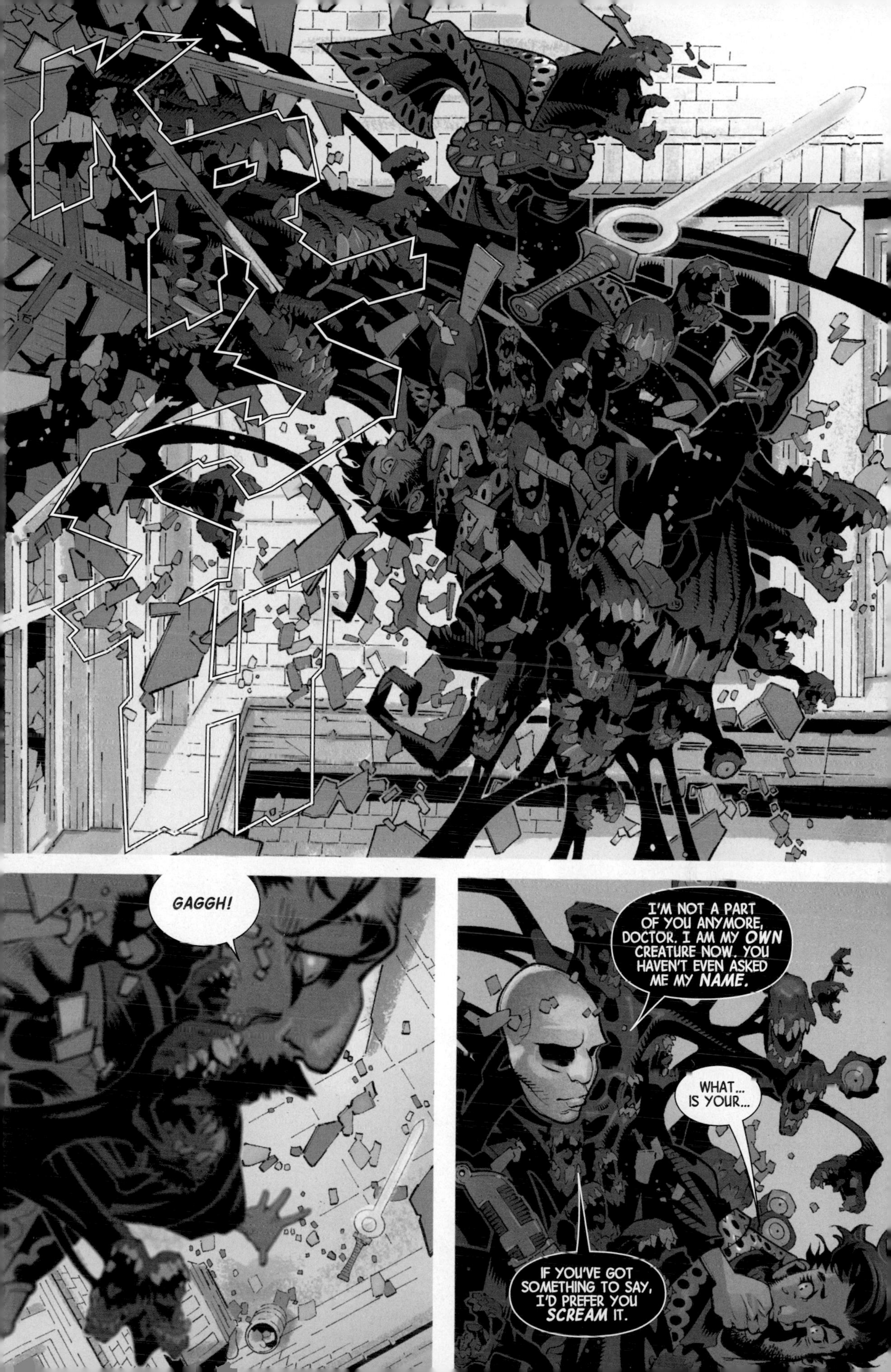
GAGGH!
I'M NOT A PART OF YOU ANYMORE, DOCTOR. I AM MY OWN CREATURE NOW. YOU HAVEN'T EVEN ASKED ME MY NAME.
WHAT... IS YOUR...
IF YOU'VE GOT SOMETHING TO SAY, I'D PREFER YOU SCREAM IT.

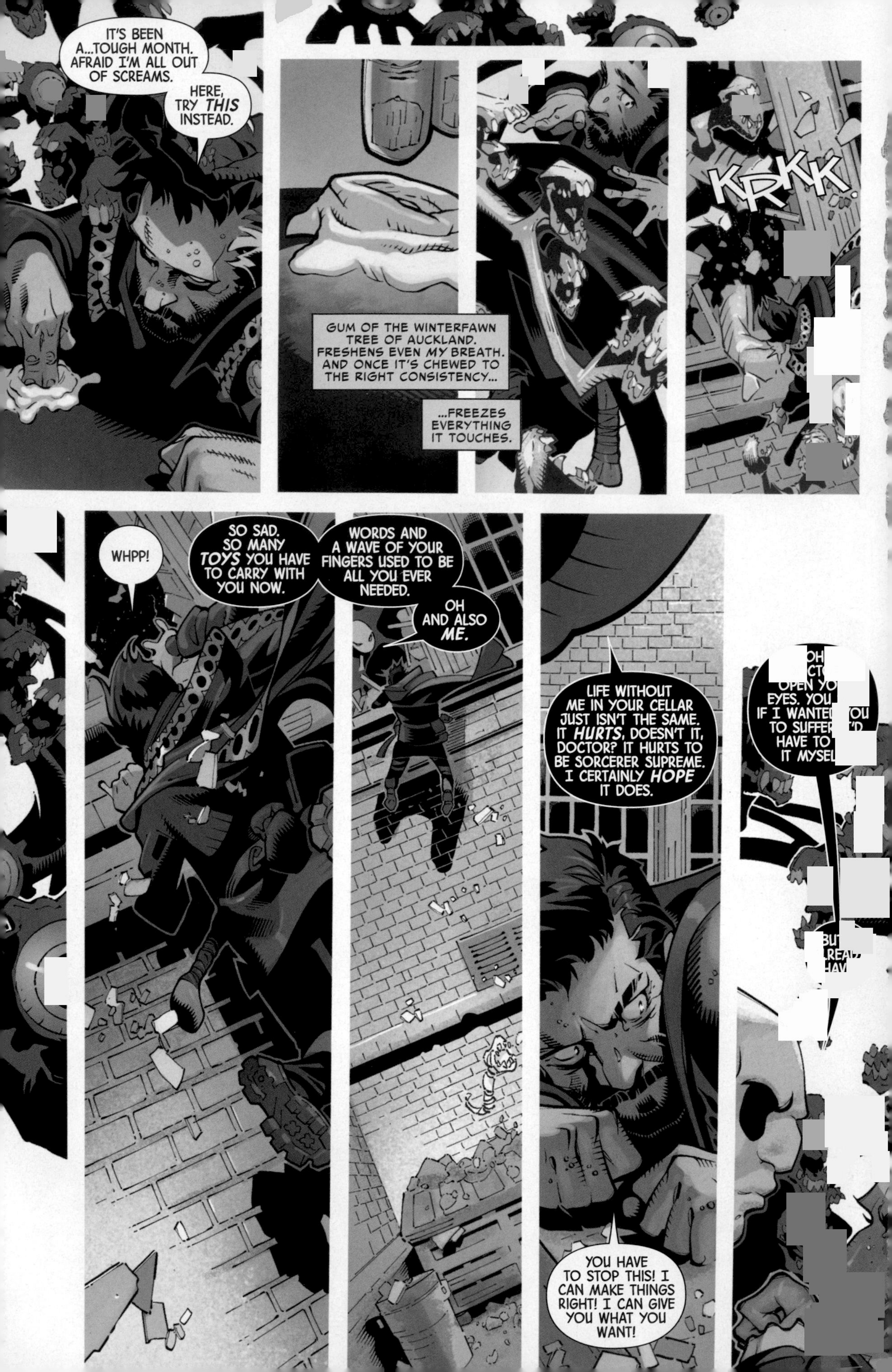

IT'S BEEN A...TOUGH MONTH. AFRAID I'M ALL OUT OF SCREAMS.
HERE, TRY *THIS* INSTEAD.
GUM OF THE WINTERFAWN TREE OF AUCKLAND. FRESHENS EVEN *MY* BREATH. AND ONCE IT'S CHEWED TO THE RIGHT CONSISTENCY...
...FREEZES EVERYTHING IT TOUCHES.
KRKK
WHPP!
SO SAD. SO MANY *TOYS* YOU HAVE TO CARRY WITH YOU NOW.
WORDS AND A WAVE OF YOUR FINGERS USED TO BE ALL YOU EVER NEEDED.
OH AND ALSO *ME.*
LIFE WITHOUT ME IN YOUR CELLAR JUST ISN'T THE SAME. IT *HURTS*, DOESN'T IT, DOCTOR? IT HURTS TO BE SORCERER SUPREME. I CERTAINLY *HOPE* IT DOES.
YOU HAVE TO STOP THIS! I CAN MAKE THINGS RIGHT! I CAN GIVE YOU WHAT YOU WANT!

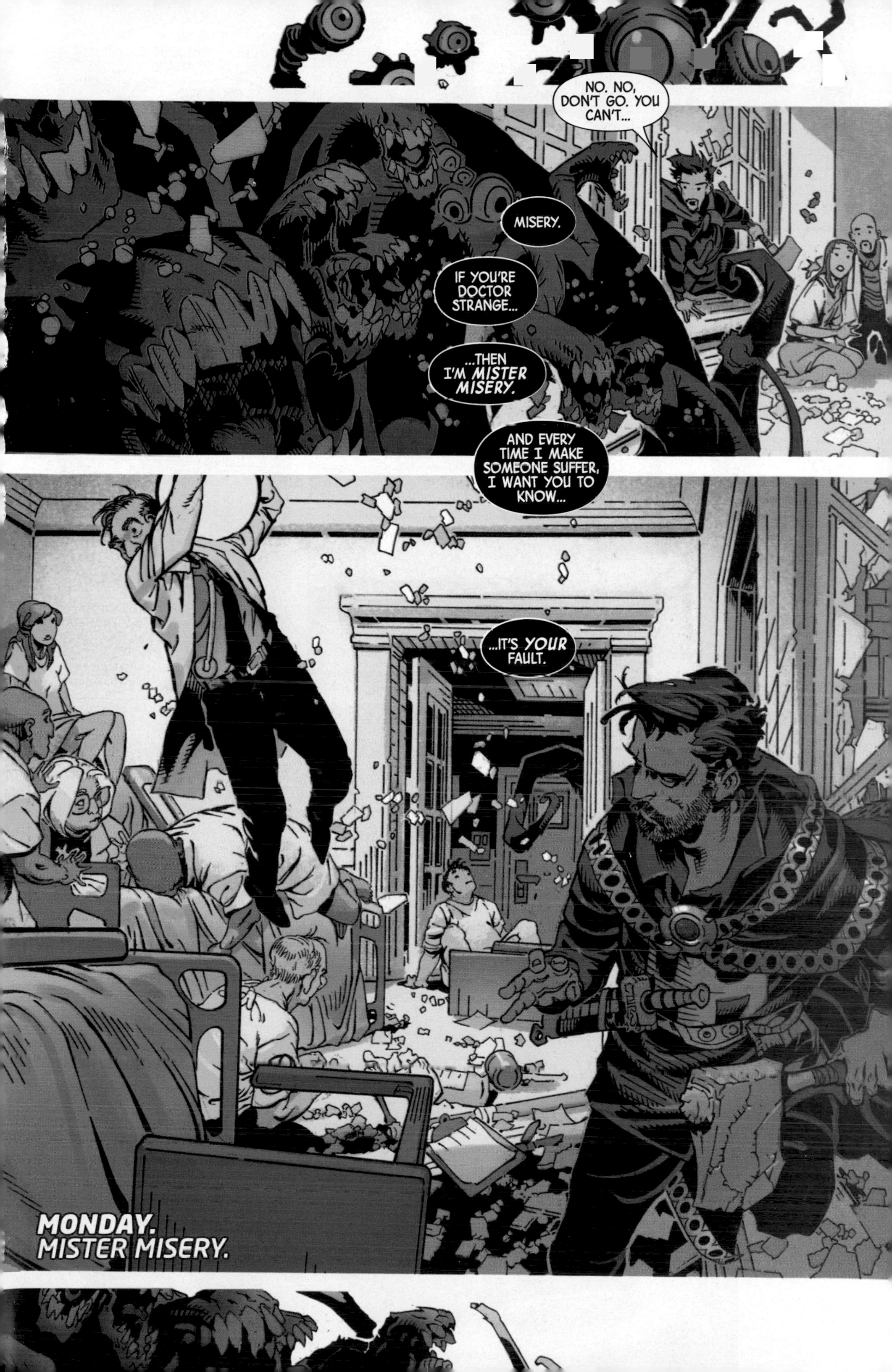
NO. NO, DON'T GO. YOU CAN'T...
MISERY.
IF YOU'RE DOCTOR STRANGE...
...THEN I'M MISTER MISERY.
AND EVERY TIME I MAKE SOMEONE SUFFER, I WANT YOU TO KNOW...
...IT'S YOUR FAULT.
MONDAY. MISTER MISERY.

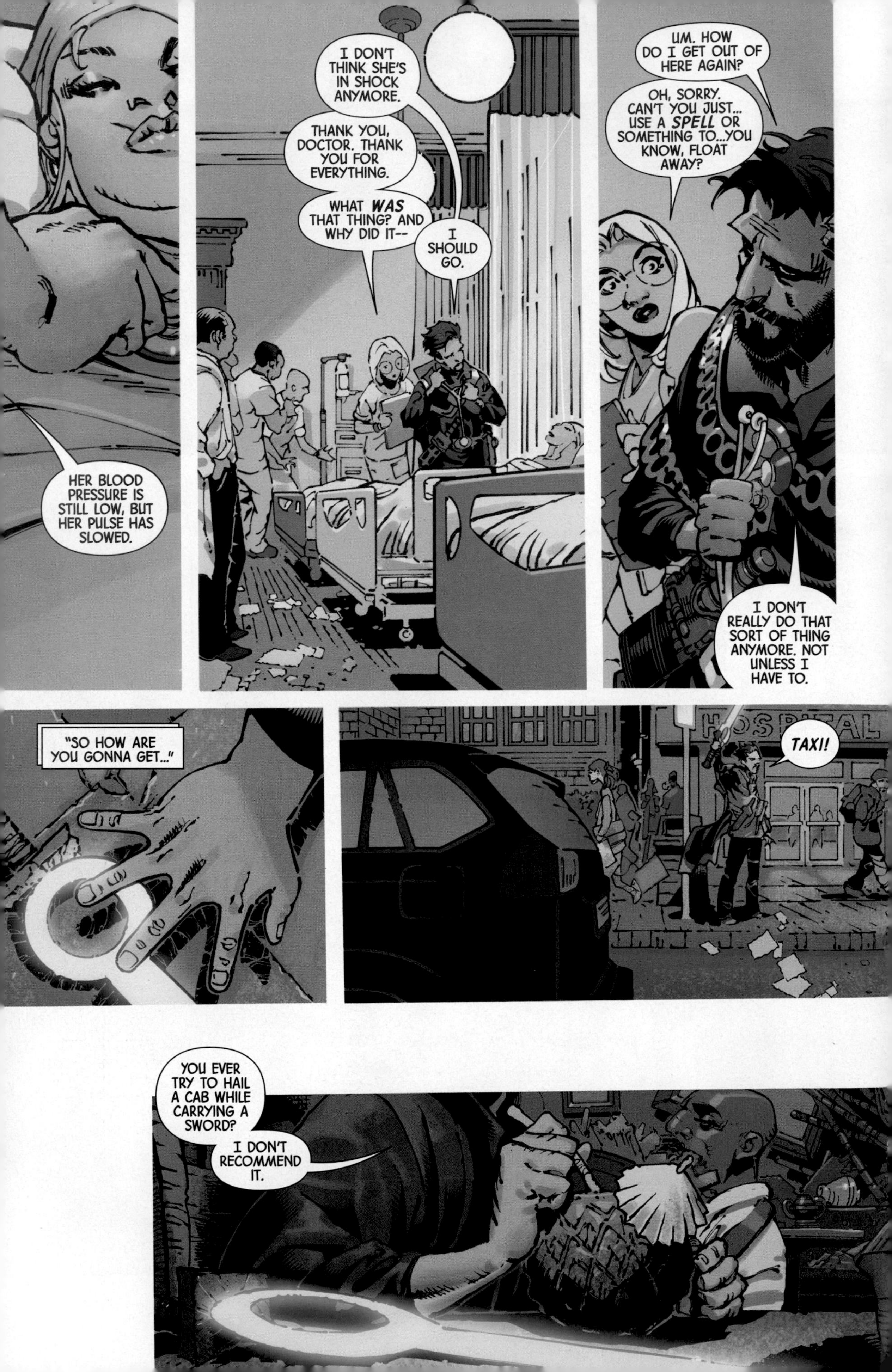

HER BLOOD PRESSURE IS STILL LOW, BUT HER PULSE HAS SLOWED.
I DON'T THINK SHE'S IN SHOCK ANYMORE.
THANK YOU, DOCTOR. THANK YOU FOR EVERYTHING.
WHAT WAS THAT THING? AND WHY DID IT--
I SHOULD GO.
UM. HOW DO I GET OUT OF HERE AGAIN?
OH, SORRY. CAN'T YOU JUST... USE A SPELL OR SOMETHING TO...YOU KNOW, FLOAT AWAY?
I DON'T REALLY DO THAT SORT OF THING ANYMORE. NOT UNLESS I HAVE TO.
"SO HOW ARE YOU GONNA GET..."
HOSPITAL
TAXI!
YOU EVER TRY TO HAIL A CAB WHILE CARRYING A SWORD?
I DON'T RECOMMEND IT.

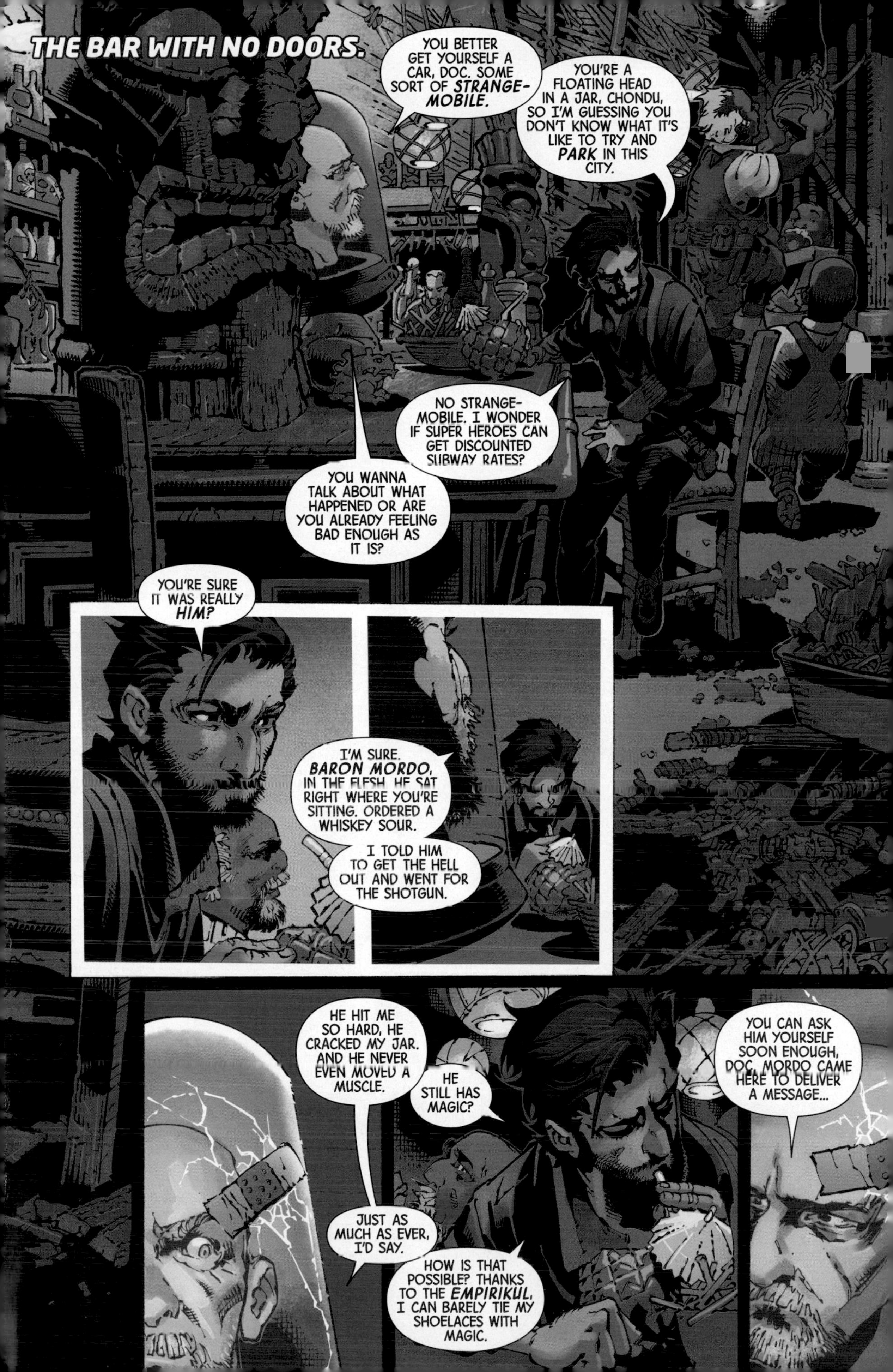
THE BAR WITH NO DOORS.
YOU BETTER GET YOURSELF A CAR, DOC. SOME SORT OF STRANGE-MOBILE.
YOU'RE A FLOATING HEAD IN A JAR, CHONDU, SO I'M GUESSING YOU DON'T KNOW WHAT IT'S LIKE TO TRY AND PARK IN THIS CITY.
NO STRANGE-MOBILE. I WONDER IF SUPER HEROES CAN GET DISCOUNTED SUBWAY RATES?
YOU WANNA TALK ABOUT WHAT HAPPENED OR ARE YOU ALREADY FEELING BAD ENOUGH AS IT IS?
YOU'RE SURE IT WAS REALLY HIM?
I'M SURE. BARON MORDO, IN THE FLESH. HE SAT RIGHT WHERE YOU'RE SITTING. ORDERED A WHISKEY SOUR.
I TOLD HIM TO GET THE HELL OUT AND WENT FOR THE SHOTGUN.
HE HIT ME SO HARD, HE CRACKED MY JAR. AND HE NEVER EVEN MOVED A MUSCLE.
HE STILL HAS MAGIC?
JUST AS MUCH AS EVER, I'D SAY.
HOW IS THAT POSSIBLE? THANKS TO THE EMPIRIKUL, I CAN BARELY TIE MY SHOELACES WITH MAGIC.
YOU CAN ASK HIM YOURSELF SOON ENOUGH, DOC. MORDO CAME HERE TO DELIVER A MESSAGE...

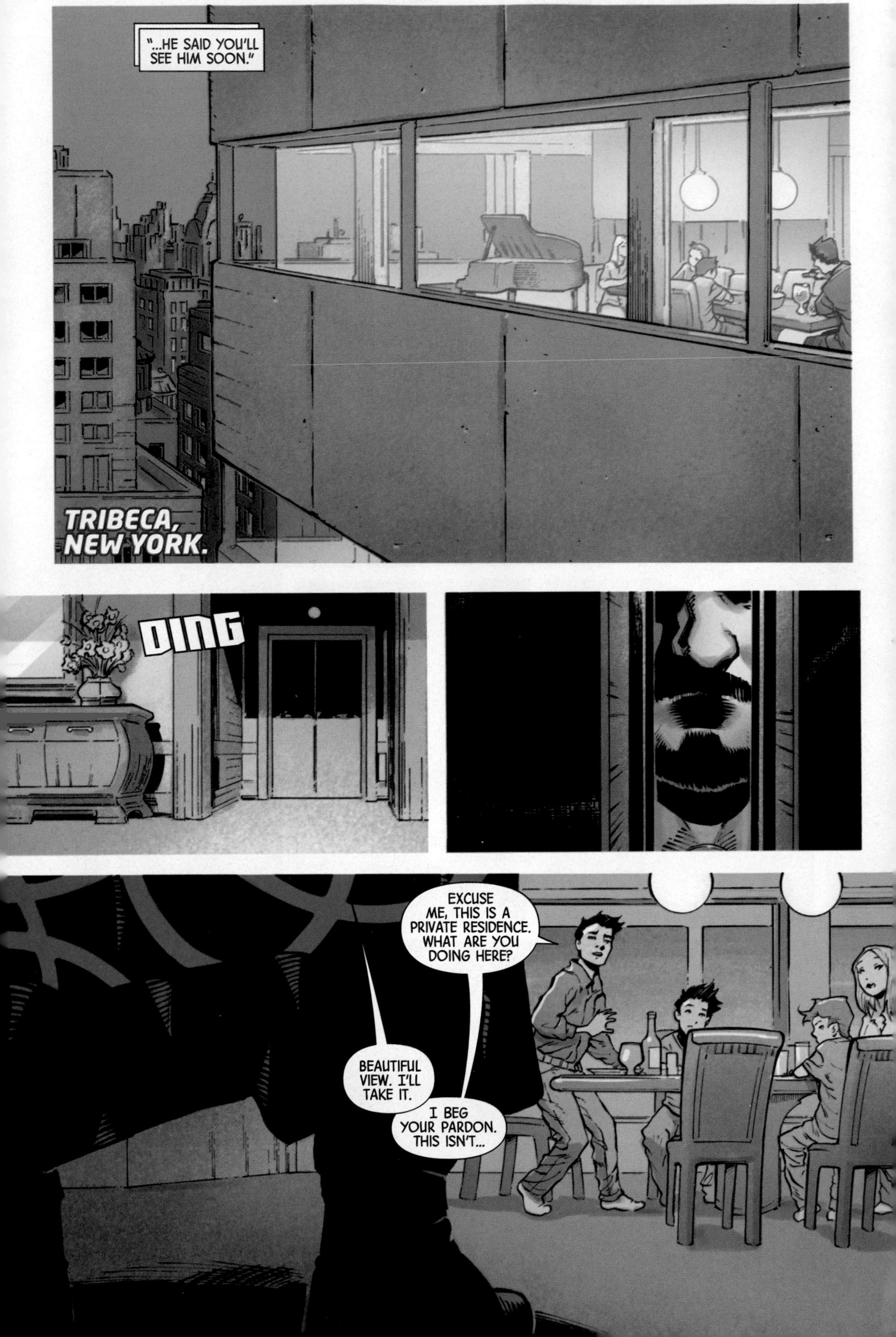
"...HE SAID YOU'LL SEE HIM SOON."
TRIBECA, NEW YORK.
DING
EXCUSE ME, THIS IS A PRIVATE RESIDENCE. WHAT ARE YOU DOING HERE?
BEAUTIFUL VIEW. I'LL TAKE IT.
I BEG YOUR PARDON. THIS ISN'T...

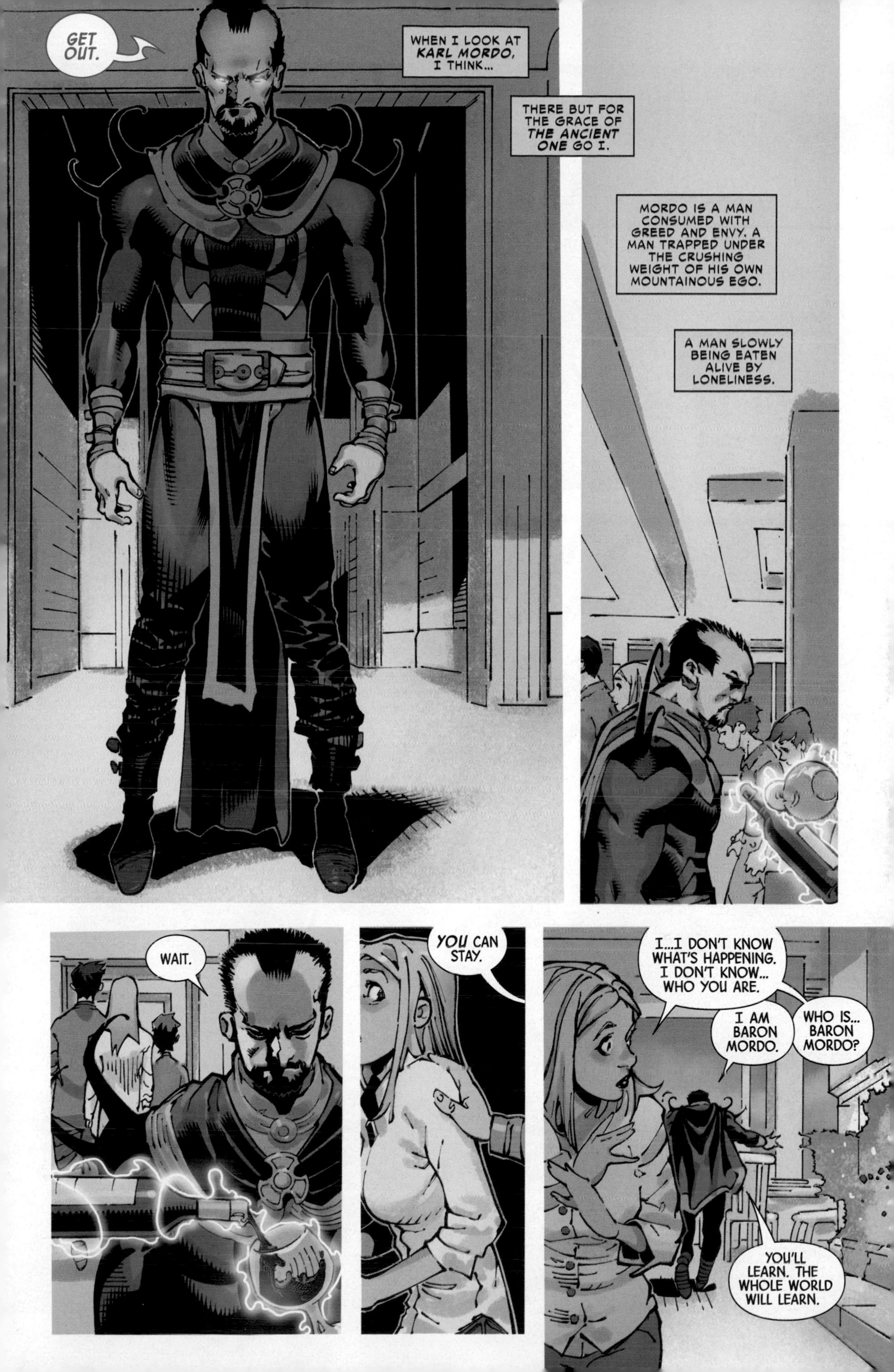
GET OUT.
WHEN I LOOK AT KARL MORDO, I THINK...
THERE BUT FOR THE GRACE OF THE ANCIENT ONE GO I.
MORDO IS A MAN CONSUMED WITH GREED AND ENVY. A MAN TRAPPED UNDER THE CRUSHING WEIGHT OF HIS OWN MOUNTAINOUS EGO.
A MAN SLOWLY BEING EATEN ALIVE BY LONELINESS.
WAIT.
YOU CAN STAY.
I...I DON'T KNOW WHAT'S HAPPENING. I DON'T KNOW... WHO YOU ARE.
I AM BARON MORDO.
WHO IS... BARON MORDO?
YOU'LL LEARN. THE WHOLE WORLD WILL LEARN.

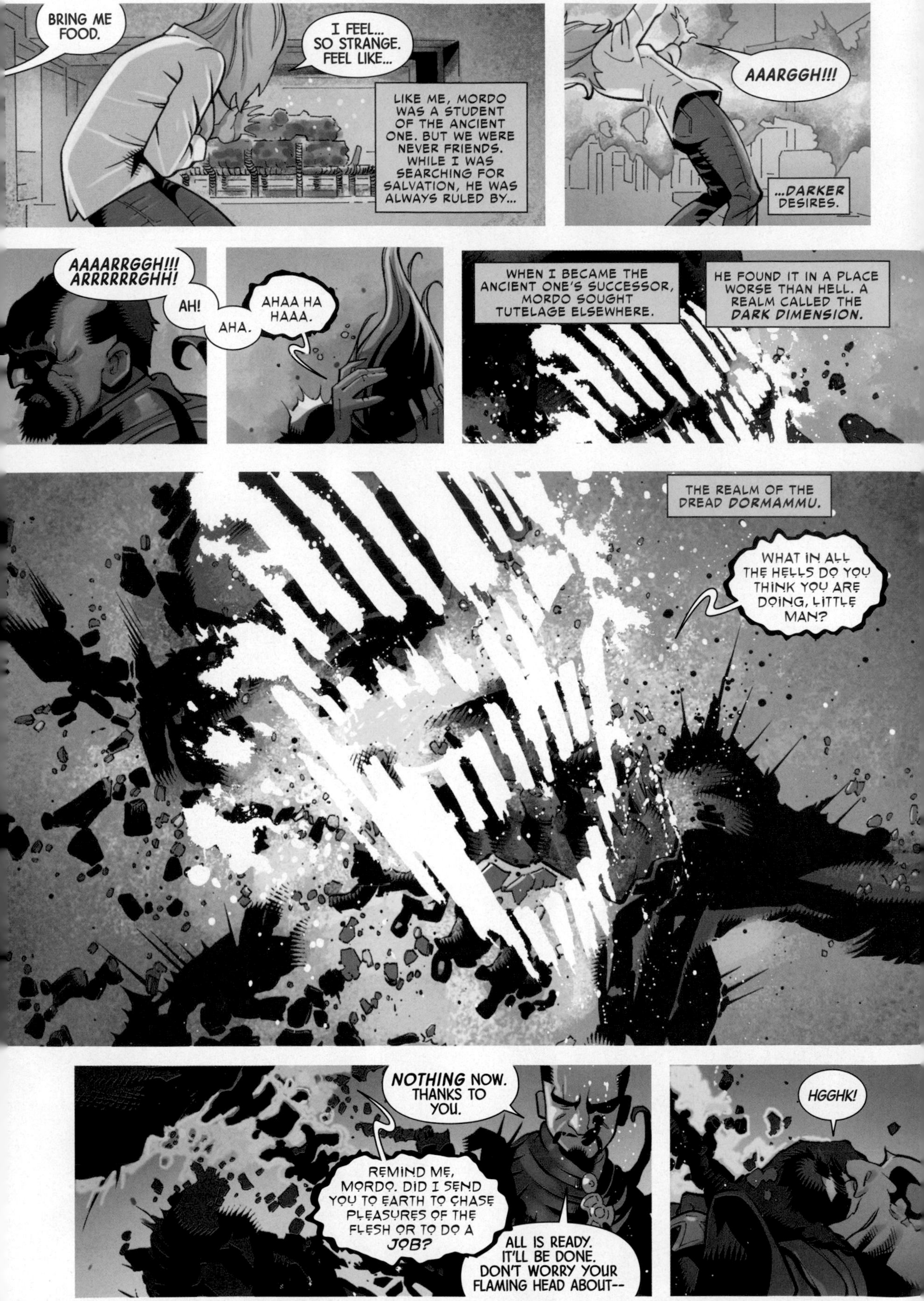
BRING ME FOOD.
I FEEL... SO STRANGE. FEEL LIKE...
LIKE ME, MORDO WAS A STUDENT OF THE ANCIENT ONE. BUT WE WERE NEVER FRIENDS. WHILE I WAS SEARCHING FOR SALVATION, HE WAS ALWAYS RULED BY...
AAARGGH!!!
...DARKER DESIRES.
AAAARRGGH!!! ARRRRRRGHH!
AH!
AHA.
AHAA HA HAAA.
WHEN I BECAME THE ANCIENT ONE'S SUCCESSOR, MORDO SOUGHT TUTELAGE ELSEWHERE.
HE FOUND IT IN A PLACE WORSE THAN HELL. A REALM CALLED THE DARK DIMENSION.
THE REALM OF THE DREAD DORMAMMU.
WHAT IN ALL THE HELLS DO YOU THINK YOU ARE DOING, LITTLE MAN?
NOTHING NOW. THANKS TO YOU.
REMIND ME, MORDO. DID I SEND YOU TO EARTH TO CHASE PLEASURES OF THE FLESH OR TO DO A JOB?
ALL IS READY. IT'LL BE DONE. DON'T WORRY YOUR FLAMING HEAD ABOUT--
HGGHK!

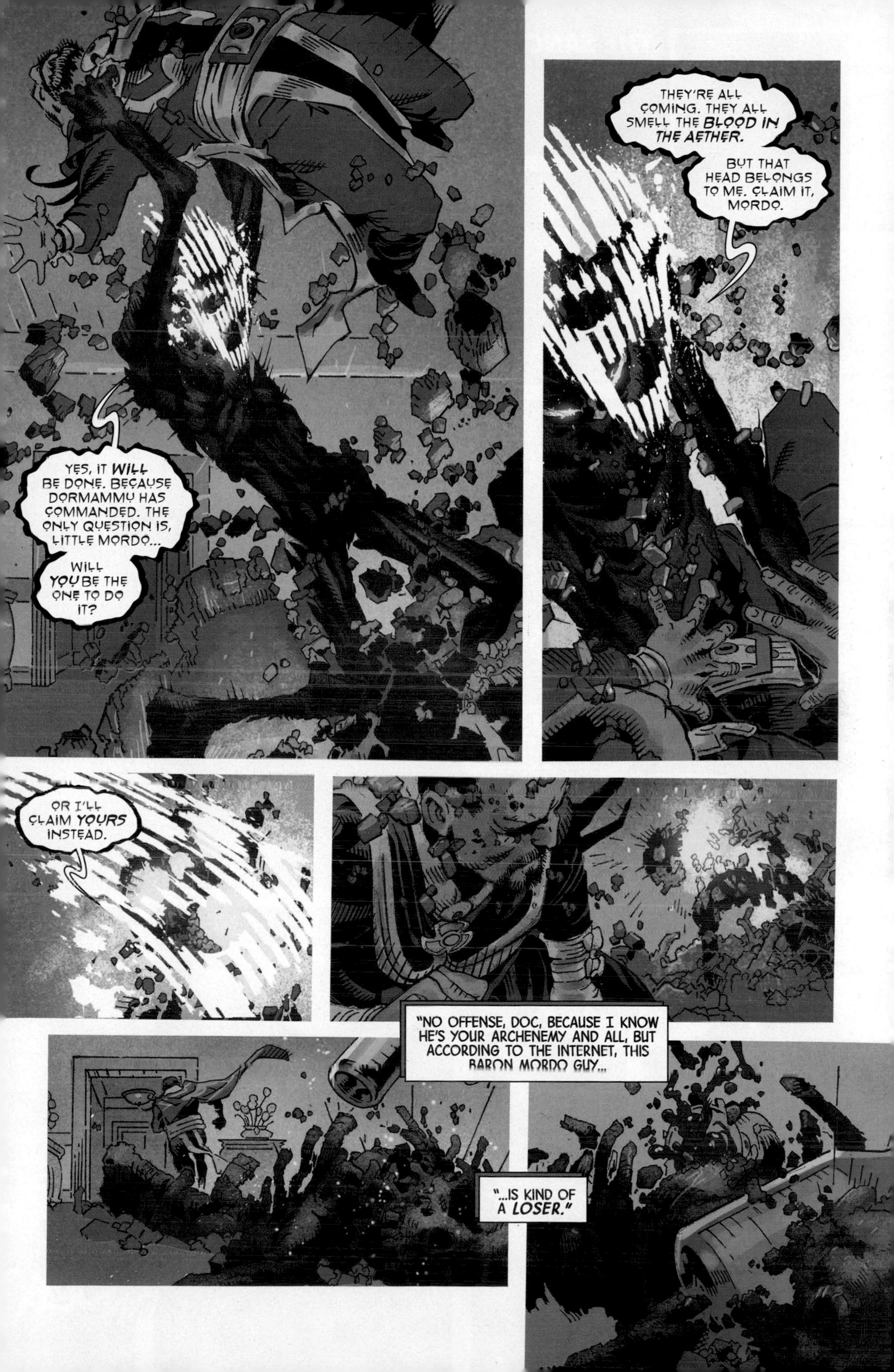
YES, IT WILL BE DONE. BECAUSE DORMAMMU HAS COMMANDED. THE ONLY QUESTION IS, LITTLE MORDO...
WILL YOU BE THE ONE TO DO IT?
THEY'RE ALL COMING. THEY ALL SMELL THE BLOOD IN THE AETHER.
BUT THAT HEAD BELONGS TO ME. CLAIM IT, MORDO.
OR I'LL CLAIM YOURS INSTEAD.
"NO OFFENSE, DOC, BECAUSE I KNOW HE'S YOUR ARCHENEMY AND ALL, BUT ACCORDING TO THE INTERNET, THIS BARON MORDO GUY...
"...IS KIND OF A LOSER."

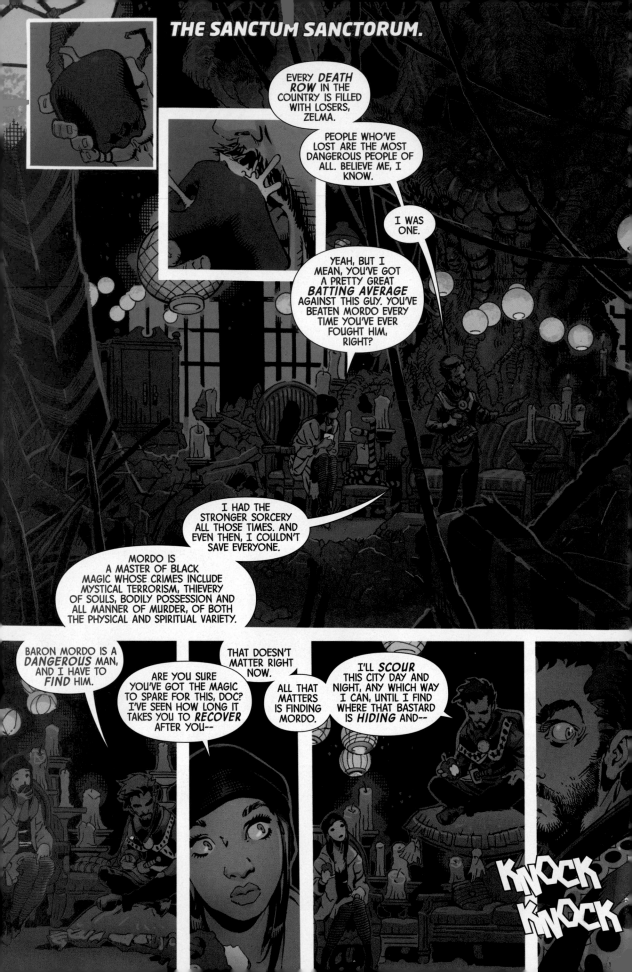

EVERY *DEATH ROW* IN THE COUNTRY IS FILLED WITH LOSERS, ZELMA.

PEOPLE WHO'VE LOST ARE THE MOST DANGEROUS PEOPLE OF ALL. BELIEVE ME, I KNOW.

I WAS ONE.

YEAH, BUT I MEAN, YOU'VE GOT A PRETTY GREAT *BATTING AVERAGE* AGAINST THIS GUY. YOU'VE BEATEN MORDO EVERY TIME YOU'VE EVER FOUGHT HIM, RIGHT?

I HAD THE STRONGER SORCERY ALL THOSE TIMES. AND EVEN THEN, I COULDN'T SAVE EVERYONE.

MORDO IS A MASTER OF BLACK MAGIC WHOSE CRIMES INCLUDE MYSTICAL TERRORISM, THIEVERY OF SOULS, BODILY POSSESSION AND ALL MANNER OF MURDER, OF BOTH THE PHYSICAL AND SPIRITUAL VARIETY.

BARON MORDO IS A *DANGEROUS* MAN, AND I HAVE TO *FIND* HIM.

ARE YOU SURE YOU'VE GOT THE MAGIC TO SPARE FOR THIS, DOC? I'VE SEEN HOW LONG IT TAKES YOU TO *RECOVER* AFTER YOU--

THAT DOESN'T MATTER RIGHT NOW.

ALL THAT MATTERS IS FINDING MORDO.

I'LL *SCOUR* THIS CITY DAY AND NIGHT, ANY WHICH WAY I CAN, UNTIL I FIND WHERE THAT BASTARD IS *HIDING* AND--

KNOCK KNOCK

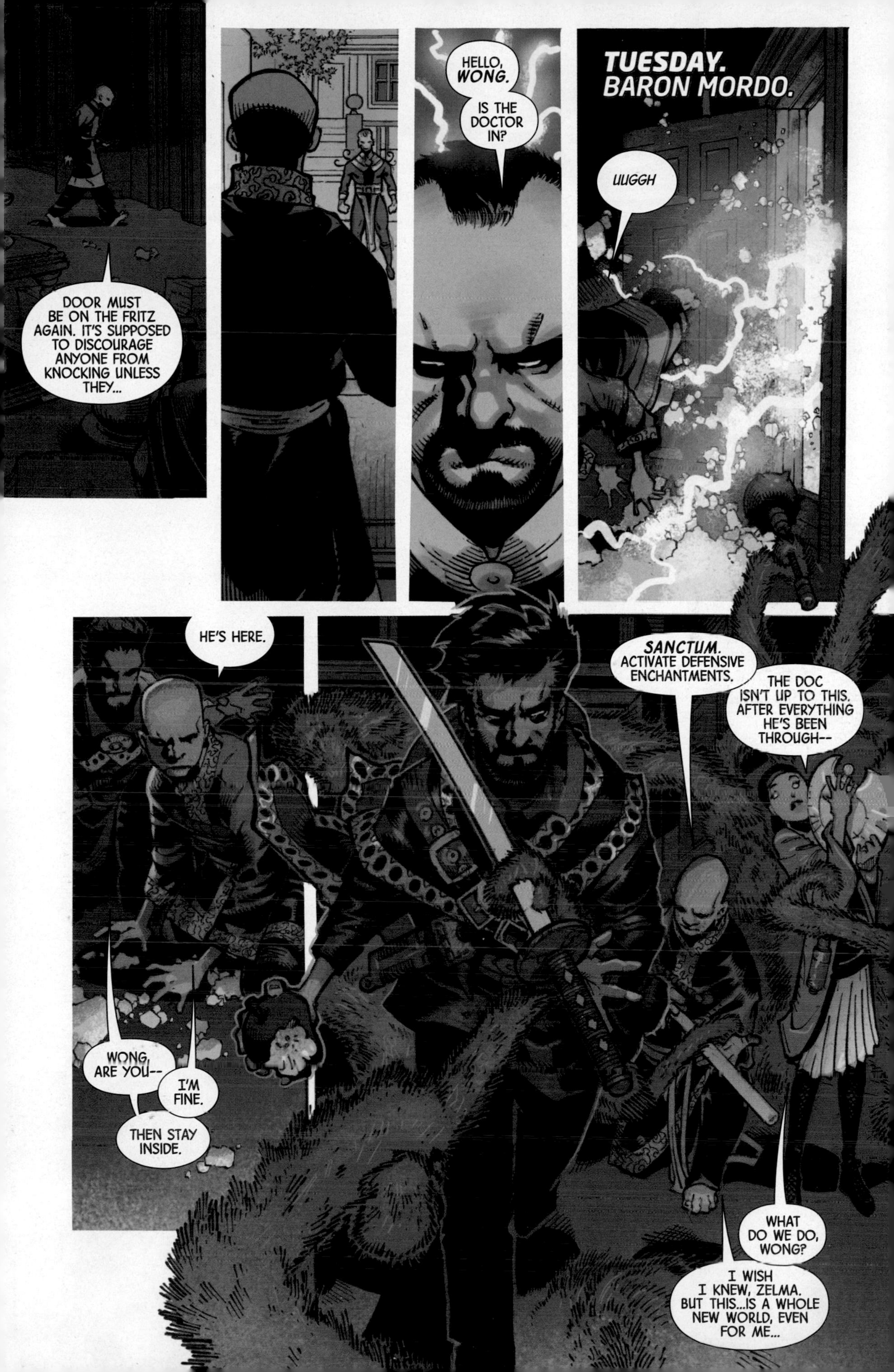
DOOR MUST BE ON THE FRITZ AGAIN. IT'S SUPPOSED TO DISCOURAGE ANYONE FROM KNOCKING UNLESS THEY...
HELLO, WONG.
IS THE DOCTOR IN?
TUESDAY. BARON MORDO.
UUGGH
HE'S HERE.
SANCTUM. ACTIVATE DEFENSIVE ENCHANTMENTS.
THE DOC ISN'T UP TO THIS. AFTER EVERYTHING HE'S BEEN THROUGH--
WONG, ARE YOU--
I'M FINE.
THEN STAY INSIDE.
WHAT DO WE DO, WONG?
I WISH I KNEW, ZELMA. BUT THIS...IS A WHOLE NEW WORLD, EVEN FOR ME...

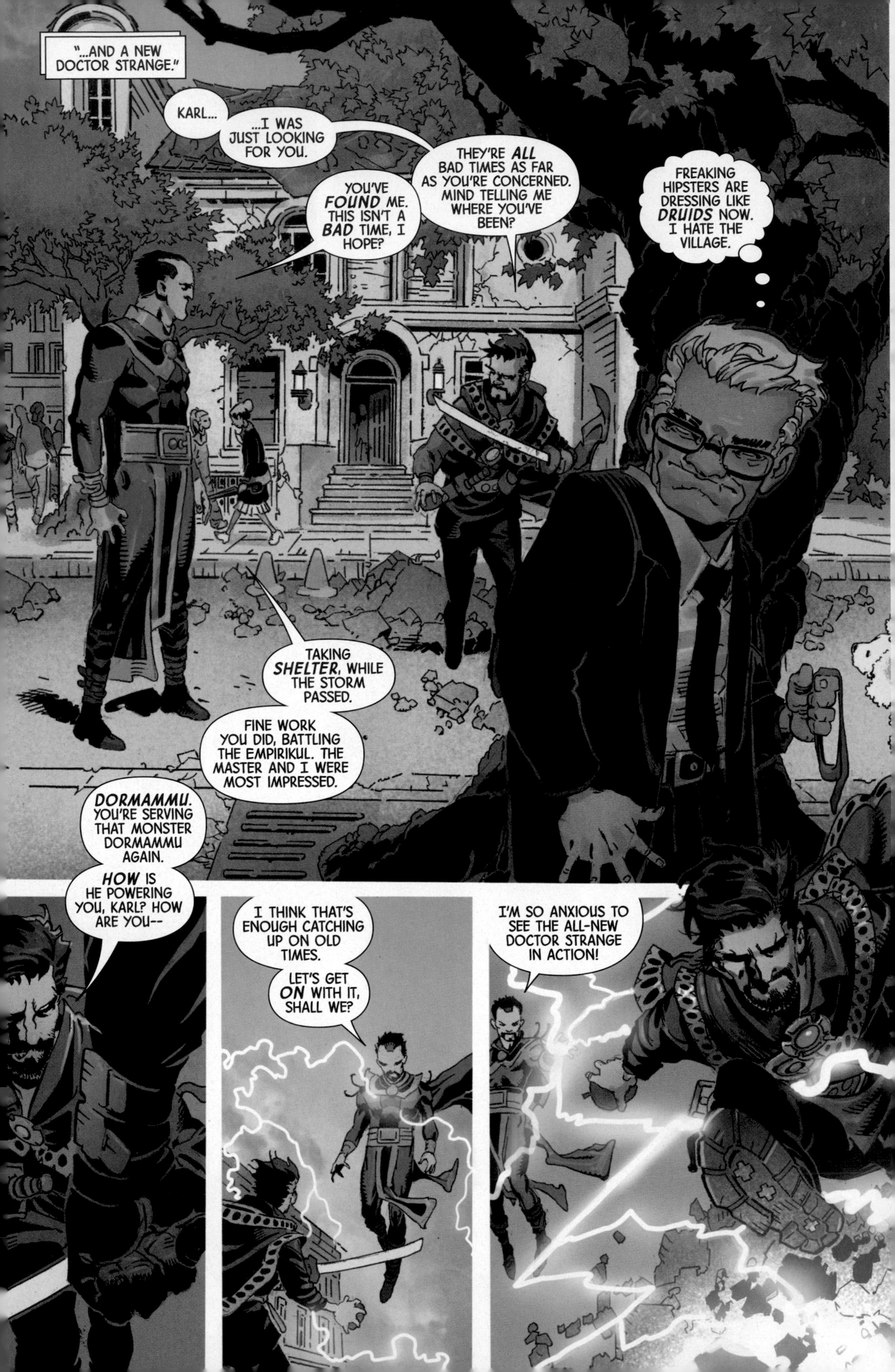
"...AND A NEW DOCTOR STRANGE."
KARL...
...I WAS JUST LOOKING FOR YOU.
YOU'VE FOUND ME. THIS ISN'T A BAD TIME, I HOPE?
THEY'RE ALL BAD TIMES AS FAR AS YOU'RE CONCERNED. MIND TELLING ME WHERE YOU'VE BEEN?
FREAKING HIPSTERS ARE DRESSING LIKE DRUIDS NOW. I HATE THE VILLAGE.
TAKING SHELTER, WHILE THE STORM PASSED.
FINE WORK YOU DID, BATTLING THE EMPIRIKUL. THE MASTER AND I WERE MOST IMPRESSED.
DORMAMMU. YOU'RE SERVING THAT MONSTER DORMAMMU AGAIN.
HOW IS HE POWERING YOU, KARL? HOW ARE YOU--
I THINK THAT'S ENOUGH CATCHING UP ON OLD TIMES.
LET'S GET ON WITH IT, SHALL WE?
I'M SO ANXIOUS TO SEE THE ALL-NEW DOCTOR STRANGE IN ACTION!

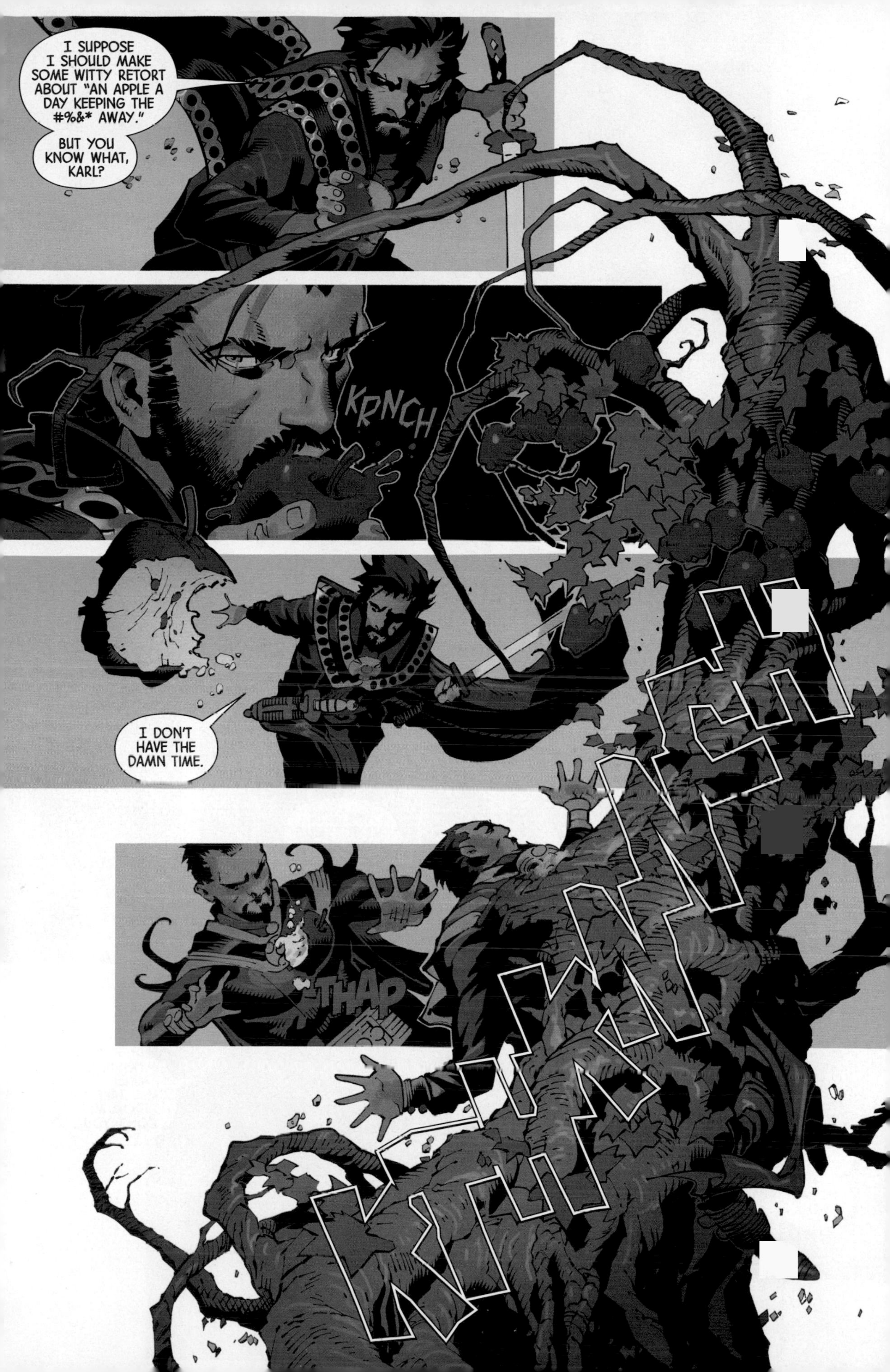
I SUPPOSE I SHOULD MAKE SOME WITTY RETORT ABOUT "AN APPLE A DAY KEEPING THE #%&* AWAY."
BUT YOU KNOW WHAT, KARL?
KRNCH
I DON'T HAVE THE DAMN TIME.
THAP

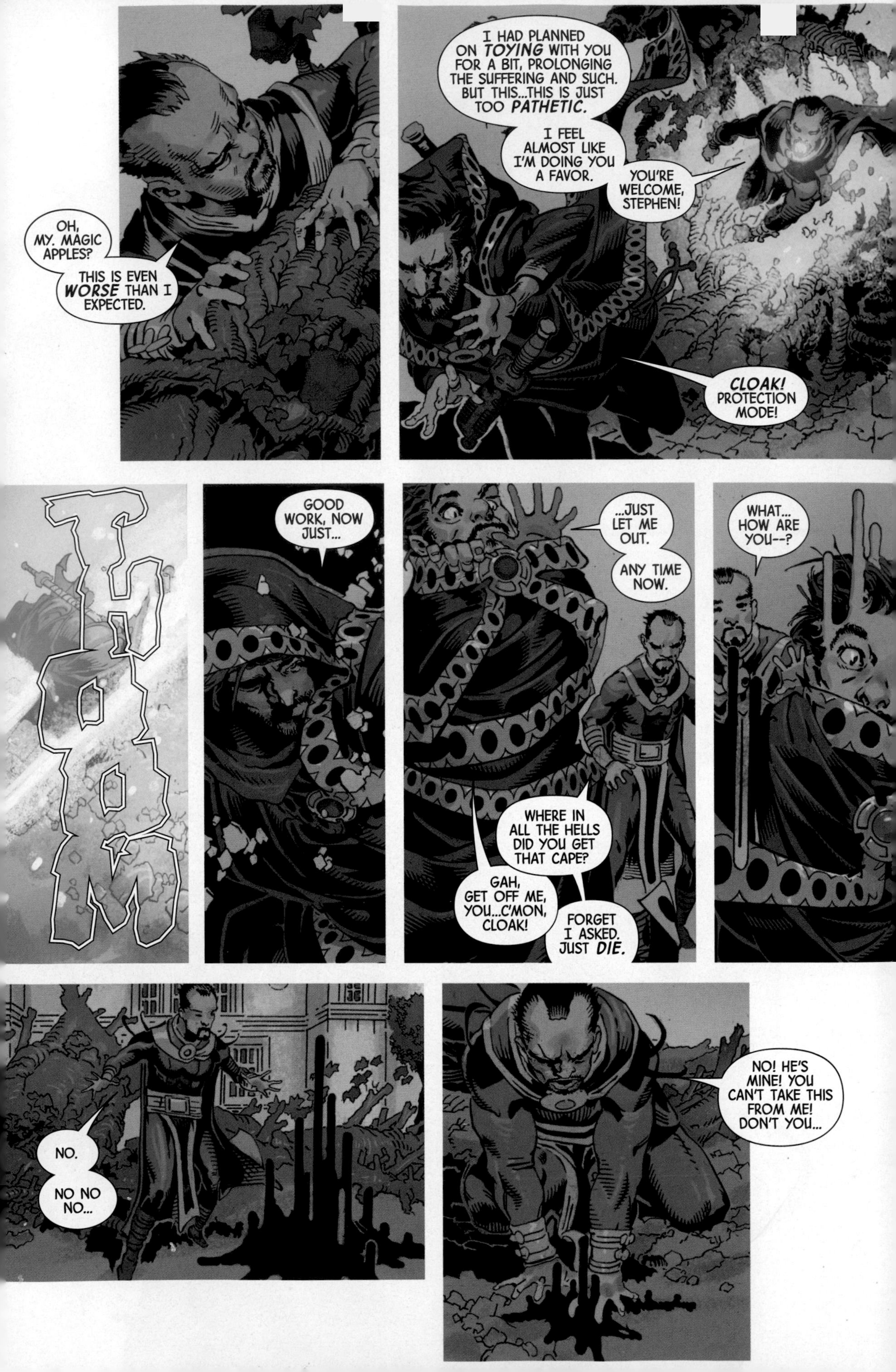
OH, MY. MAGIC APPLES?
THIS IS EVEN WORSE THAN I EXPECTED.
I HAD PLANNED ON TOYING WITH YOU FOR A BIT, PROLONGING THE SUFFERING AND SUCH. BUT THIS...THIS IS JUST TOO PATHETIC.
I FEEL ALMOST LIKE I'M DOING YOU A FAVOR.
YOU'RE WELCOME, STEPHEN!
CLOAK! PROTECTION MODE!
GOOD WORK, NOW JUST...
...JUST LET ME OUT.
ANY TIME NOW.
WHERE IN ALL THE HELLS DID YOU GET THAT CAPE?
GAH, GET OFF ME, YOU...C'MON, CLOAK!
FORGET I ASKED. JUST DIE.
WHAT... HOW ARE YOU--?
NO.
NO NO NO...
NO! HE'S MINE! YOU CAN'T TAKE THIS FROM ME! DON'T YOU...

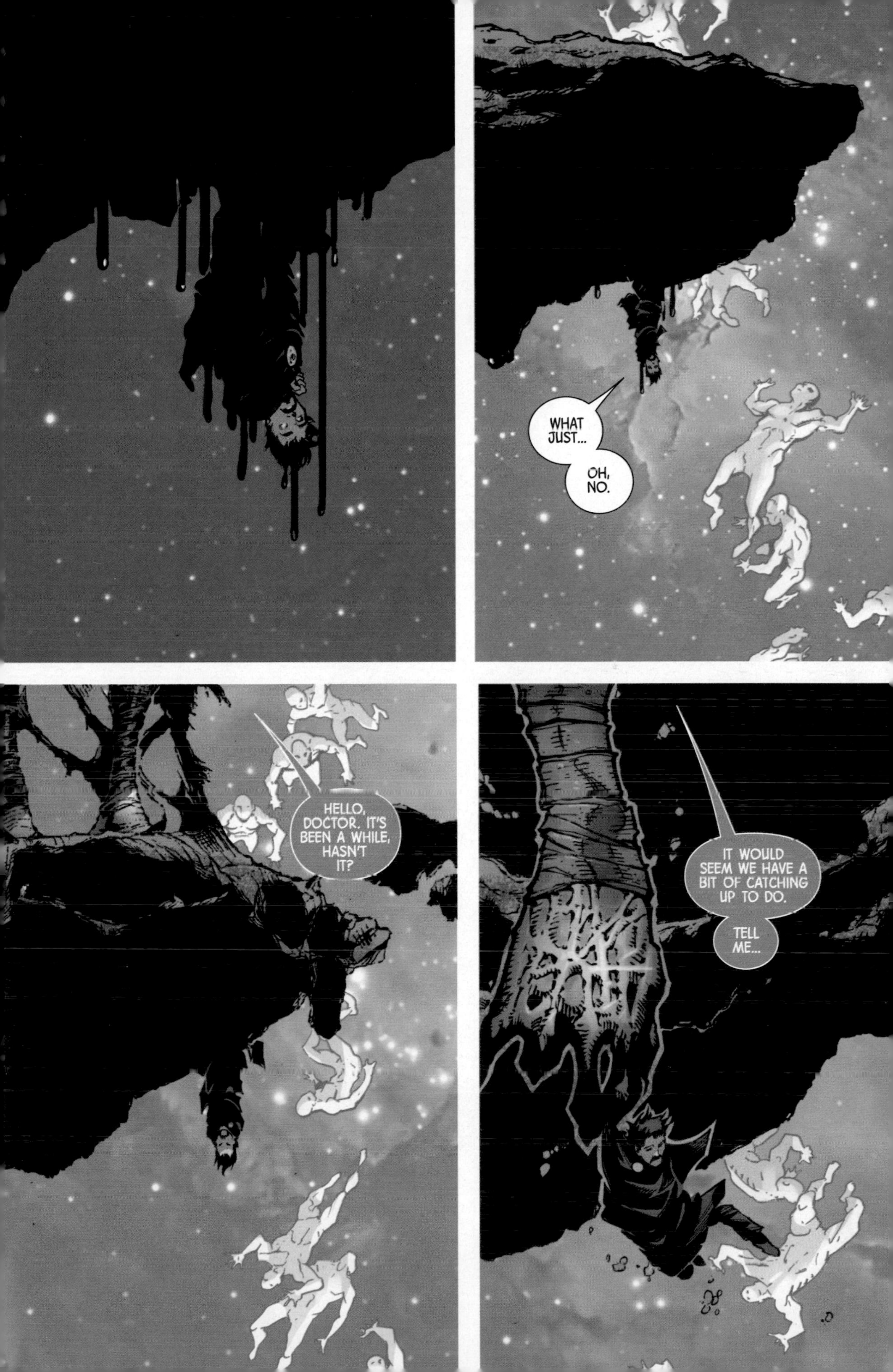
WHAT JUST...
OH, NO.
HELLO, DOCTOR. IT'S BEEN A WHILE, HASN'T IT?
IT WOULD SEEM WE HAVE A BIT OF CATCHING UP TO DO.
TELL ME...

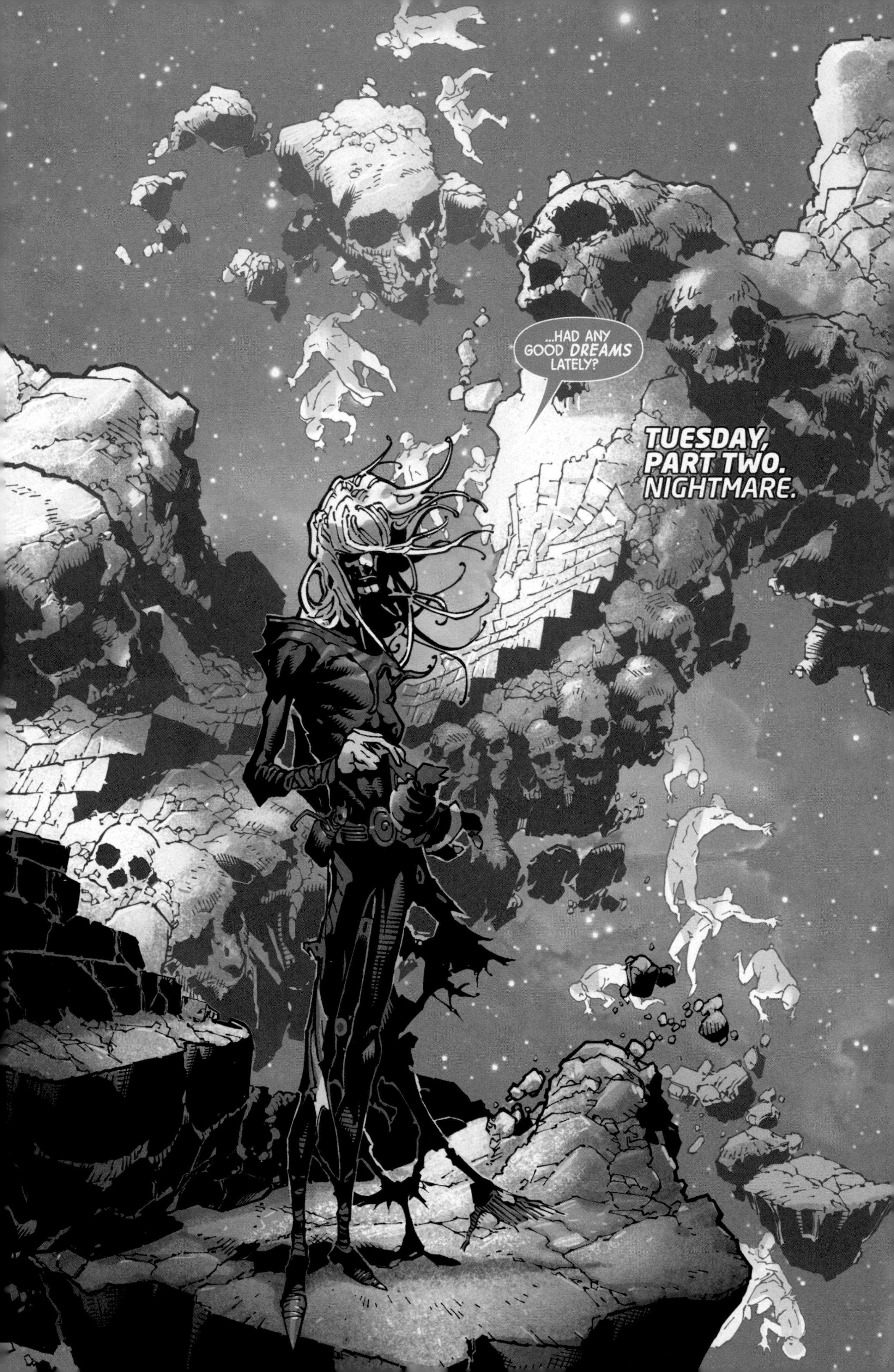

...HAD ANY GOOD DREAMS LATELY?
TUESDAY, PART TWO. NIGHTMARE.

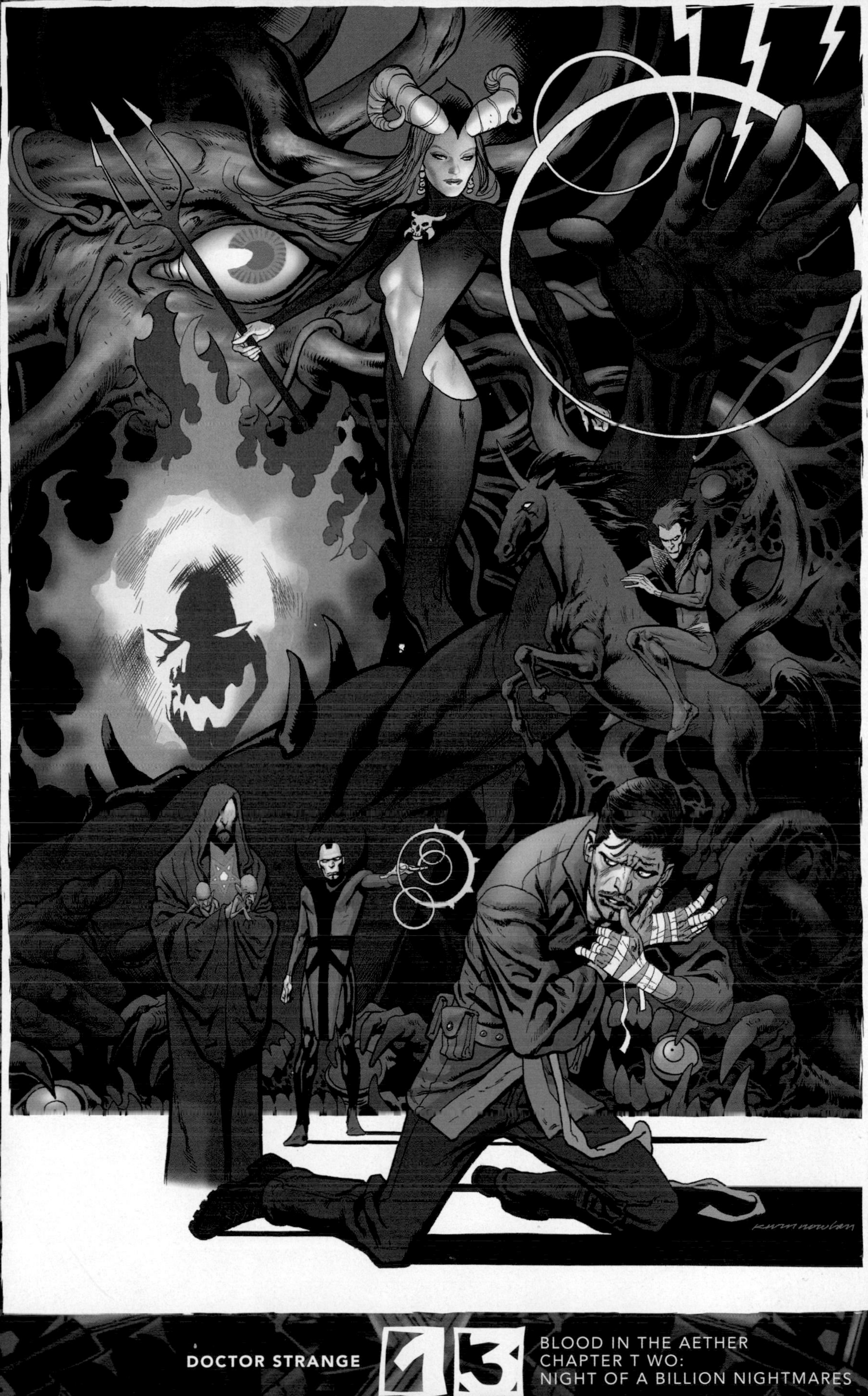
kevin nowlan

DOCTOR STRANGE 13

BLOOD IN THE AETHER
CHAPTER TWO:
NIGHT OF A BILLION NIGHTMARES

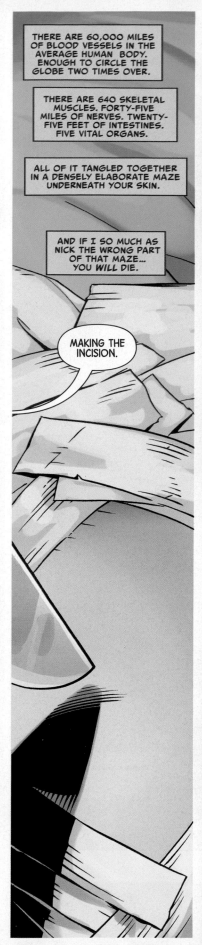

THERE ARE 60,000 MILES OF BLOOD VESSELS IN THE AVERAGE HUMAN BODY. ENOUGH TO CIRCLE THE GLOBE TWO TIMES OVER.

THERE ARE 640 SKELETAL MUSCLES. FORTY-FIVE MILES OF NERVES. TWENTY-FIVE FEET OF INTESTINES. FIVE VITAL ORGANS.

ALL OF IT TANGLED TOGETHER IN A DENSELY ELABORATE MAZE UNDERNEATH YOUR SKIN.

AND IF I SO MUCH AS NICK THE WRONG PART OF THAT MAZE... YOU *WILL* DIE.

MAKING THE INCISION.

YET I NAVIGATE THAT LABYRINTH MULTIPLE TIMES EVERY WEEK.

AND I'VE NEVER ONCE FAILED TO DETERMINE THE CORRECT OPERATIVE LOCATION. AND MAKE THE INCISION THAT *SAVES* YOUR LIFE INSTEAD OF ENDS IT.

I PUT MY PANTS ON THE SAME AS ANYONE. EXCEPT ONCE THEY'RE ON...I CUT PEOPLE OPEN AND READ THEIR INSIDES THE WAY OTHERS READ A BOOK.

I'M DOCTOR STEPHEN STRANGE, *THE WORLD'S GREATEST SURGEON.*

AND THIS IS WHAT I WAS BORN TO DO.

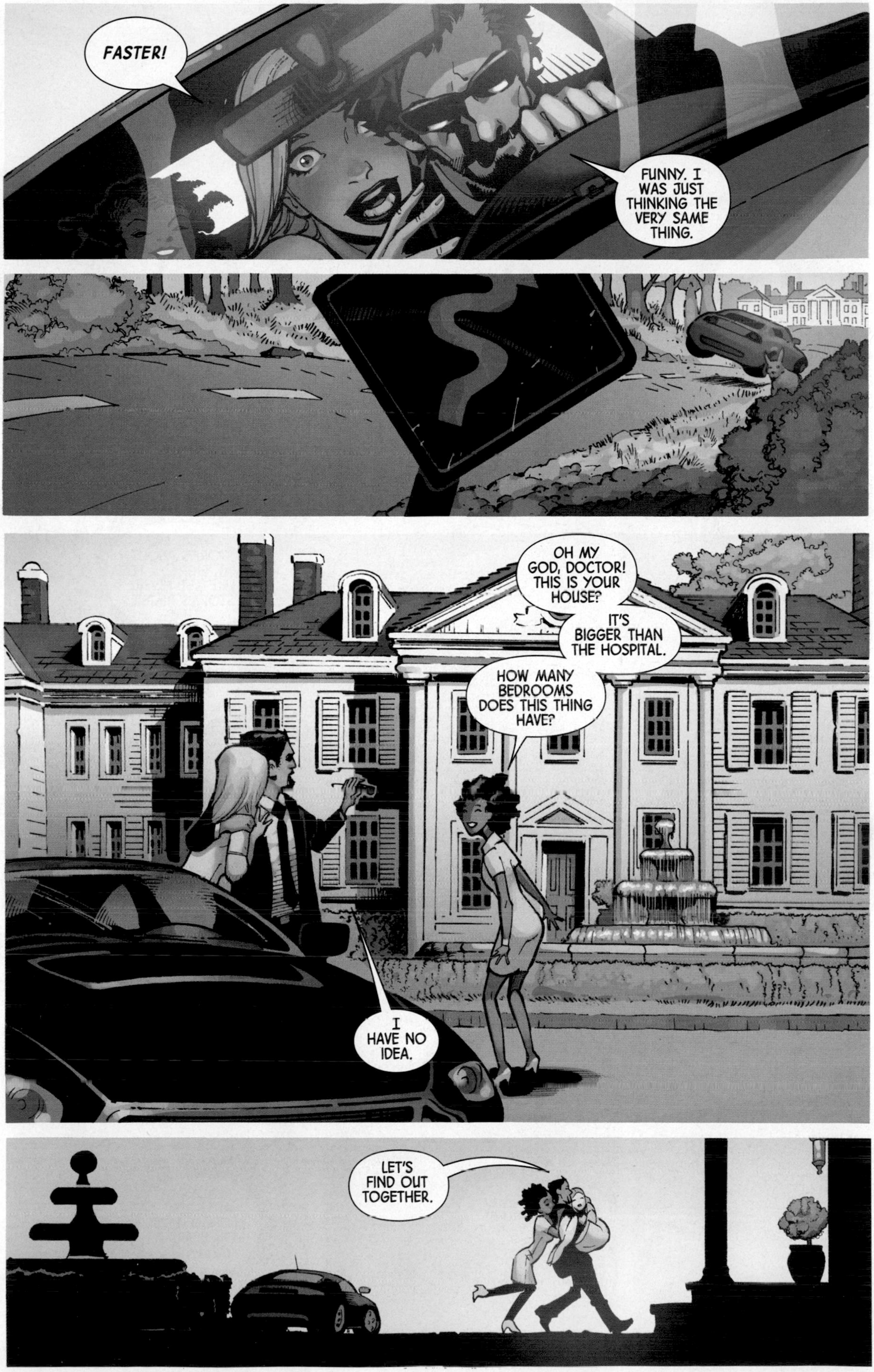
FASTER!
FUNNY. I WAS JUST THINKING THE VERY SAME THING.
OH MY GOD, DOCTOR! THIS IS YOUR HOUSE?
IT'S BIGGER THAN THE HOSPITAL.
HOW MANY BEDROOMS DOES THIS THING HAVE?
I HAVE NO IDEA.
LET'S FIND OUT TOGETHER.

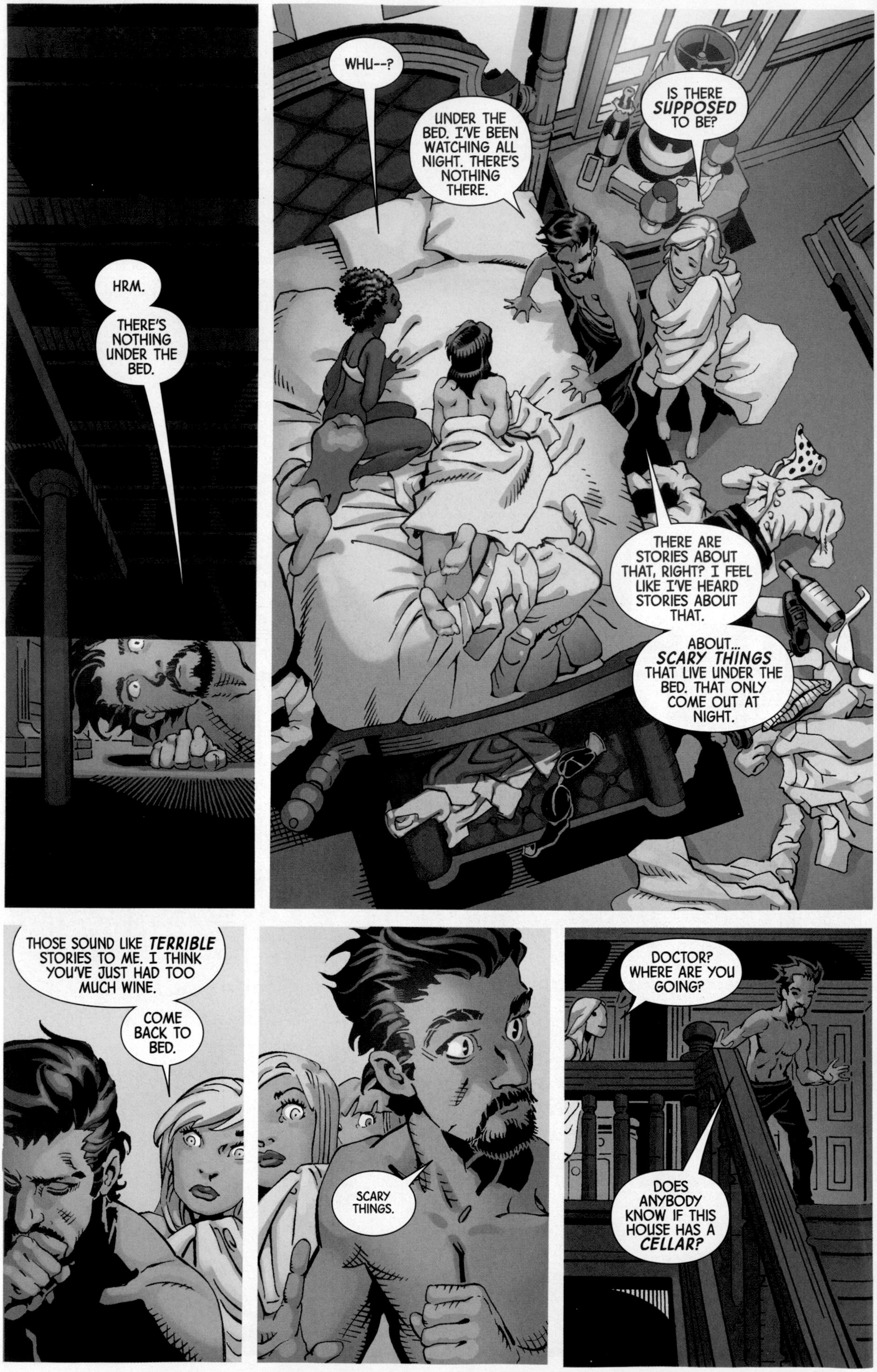
HRM.
THERE'S NOTHING UNDER THE BED.
WHU--?
UNDER THE BED. I'VE BEEN WATCHING ALL NIGHT. THERE'S NOTHING THERE.
IS THERE SUPPOSED TO BE?
THERE ARE STORIES ABOUT THAT, RIGHT? I FEEL LIKE I'VE HEARD STORIES ABOUT THAT.
ABOUT... SCARY THINGS THAT LIVE UNDER THE BED. THAT ONLY COME OUT AT NIGHT.
THOSE SOUND LIKE TERRIBLE STORIES TO ME. I THINK YOU'VE JUST HAD TOO MUCH WINE.
COME BACK TO BED.
SCARY THINGS.
DOCTOR? WHERE ARE YOU GOING?
DOES ANYBODY KNOW IF THIS HOUSE HAS A CELLAR?

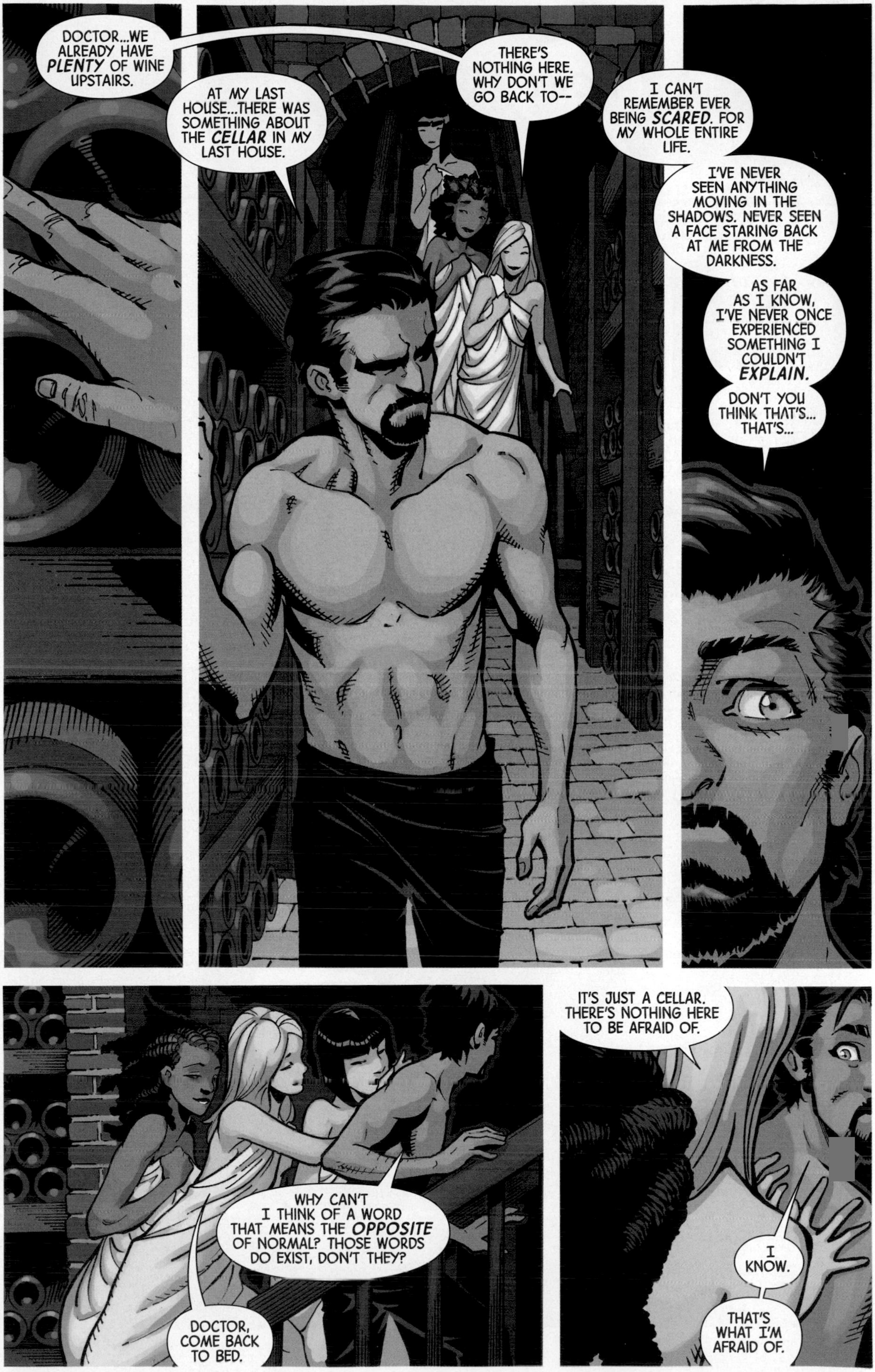
DOCTOR...WE ALREADY HAVE PLENTY OF WINE UPSTAIRS.
AT MY LAST HOUSE...THERE WAS SOMETHING ABOUT THE CELLAR IN MY LAST HOUSE.
THERE'S NOTHING HERE. WHY DON'T WE GO BACK TO--
I CAN'T REMEMBER EVER BEING SCARED. FOR MY WHOLE ENTIRE LIFE.
I'VE NEVER SEEN ANYTHING MOVING IN THE SHADOWS. NEVER SEEN A FACE STARING BACK AT ME FROM THE DARKNESS.
AS FAR AS I KNOW, I'VE NEVER ONCE EXPERIENCED SOMETHING I COULDN'T EXPLAIN.
DON'T YOU THINK THAT'S... THAT'S...
WHY CAN'T I THINK OF A WORD THAT MEANS THE OPPOSITE OF NORMAL? THOSE WORDS DO EXIST, DON'T THEY?
DOCTOR, COME BACK TO BED.
IT'S JUST A CELLAR. THERE'S NOTHING HERE TO BE AFRAID OF.
I KNOW.
THAT'S WHAT I'M AFRAID OF.

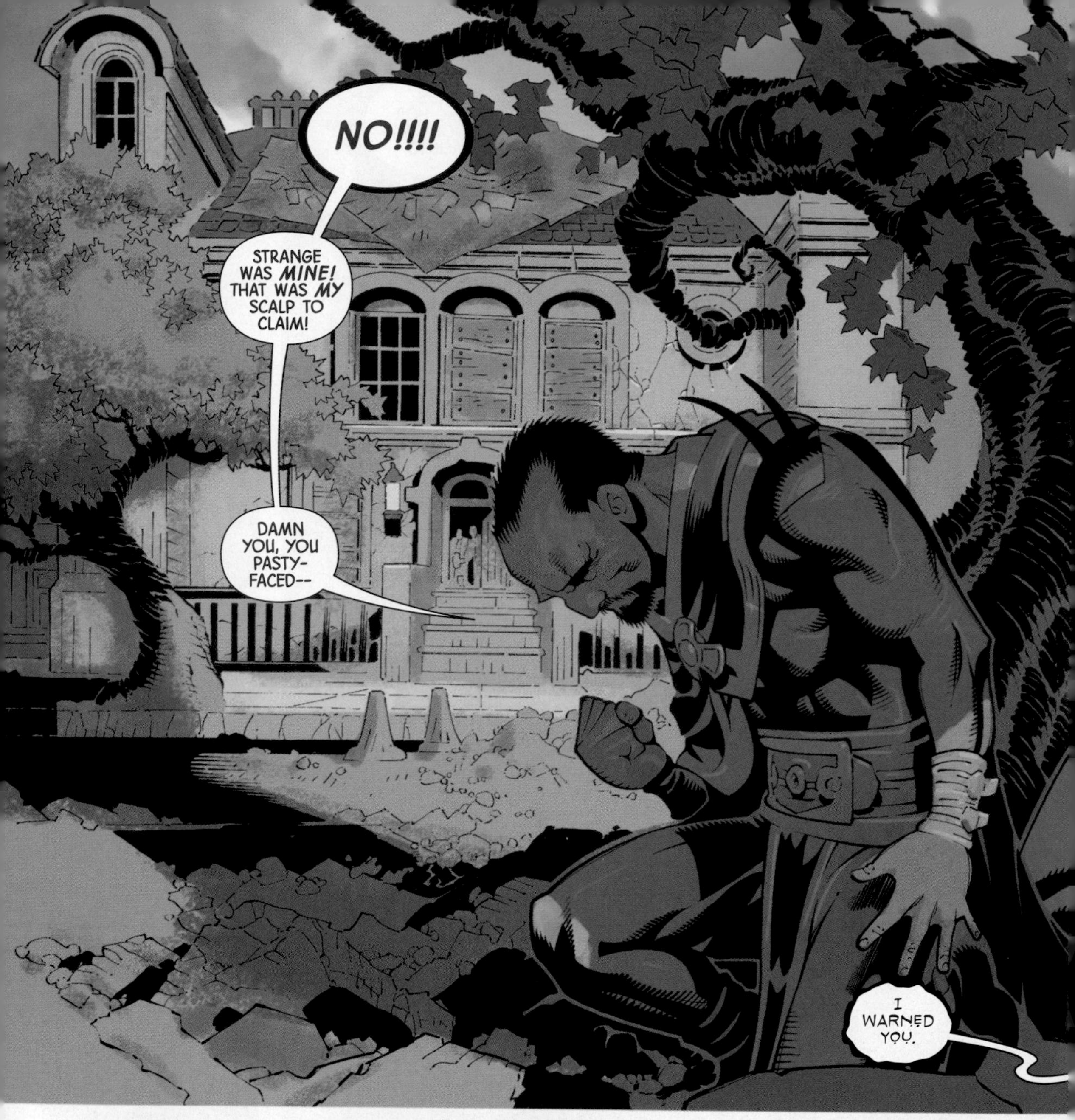
NO!!!!
STRANGE WAS MINE! THAT WAS MY SCALP TO CLAIM!
DAMN YOU, YOU PASTY-FACED--
I WARNED YOU.

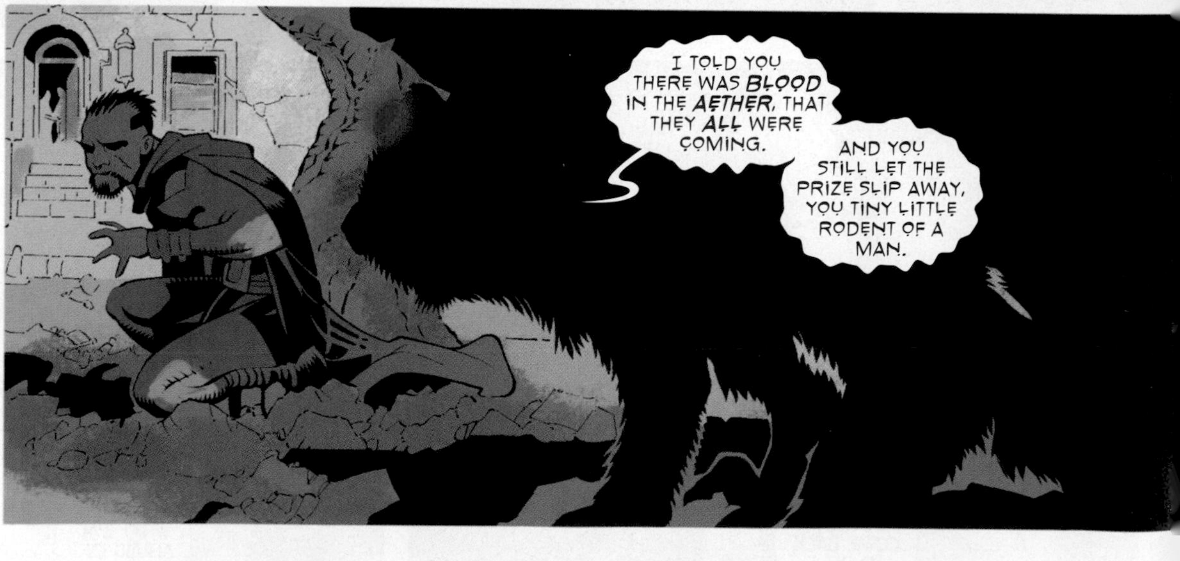
I TOLD YOU THERE WAS BLOOD IN THE AETHER, THAT THEY ALL WERE COMING.
AND YOU STILL LET THE PRIZE SLIP AWAY, YOU TINY LITTLE RODENT OF A MAN.

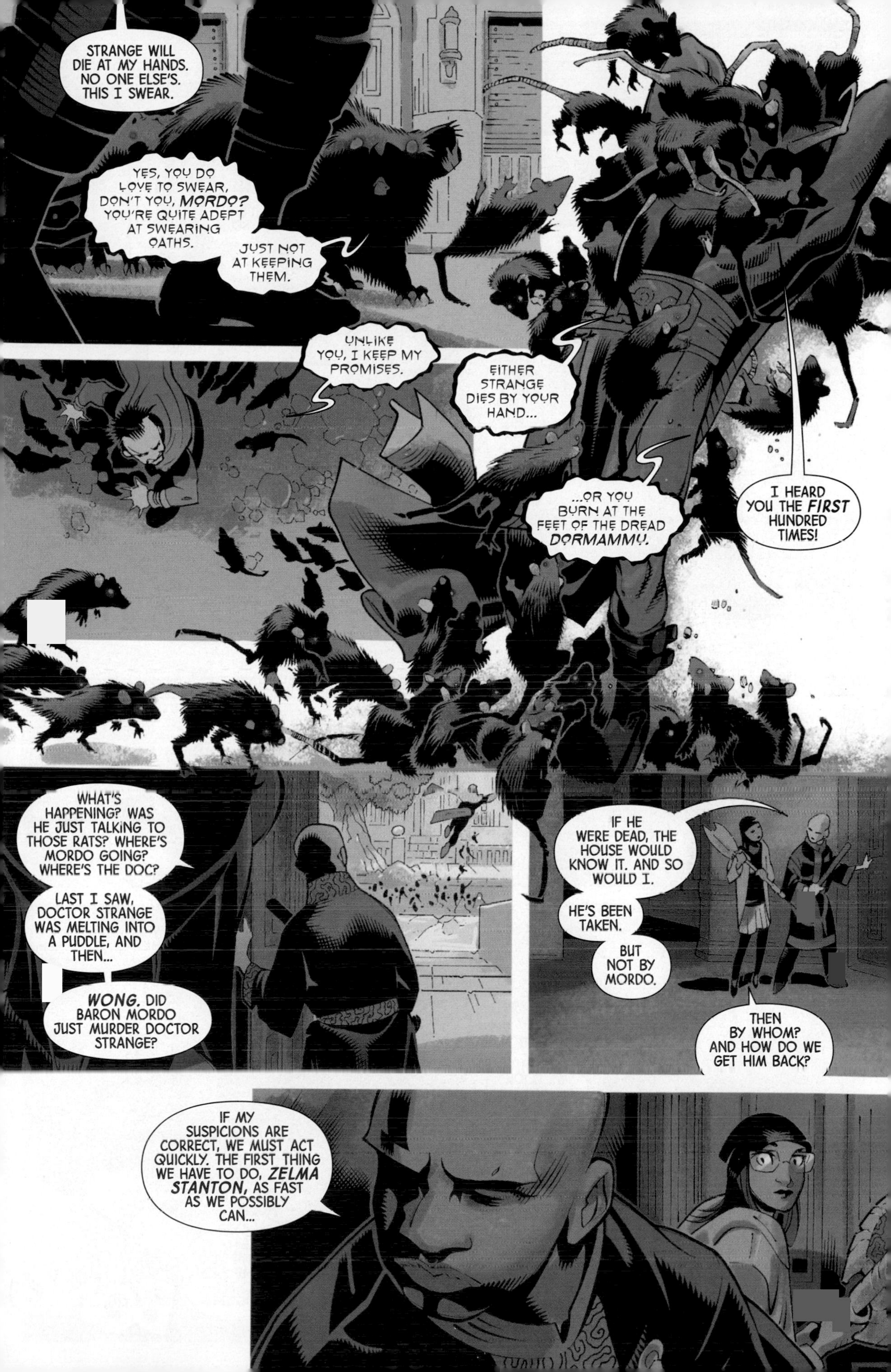

STRANGE WILL DIE AT MY HANDS. NO ONE ELSE'S. THIS I SWEAR.
YES, YOU DO LOVE TO SWEAR, DON'T YOU, MORDO? YOU'RE QUITE ADEPT AT SWEARING OATHS.
JUST NOT AT KEEPING THEM.
UNLIKE YOU, I KEEP MY PROMISES.
EITHER STRANGE DIES BY YOUR HAND...
...OR YOU BURN AT THE FEET OF THE DREAD DORMAMMU.
I HEARD YOU THE FIRST HUNDRED TIMES!
WHAT'S HAPPENING? WAS HE JUST TALKING TO THOSE RATS? WHERE'S MORDO GOING? WHERE'S THE DOC?
LAST I SAW, DOCTOR STRANGE WAS MELTING INTO A PUDDLE, AND THEN...
WONG. DID BARON MORDO JUST MURDER DOCTOR STRANGE?
IF HE WERE DEAD, THE HOUSE WOULD KNOW IT. AND SO WOULD I.
HE'S BEEN TAKEN.
BUT NOT BY MORDO.
THEN BY WHOM? AND HOW DO WE GET HIM BACK?
IF MY SUSPICIONS ARE CORRECT, WE MUST ACT QUICKLY. THE FIRST THING WE HAVE TO DO, ZELMA STANTON, AS FAST AS WE POSSIBLY CAN...

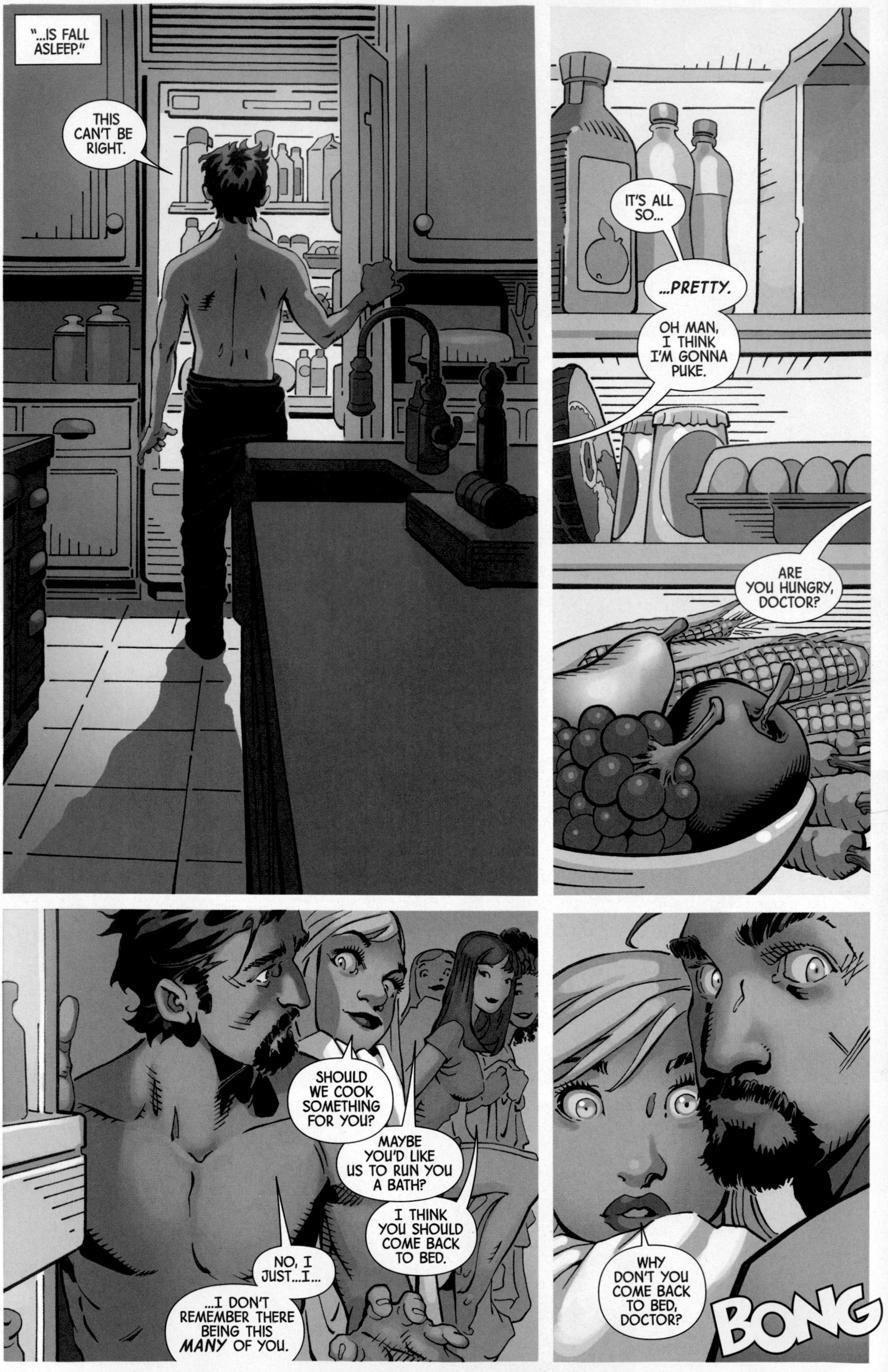
"...IS FALL ASLEEP."
THIS CAN'T BE RIGHT.
IT'S ALL SO...
...PRETTY.
OH MAN, I THINK I'M GONNA PUKE.
ARE YOU HUNGRY, DOCTOR?
SHOULD WE COOK SOMETHING FOR YOU?
MAYBE YOU'D LIKE US TO RUN YOU A BATH?
I THINK YOU SHOULD COME BACK TO BED.
NO, I JUST...I...
...I DON'T REMEMBER THERE BEING THIS *MANY* OF YOU.
WHY DON'T YOU COME BACK TO BED, DOCTOR?
BONG

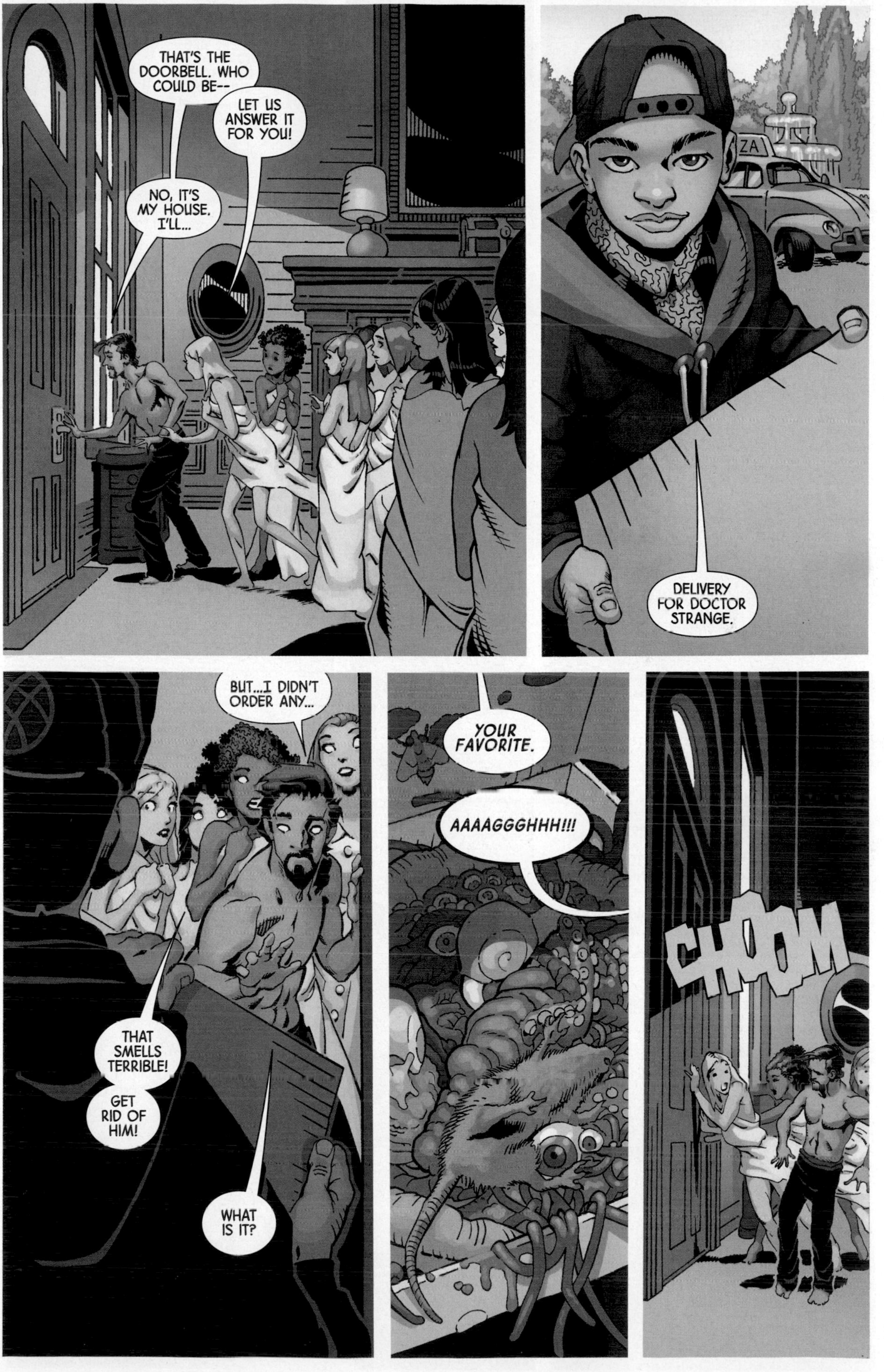
THAT'S THE DOORBELL. WHO COULD BE--
LET US ANSWER IT FOR YOU!
NO, IT'S MY HOUSE. I'LL...
ZA
DELIVERY FOR DOCTOR STRANGE.
BUT...I DIDN'T ORDER ANY...
THAT SMELLS TERRIBLE!
GET RID OF HIM!
WHAT IS IT?
YOUR FAVORITE.
AAAAGGGHHH!!!
CHOOM

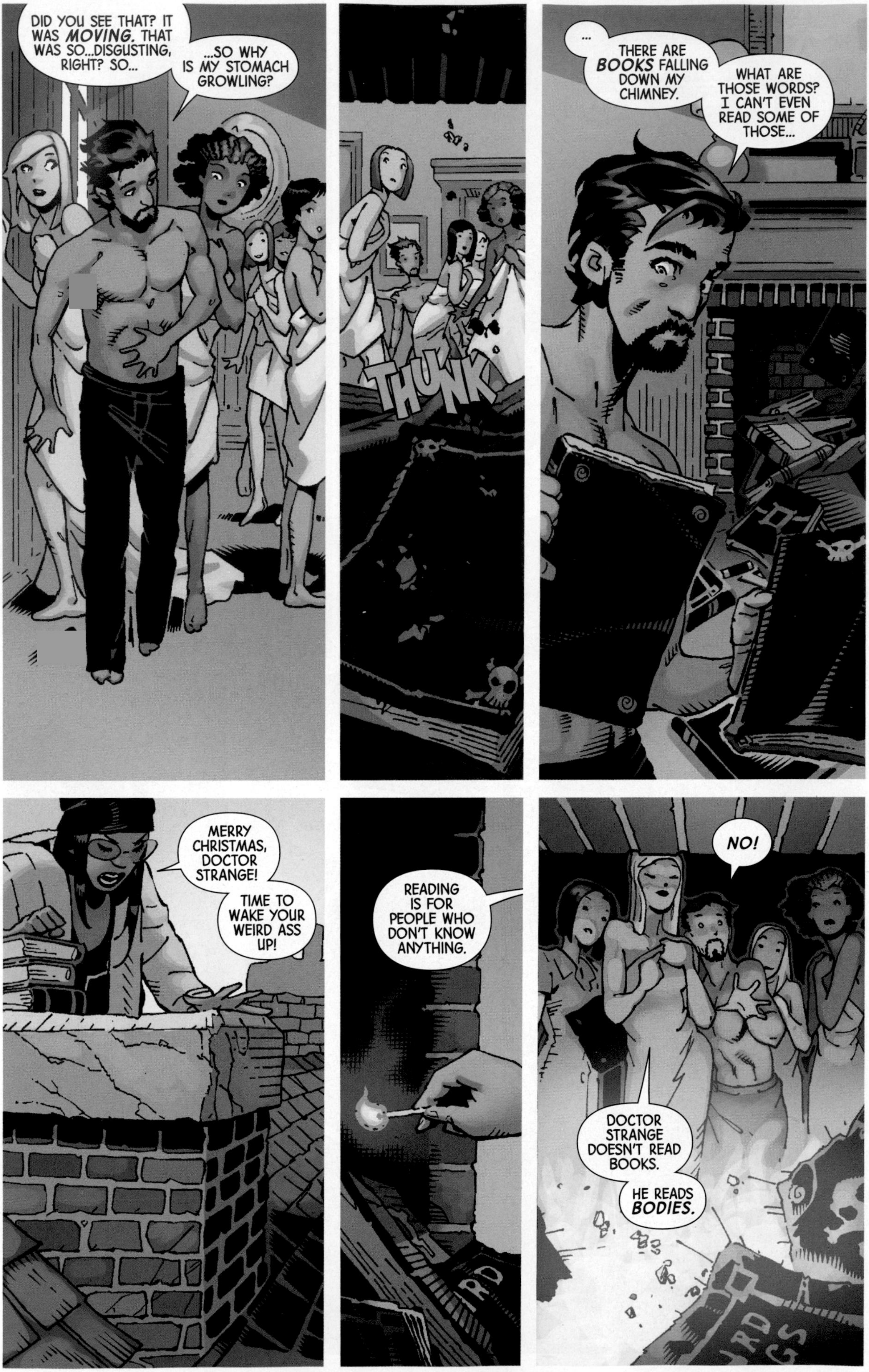
DID YOU SEE THAT? IT WAS MOVING. THAT WAS SO...DISGUSTING, RIGHT? SO...
...SO WHY IS MY STOMACH GROWLING?
THUNK
...
THERE ARE BOOKS FALLING DOWN MY CHIMNEY.
WHAT ARE THOSE WORDS? I CAN'T EVEN READ SOME OF THOSE...
MERRY CHRISTMAS, DOCTOR STRANGE!
TIME TO WAKE YOUR WEIRD ASS UP!
READING IS FOR PEOPLE WHO DON'T KNOW ANYTHING.
NO!
DOCTOR STRANGE DOESN'T READ BOOKS.
HE READS BODIES.

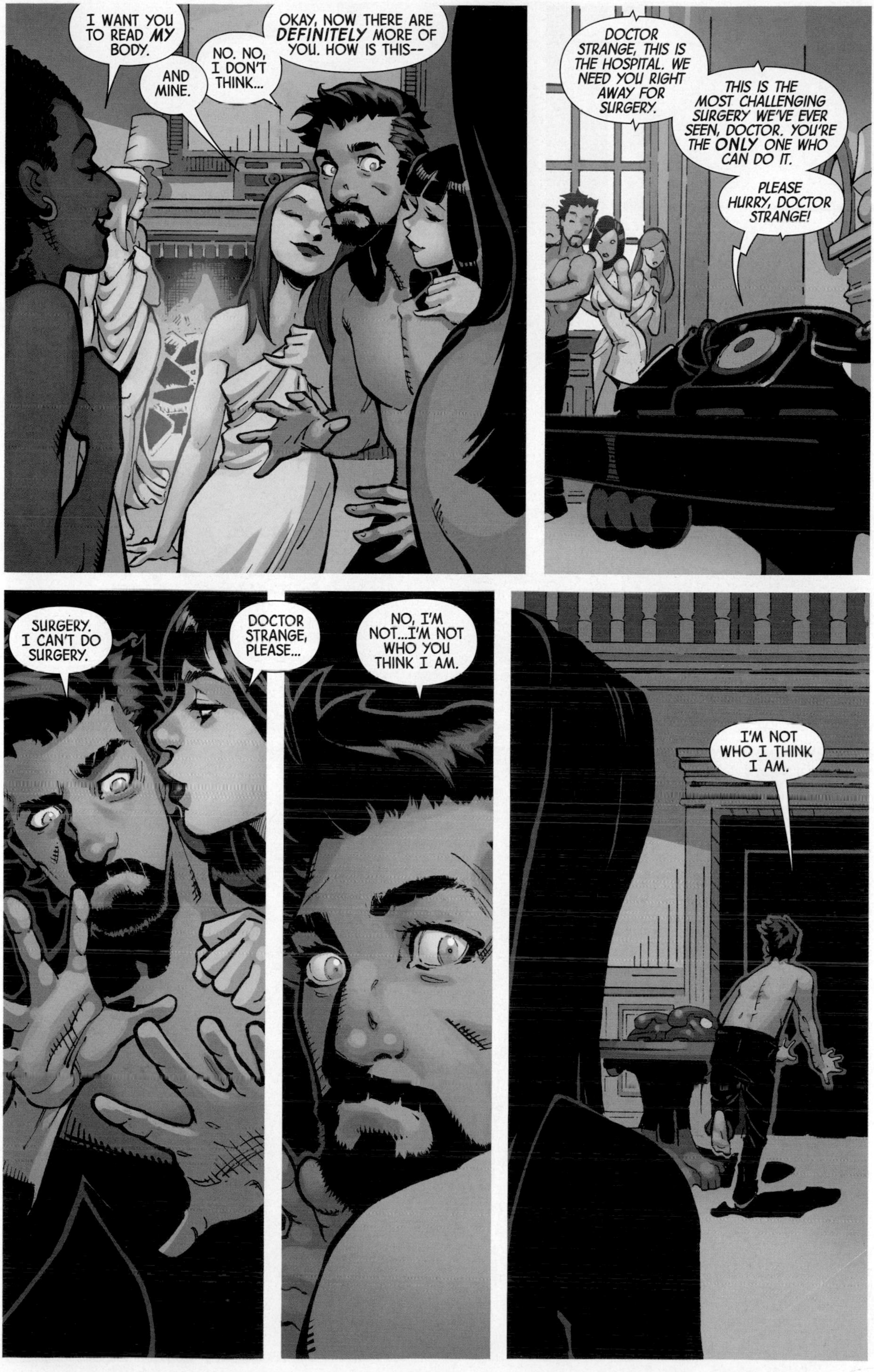
I WANT YOU TO READ MY BODY.
AND MINE.
NO. NO, I DON'T THINK...
OKAY, NOW THERE ARE DEFINITELY MORE OF YOU. HOW IS THIS--
DOCTOR STRANGE, THIS IS THE HOSPITAL. WE NEED YOU RIGHT AWAY FOR SURGERY.
THIS IS THE MOST CHALLENGING SURGERY WE'VE EVER SEEN, DOCTOR. YOU'RE THE ONLY ONE WHO CAN DO IT.
PLEASE HURRY, DOCTOR STRANGE!
SURGERY. I CAN'T DO SURGERY.
DOCTOR STRANGE, PLEASE...
NO, I'M NOT...I'M NOT WHO YOU THINK I AM.
I'M NOT WHO I THINK I AM.

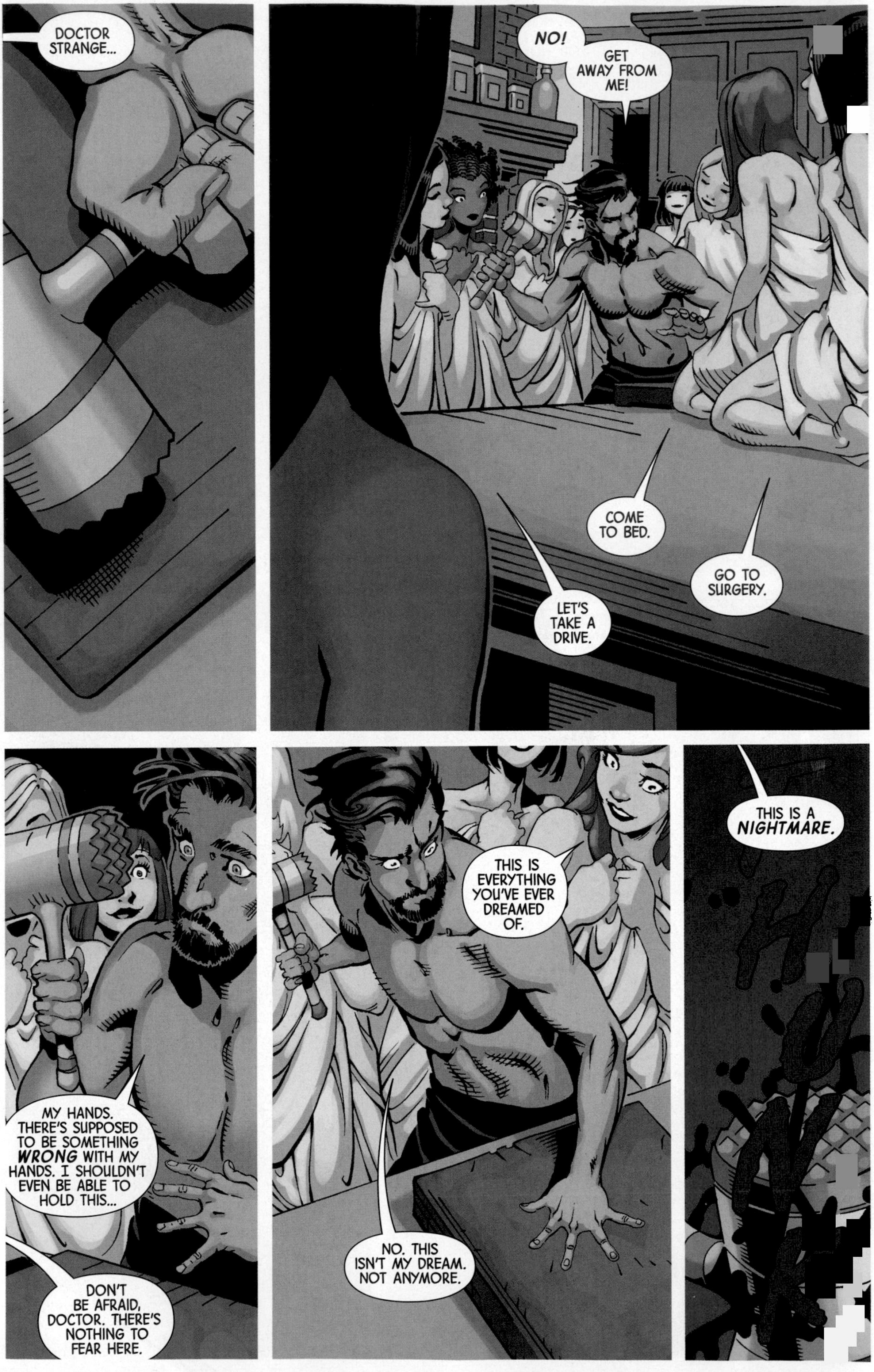
DOCTOR STRANGE...
NO!
GET AWAY FROM ME!
COME TO BED.
LET'S TAKE A DRIVE.
GO TO SURGERY.
MY HANDS. THERE'S SUPPOSED TO BE SOMETHING WRONG WITH MY HANDS. I SHOULDN'T EVEN BE ABLE TO HOLD THIS...
DON'T BE AFRAID, DOCTOR. THERE'S NOTHING TO FEAR HERE.
THIS IS EVERYTHING YOU'VE EVER DREAMED OF.
NO. THIS ISN'T MY DREAM. NOT ANYMORE.
THIS IS A NIGHTMARE.

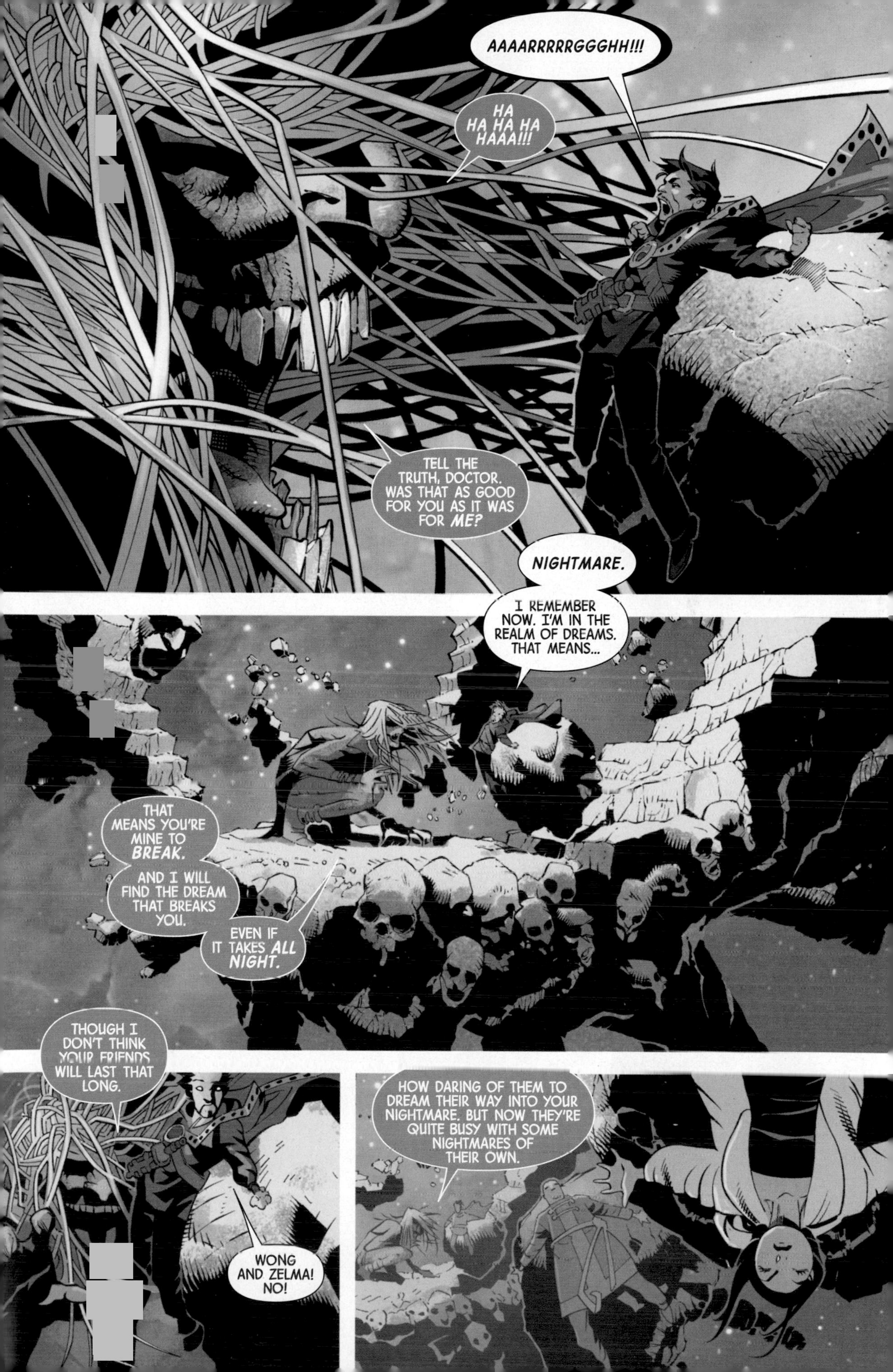
AAAARRRRRGGGHH!!!
HA HA HA HA HAAA!!!
TELL THE TRUTH, DOCTOR. WAS THAT AS GOOD FOR YOU AS IT WAS FOR ME?
NIGHTMARE.
I REMEMBER NOW. I'M IN THE REALM OF DREAMS. THAT MEANS...
THAT MEANS YOU'RE MINE TO BREAK.
AND I WILL FIND THE DREAM THAT BREAKS YOU.
EVEN IF IT TAKES ALL NIGHT.
THOUGH I DON'T THINK YOUR FRIENDS WILL LAST THAT LONG.
WONG AND ZELMA! NO!
HOW DARING OF THEM TO DREAM THEIR WAY INTO YOUR NIGHTMARE. BUT NOW THEY'RE QUITE BUSY WITH SOME NIGHTMARES OF THEIR OWN.

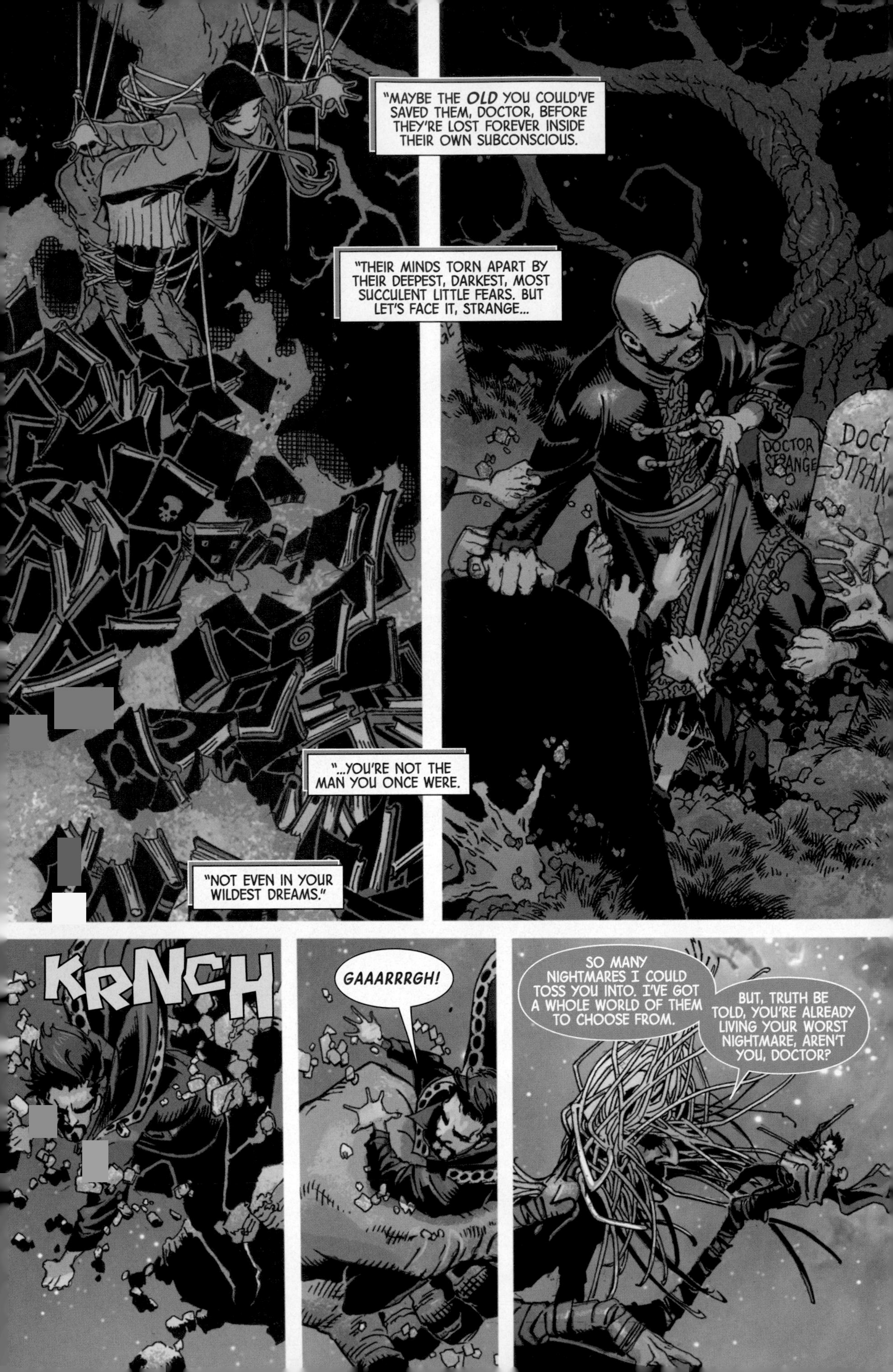
"MAYBE THE *OLD* YOU COULD'VE SAVED THEM, DOCTOR, BEFORE THEY'RE LOST FOREVER INSIDE THEIR OWN SUBCONSCIOUS.
"THEIR MINDS TORN APART BY THEIR DEEPEST, DARKEST, MOST SUCCULENT LITTLE FEARS. BUT LET'S FACE IT, STRANGE...
DOCTOR STRANGE
"...YOU'RE NOT THE MAN YOU ONCE WERE.
"NOT EVEN IN YOUR WILDEST DREAMS."
KRNCH
GAAARRRGH!
SO MANY NIGHTMARES I COULD TOSS YOU INTO. I'VE GOT A WHOLE WORLD OF THEM TO CHOOSE FROM.
BUT, TRUTH BE TOLD, YOU'RE ALREADY LIVING YOUR WORST NIGHTMARE, AREN'T YOU, DOCTOR?

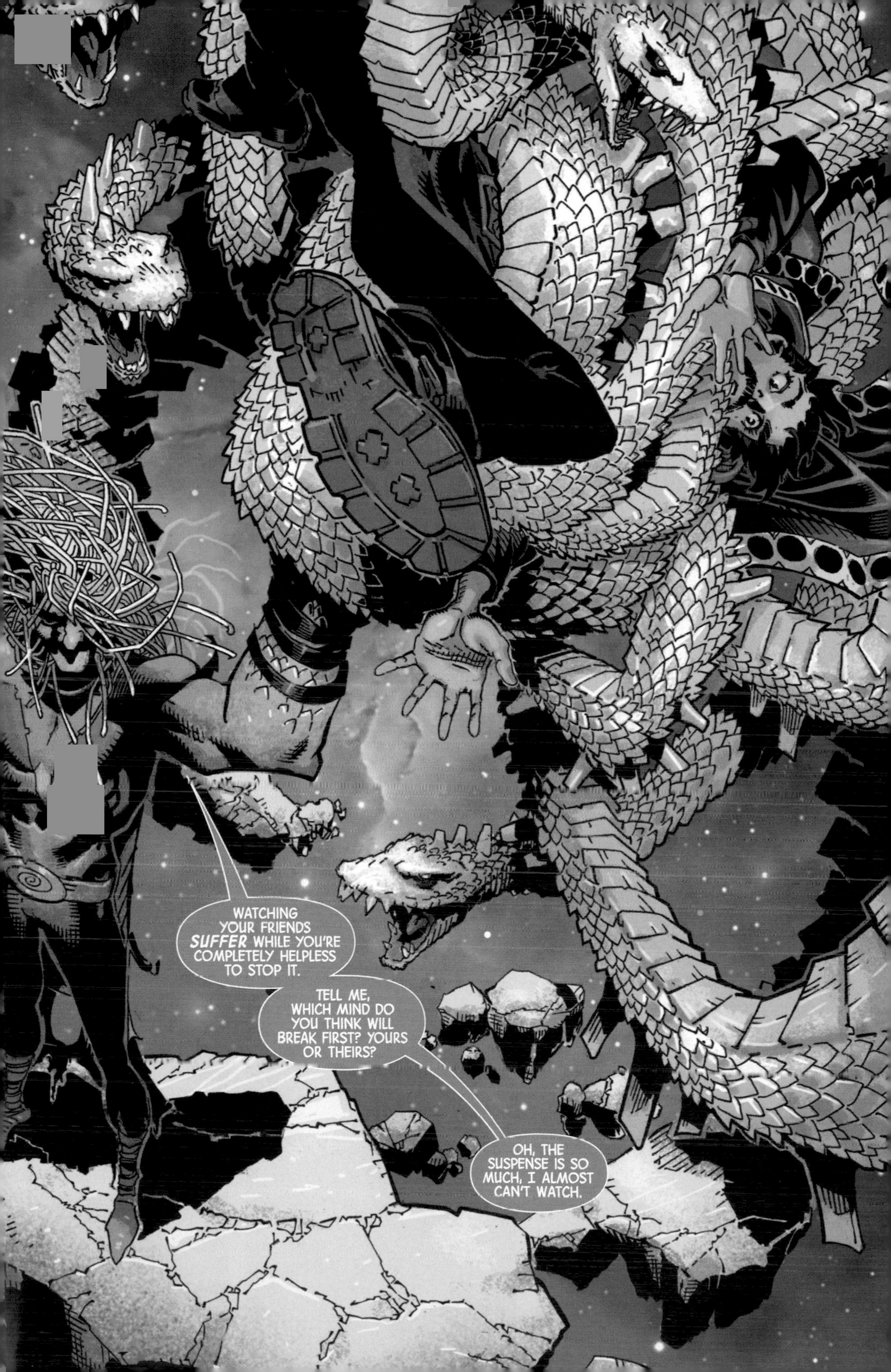
WATCHING YOUR FRIENDS SUFFER WHILE YOU'RE COMPLETELY HELPLESS TO STOP IT.
TELL ME, WHICH MIND DO YOU THINK WILL BREAK FIRST? YOURS OR THEIRS?
OH, THE SUSPENSE IS SO MUCH, I ALMOST CAN'T WATCH.

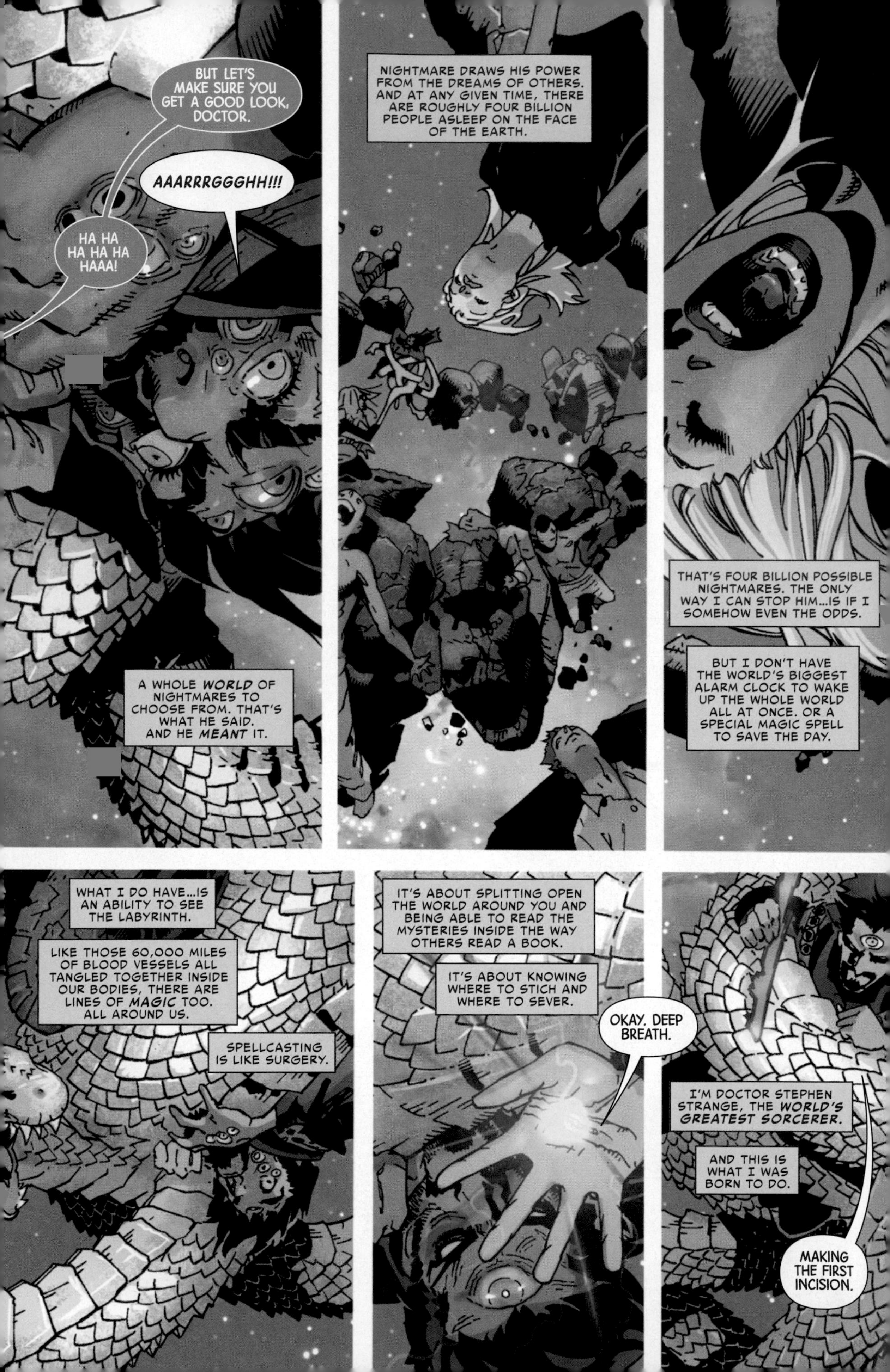
BUT LET'S MAKE SURE YOU GET A GOOD LOOK, DOCTOR.
AAARRRGGGHH!!!
HA HA HA HA HA HAAA!
A WHOLE WORLD OF NIGHTMARES TO CHOOSE FROM. THAT'S WHAT HE SAID. AND HE MEANT IT.
NIGHTMARE DRAWS HIS POWER FROM THE DREAMS OF OTHERS. AND AT ANY GIVEN TIME, THERE ARE ROUGHLY FOUR BILLION PEOPLE ASLEEP ON THE FACE OF THE EARTH.
THAT'S FOUR BILLION POSSIBLE NIGHTMARES. THE ONLY WAY I CAN STOP HIM...IS IF I SOMEHOW EVEN THE ODDS.
BUT I DON'T HAVE THE WORLD'S BIGGEST ALARM CLOCK TO WAKE UP THE WHOLE WORLD ALL AT ONCE. OR A SPECIAL MAGIC SPELL TO SAVE THE DAY.
WHAT I DO HAVE...IS AN ABILITY TO SEE THE LABYRINTH.
LIKE THOSE 60,000 MILES OF BLOOD VESSELS ALL TANGLED TOGETHER INSIDE OUR BODIES, THERE ARE LINES OF MAGIC TOO. ALL AROUND US.
SPELLCASTING IS LIKE SURGERY.
IT'S ABOUT SPLITTING OPEN THE WORLD AROUND YOU AND BEING ABLE TO READ THE MYSTERIES INSIDE THE WAY OTHERS READ A BOOK.
IT'S ABOUT KNOWING WHERE TO STICH AND WHERE TO SEVER.
OKAY. DEEP BREATH.
I'M DOCTOR STEPHEN STRANGE, THE WORLD'S GREATEST SORCERER.
AND THIS IS WHAT I WAS BORN TO DO.
MAKING THE FIRST INCISION.

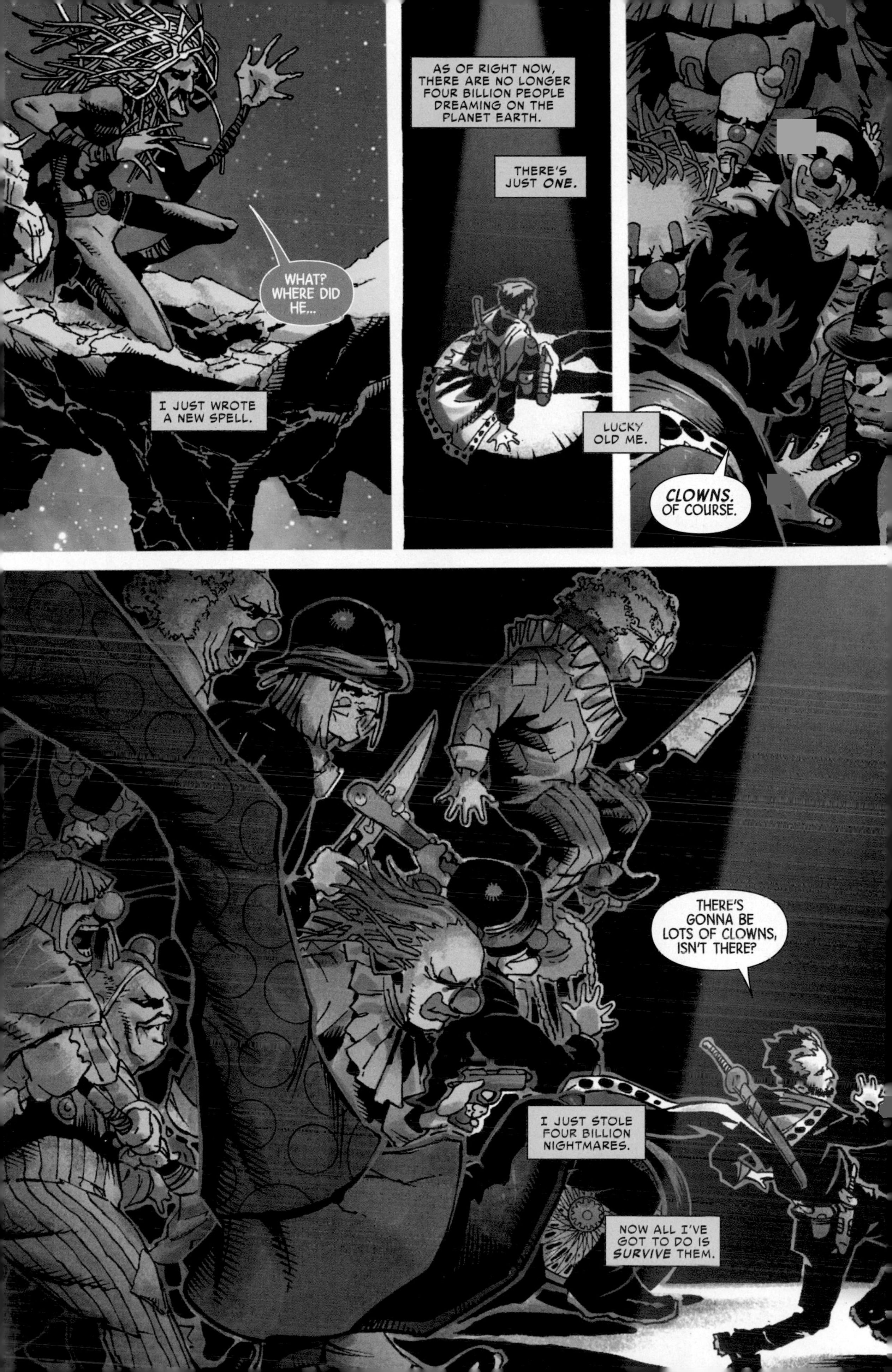
WHAT? WHERE DID HE...
I JUST WROTE A NEW SPELL.
AS OF RIGHT NOW, THERE ARE NO LONGER FOUR BILLION PEOPLE DREAMING ON THE PLANET EARTH.
THERE'S JUST *ONE.*
LUCKY OLD ME.
CLOWNS. OF COURSE.
THERE'S GONNA BE LOTS OF CLOWNS, ISN'T THERE?
I JUST STOLE FOUR BILLION NIGHTMARES.
NOW ALL I'VE GOT TO DO IS *SURVIVE* THEM.

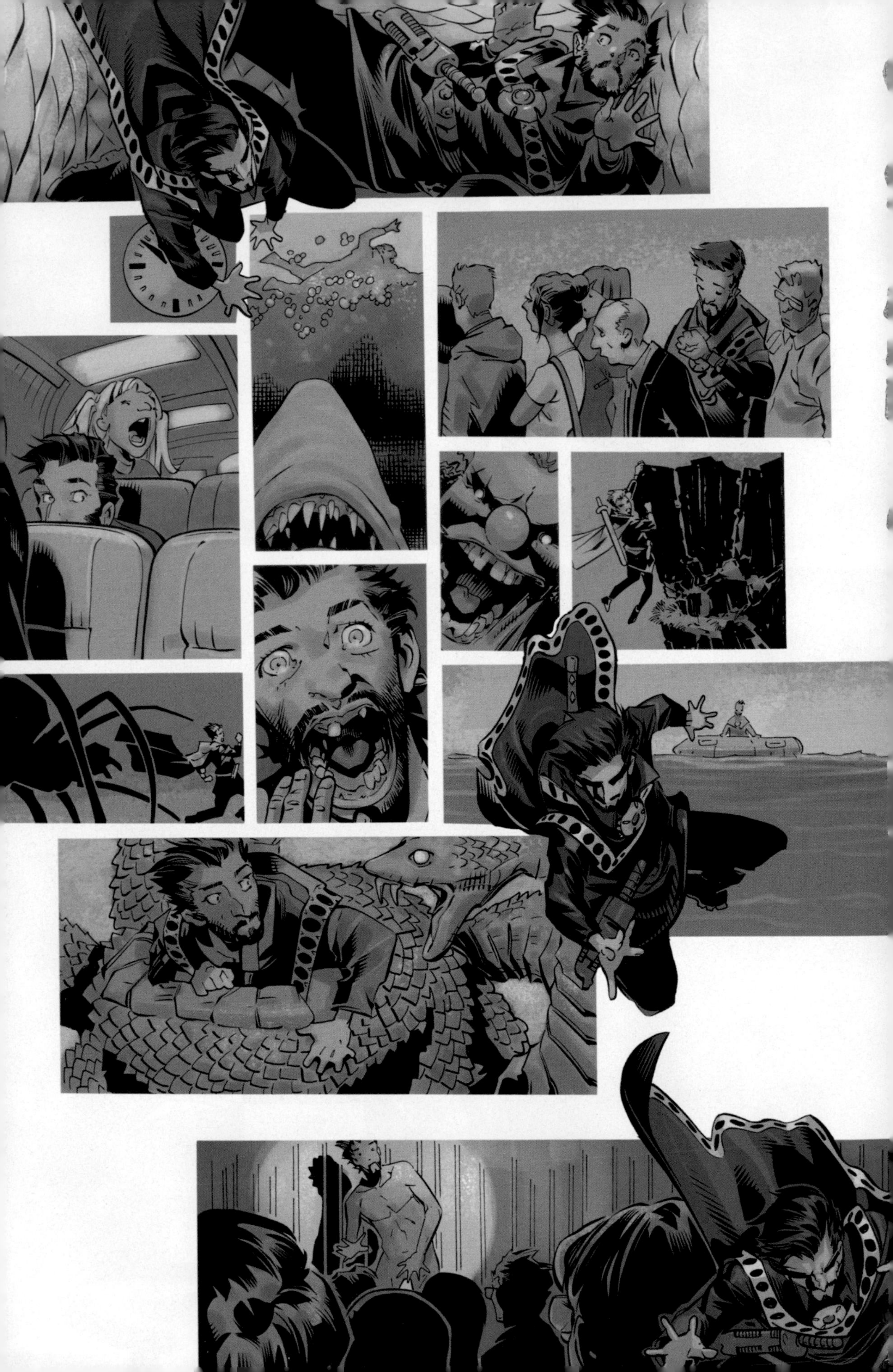

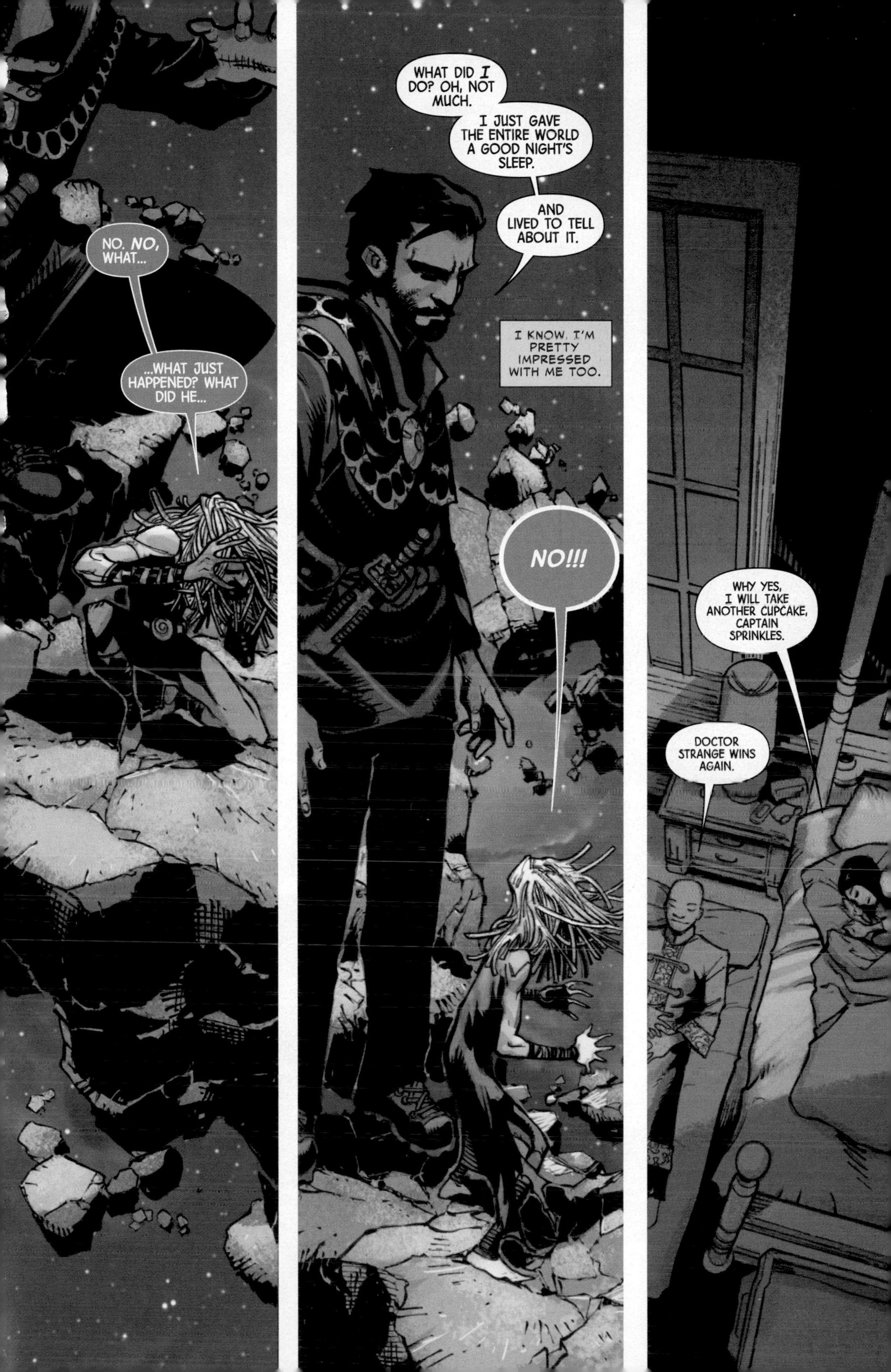
NO. NO, WHAT...
...WHAT JUST HAPPENED? WHAT DID HE...
WHAT DID I DO? OH, NOT MUCH.
I JUST GAVE THE ENTIRE WORLD A GOOD NIGHT'S SLEEP.
AND LIVED TO TELL ABOUT IT.
I KNOW. I'M PRETTY IMPRESSED WITH ME TOO.
NO!!!
WHY YES, I WILL TAKE ANOTHER CUPCAKE, CAPTAIN SPRINKLES.
DOCTOR STRANGE WINS AGAIN.

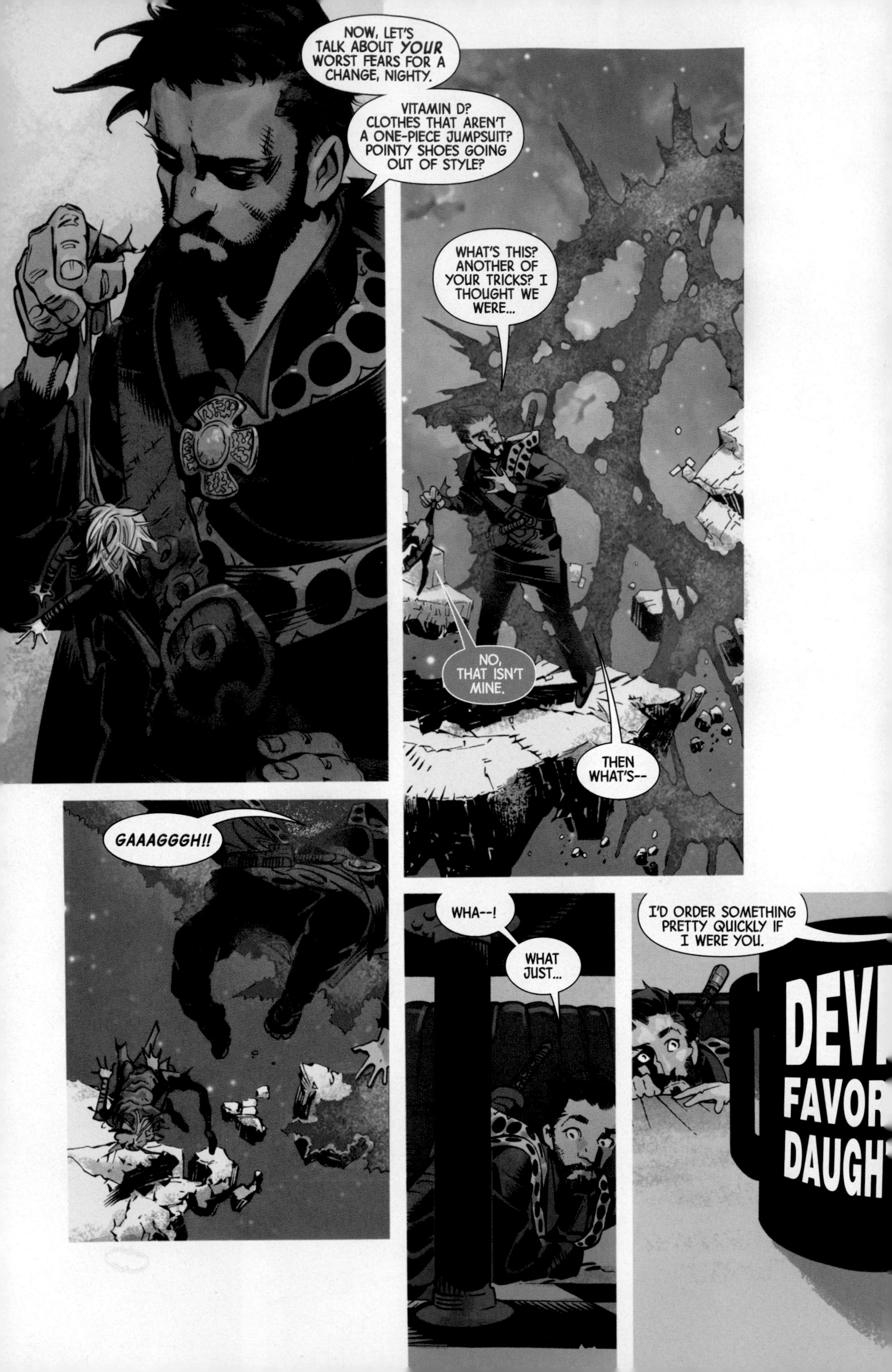
NOW, LET'S TALK ABOUT YOUR WORST FEARS FOR A CHANGE, NIGHTY.
VITAMIN D? CLOTHES THAT AREN'T A ONE-PIECE JUMPSUIT? POINTY SHOES GOING OUT OF STYLE?
WHAT'S THIS? ANOTHER OF YOUR TRICKS? I THOUGHT WE WERE...
NO, THAT ISN'T MINE.
THEN WHAT'S--
GAAAGGGH!!
WHA--!
WHAT JUST...
I'D ORDER SOMETHING PRETTY QUICKLY IF I WERE YOU.
DEV
FAVOR
DAUGH

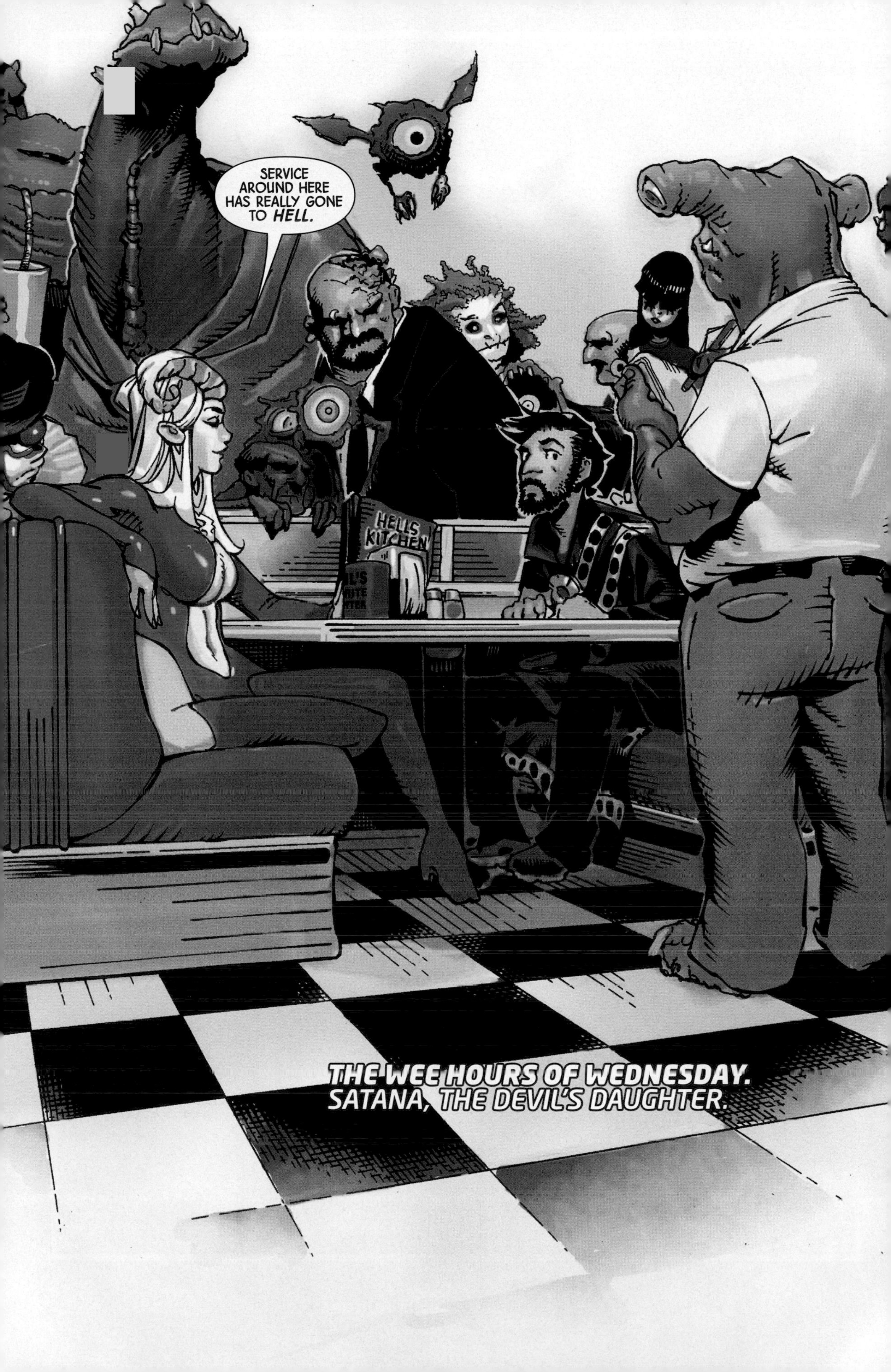
SERVICE AROUND HERE HAS REALLY GONE TO HELL.
HELLS KITCHEN
THE WEE HOURS OF WEDNESDAY.
SATANA, THE DEVIL'S DAUGHTER.

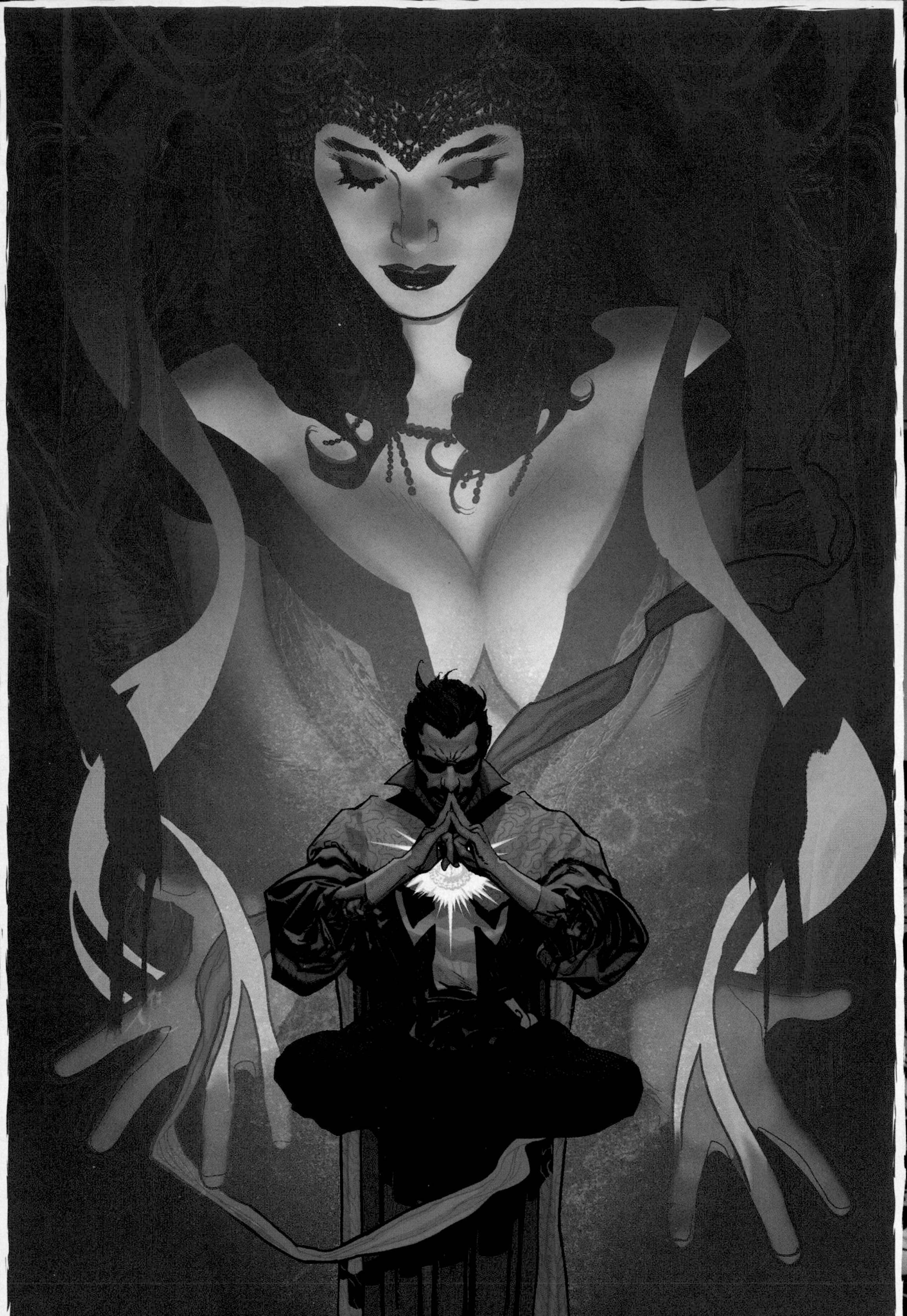

#11 VARIANT BY **ADAM HUGHES**

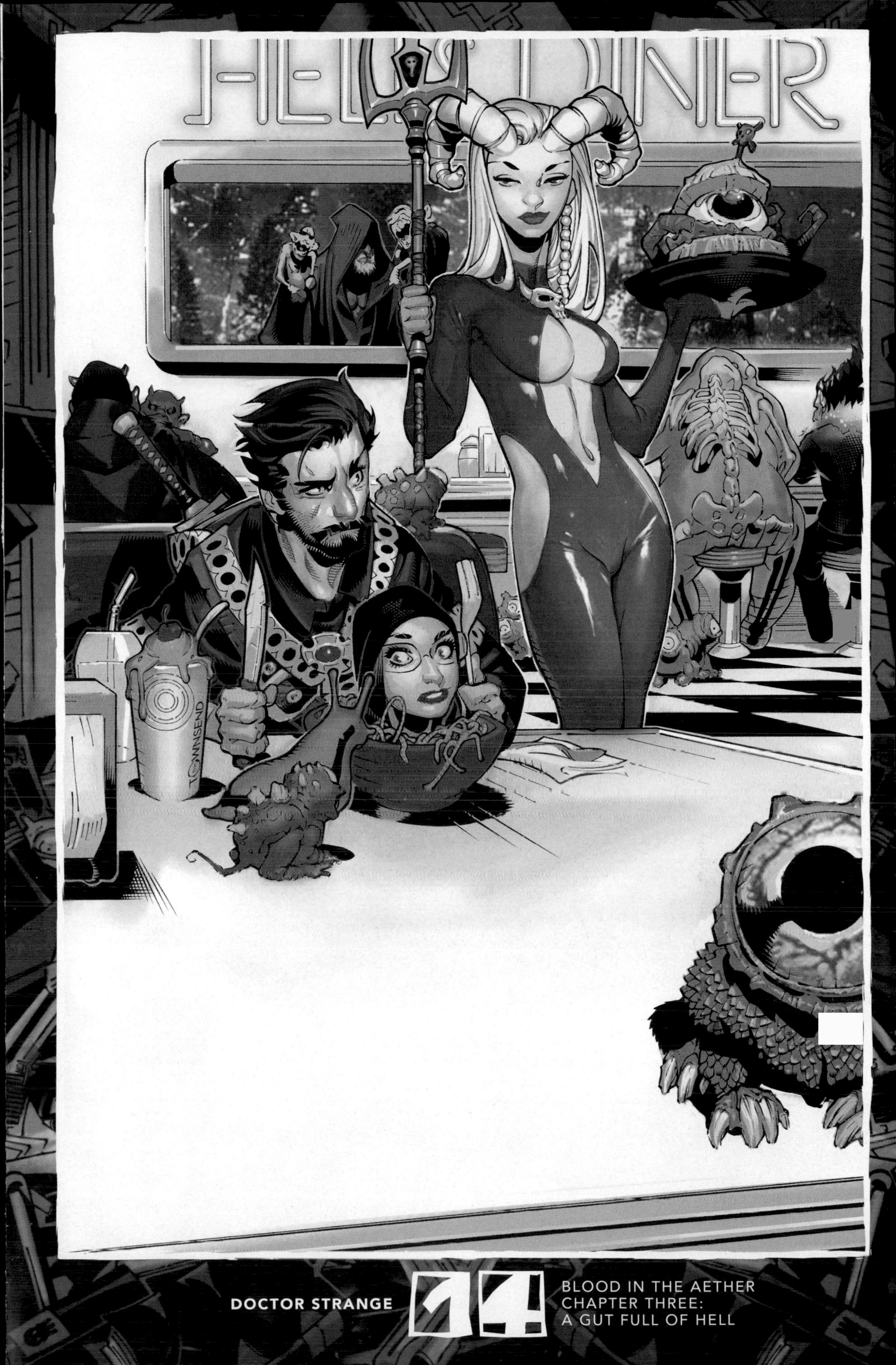
HELL'S DINER
TOWNSEND
DOCTOR STRANGE
14
BLOOD IN THE AETHER
CHAPTER THREE:
A GUT FULL OF HELL

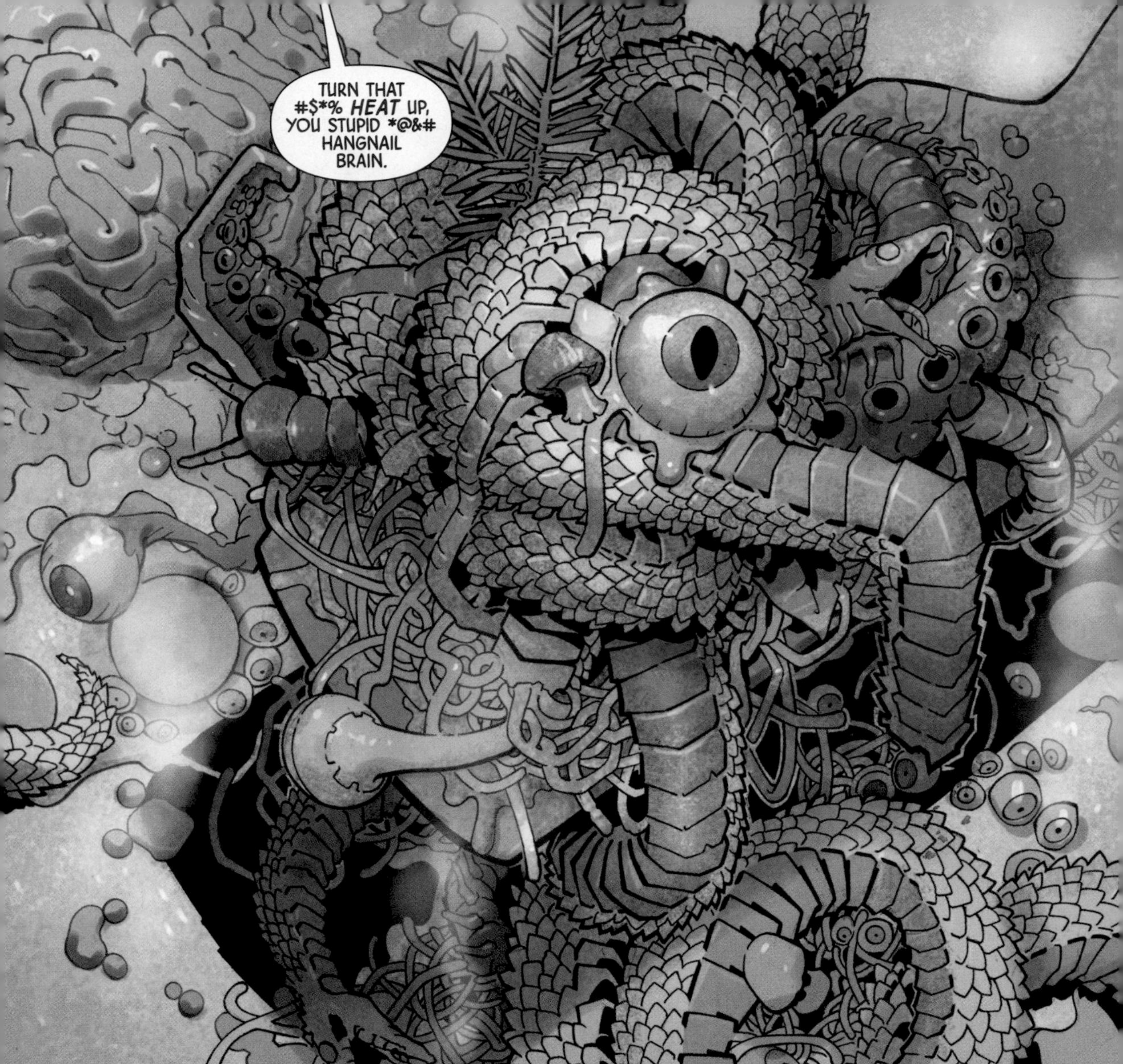
TURN THAT #$*% HEAT UP, YOU STUPID *@&# HANGNAIL BRAIN.

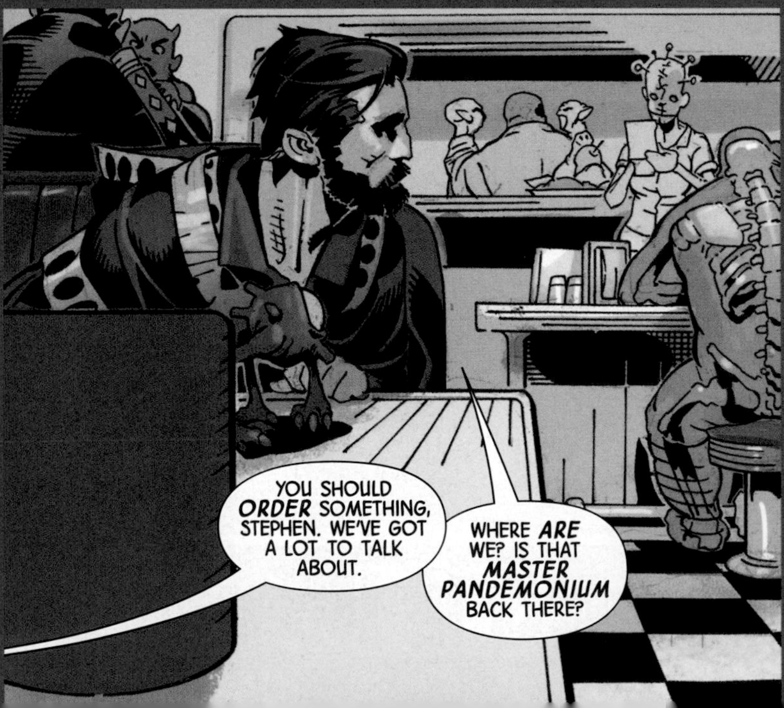
YOU SHOULD ORDER SOMETHING, STEPHEN. WE'VE GOT A LOT TO TALK ABOUT.
WHERE ARE WE? IS THAT MASTER PANDEMONIUM BACK THERE?

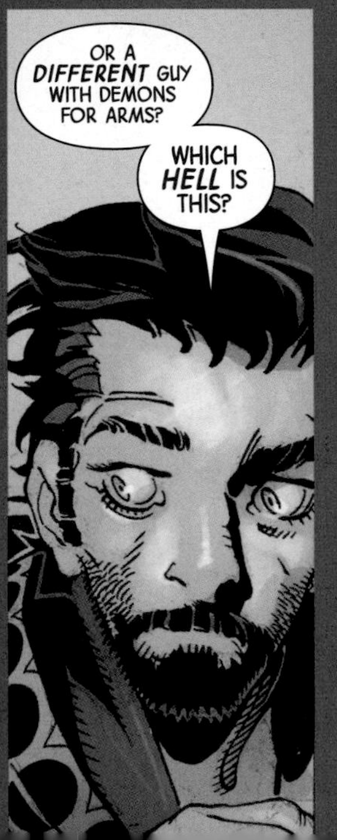
OR A DIFFERENT GUY WITH DEMONS FOR ARMS?
WHICH HELL IS THIS?

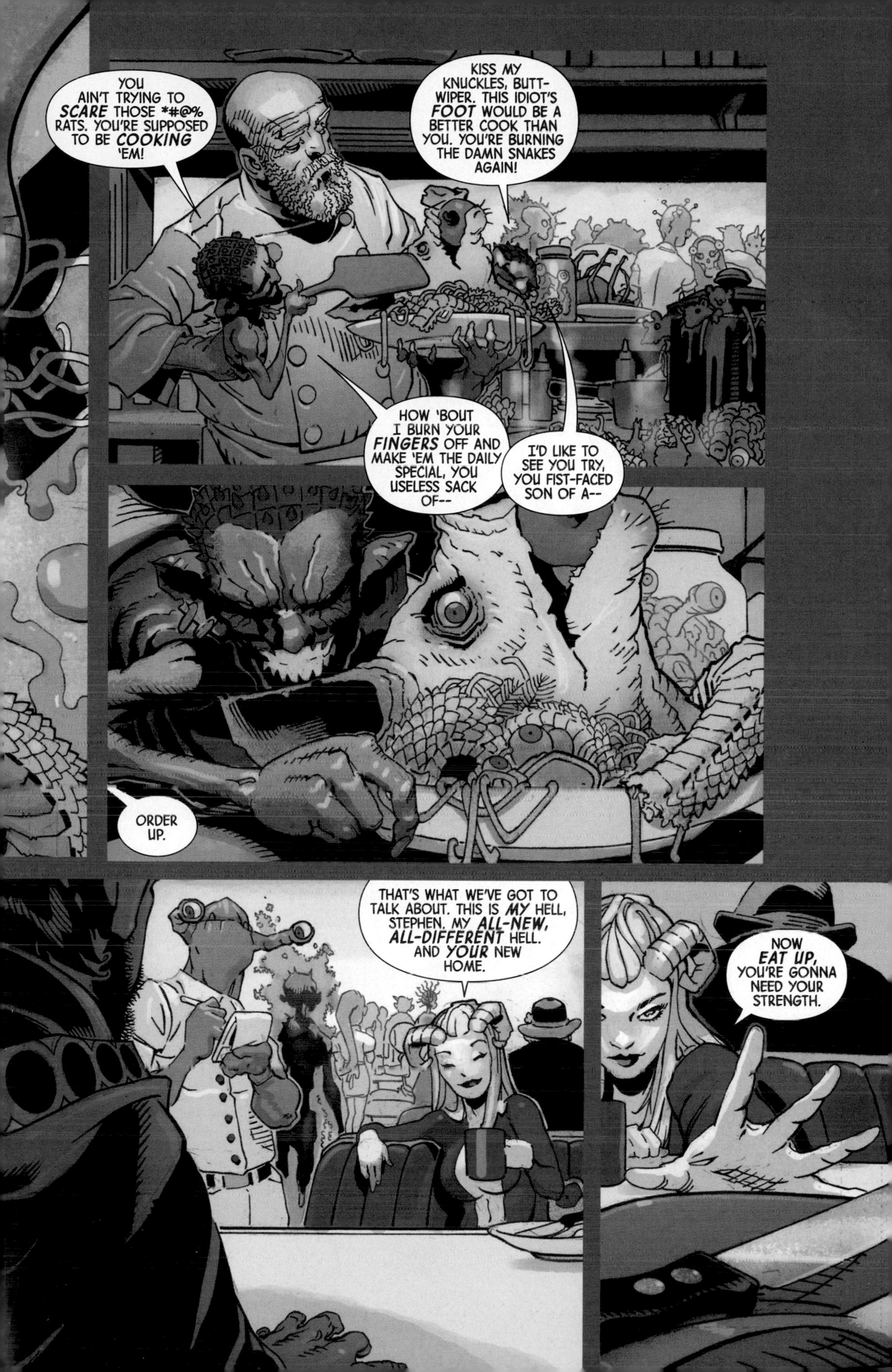
YOU AIN'T TRYING TO SCARE THOSE *#@% RATS. YOU'RE SUPPOSED TO BE COOKING 'EM!
KISS MY KNUCKLES, BUTT-WIPER. THIS IDIOT'S FOOT WOULD BE A BETTER COOK THAN YOU. YOU'RE BURNING THE DAMN SNAKES AGAIN!
HOW 'BOUT I BURN YOUR FINGERS OFF AND MAKE 'EM THE DAILY SPECIAL, YOU USELESS SACK OF--
I'D LIKE TO SEE YOU TRY, YOU FIST-FACED SON OF A--
ORDER UP.
THAT'S WHAT WE'VE GOT TO TALK ABOUT. THIS IS MY HELL, STEPHEN. MY ALL-NEW, ALL-DIFFERENT HELL. AND YOUR NEW HOME.
NOW EAT UP, YOU'RE GONNA NEED YOUR STRENGTH.

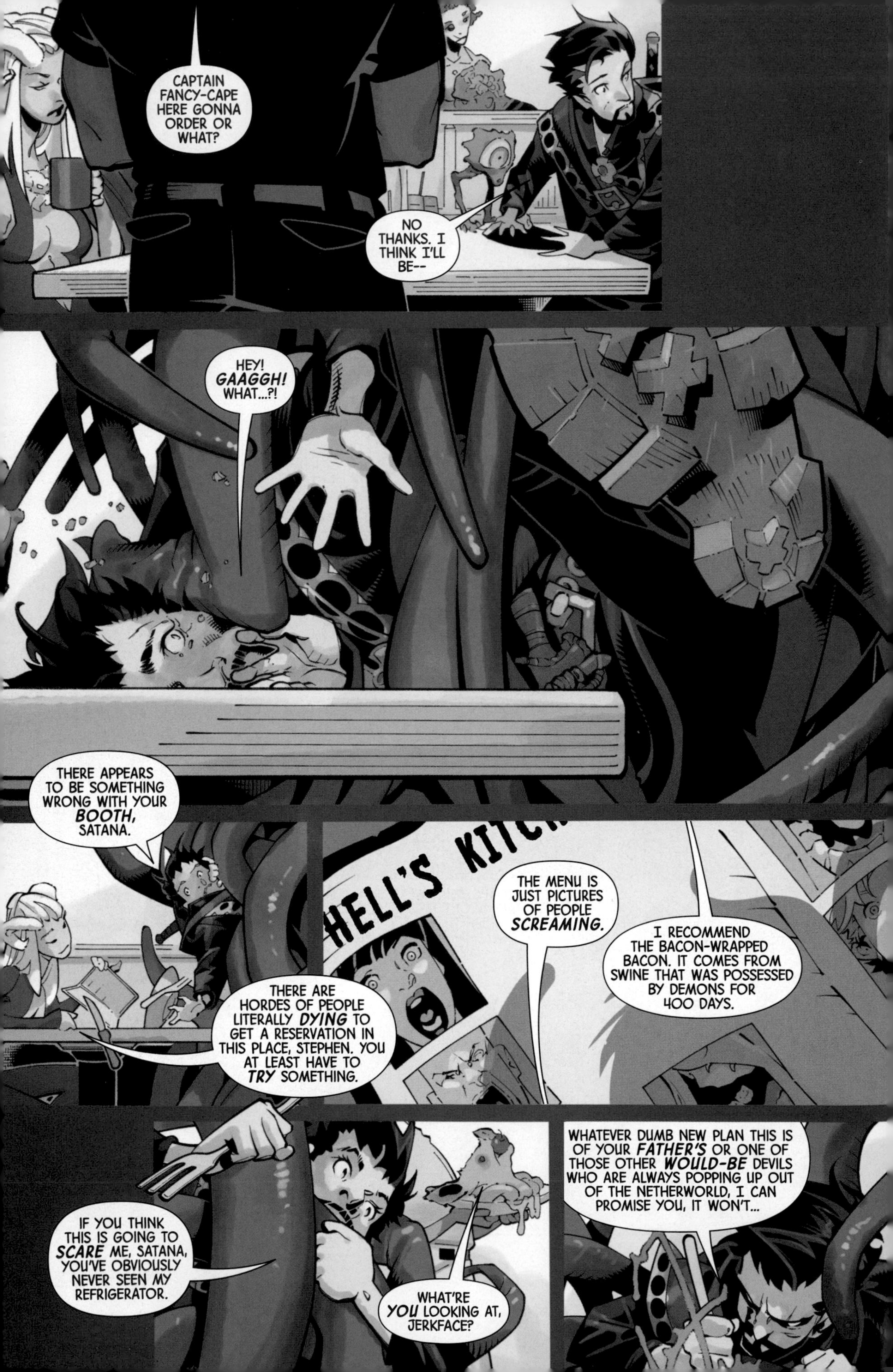
CAPTAIN FANCY-CAPE HERE GONNA ORDER OR WHAT?
NO THANKS. I THINK I'LL BE--
HEY! GAAGGH! WHAT...?!
THERE APPEARS TO BE SOMETHING WRONG WITH YOUR BOOTH, SATANA.
HELL'S KITCH
THERE ARE HORDES OF PEOPLE LITERALLY DYING TO GET A RESERVATION IN THIS PLACE, STEPHEN. YOU AT LEAST HAVE TO TRY SOMETHING.
THE MENU IS JUST PICTURES OF PEOPLE SCREAMING.
I RECOMMEND THE BACON-WRAPPED BACON. IT COMES FROM SWINE THAT WAS POSSESSED BY DEMONS FOR 400 DAYS.
IF YOU THINK THIS IS GOING TO SCARE ME, SATANA, YOU'VE OBVIOUSLY NEVER SEEN MY REFRIGERATOR.
WHAT'RE YOU LOOKING AT, JERKFACE?
WHATEVER DUMB NEW PLAN THIS IS OF YOUR FATHER'S OR ONE OF THOSE OTHER WOULD-BE DEVILS WHO ARE ALWAYS POPPING UP OUT OF THE NETHERWORLD, I CAN PROMISE YOU, IT WON'T...

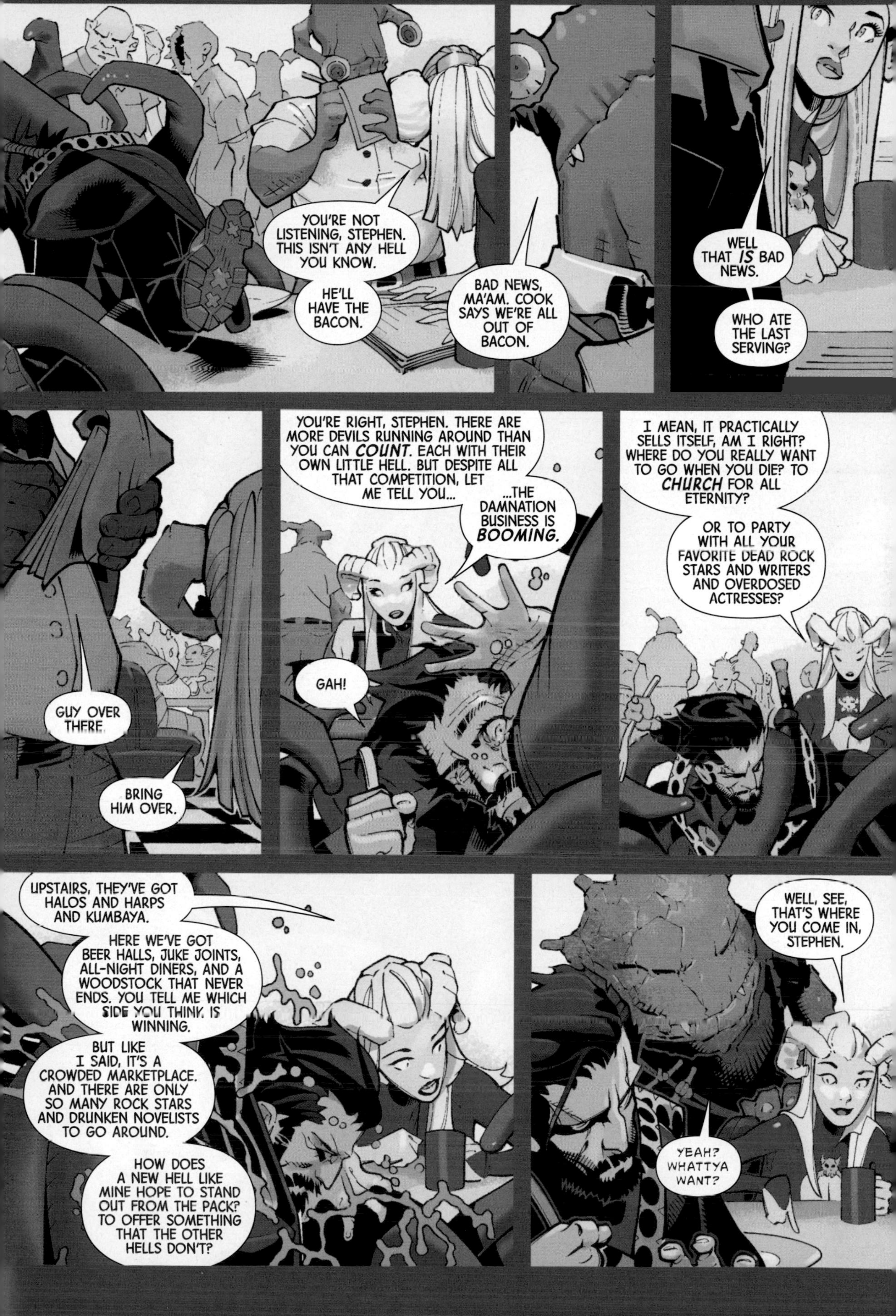

YOU'RE NOT LISTENING, STEPHEN. THIS ISN'T ANY HELL YOU KNOW.
HE'LL HAVE THE BACON.
BAD NEWS, MA'AM. COOK SAYS WE'RE ALL OUT OF BACON.
WELL THAT IS BAD NEWS.
WHO ATE THE LAST SERVING?
GUY OVER THERE.
BRING HIM OVER.
YOU'RE RIGHT, STEPHEN. THERE ARE MORE DEVILS RUNNING AROUND THAN YOU CAN COUNT. EACH WITH THEIR OWN LITTLE HELL. BUT DESPITE ALL THAT COMPETITION, LET ME TELL YOU...
...THE DAMNATION BUSINESS IS BOOMING.
GAH!
I MEAN, IT PRACTICALLY SELLS ITSELF, AM I RIGHT? WHERE DO YOU REALLY WANT TO GO WHEN YOU DIE? TO CHURCH FOR ALL ETERNITY?
OR TO PARTY WITH ALL YOUR FAVORITE DEAD ROCK STARS AND WRITERS AND OVERDOSED ACTRESSES?
UPSTAIRS, THEY'VE GOT HALOS AND HARPS AND KUMBAYA.
HERE WE'VE GOT BEER HALLS, JUKE JOINTS, ALL-NIGHT DINERS, AND A WOODSTOCK THAT NEVER ENDS. YOU TELL ME WHICH SIDE YOU THINK IS WINNING.
BUT LIKE I SAID, IT'S A CROWDED MARKETPLACE. AND THERE ARE ONLY SO MANY ROCK STARS AND DRUNKEN NOVELISTS TO GO AROUND.
HOW DOES A NEW HELL LIKE MINE HOPE TO STAND OUT FROM THE PACK? TO OFFER SOMETHING THAT THE OTHER HELLS DON'T?
WELL, SEE, THAT'S WHERE YOU COME IN, STEPHEN.
YEAH? WHATTYA WANT?

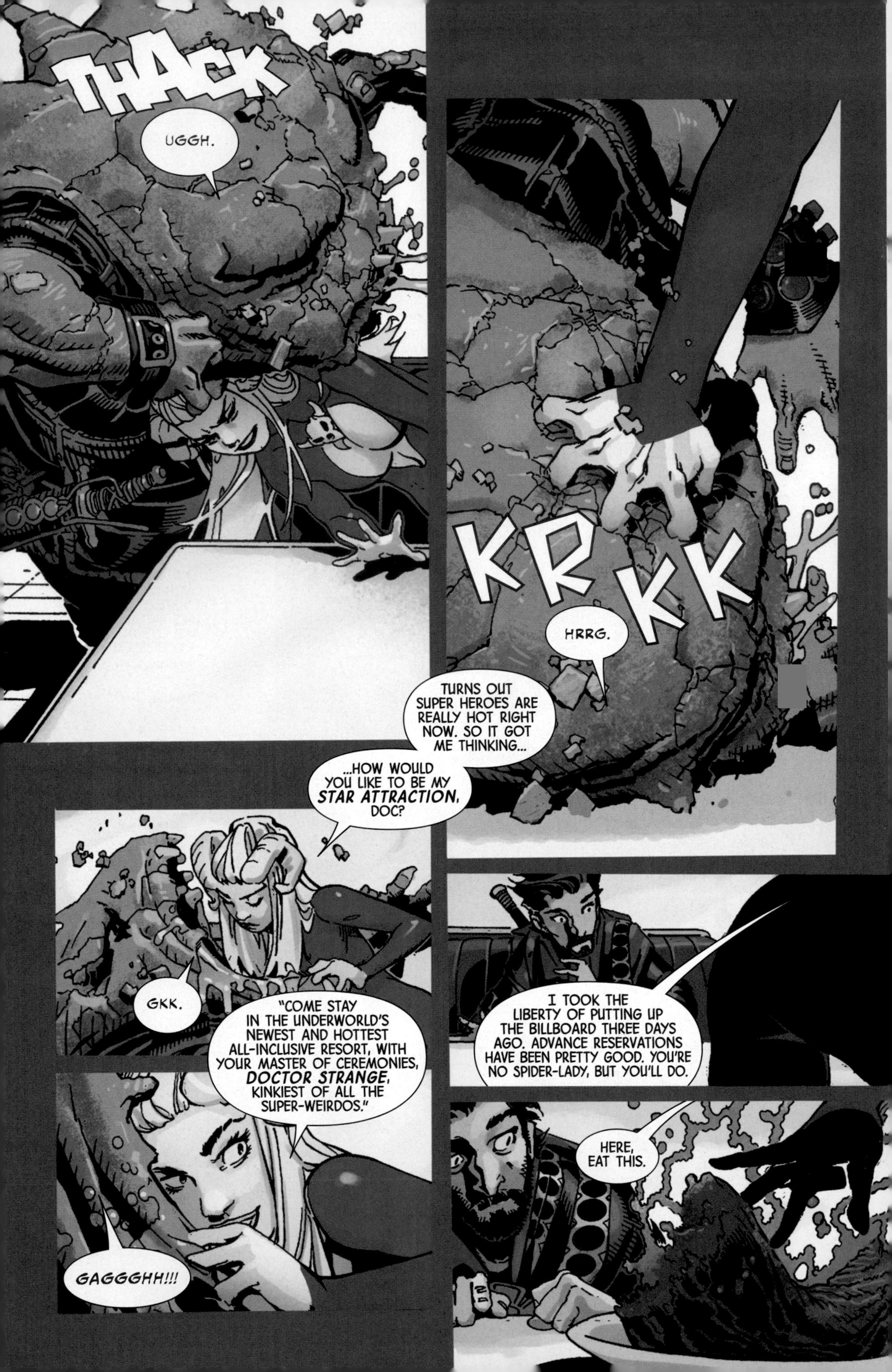
THACK
UGGH.
KRKK
HRRG.
TURNS OUT SUPER HEROES ARE REALLY HOT RIGHT NOW. SO IT GOT ME THINKING...
...HOW WOULD YOU LIKE TO BE MY STAR ATTRACTION, DOC?
GKK.
"COME STAY IN THE UNDERWORLD'S NEWEST AND HOTTEST ALL-INCLUSIVE RESORT, WITH YOUR MASTER OF CEREMONIES, DOCTOR STRANGE, KINKIEST OF ALL THE SUPER-WEIRDOS."
GAGGGHH!!!
I TOOK THE LIBERTY OF PUTTING UP THE BILLBOARD THREE DAYS AGO. ADVANCE RESERVATIONS HAVE BEEN PRETTY GOOD. YOU'RE NO SPIDER-LADY, BUT YOU'LL DO.
HERE, EAT THIS.

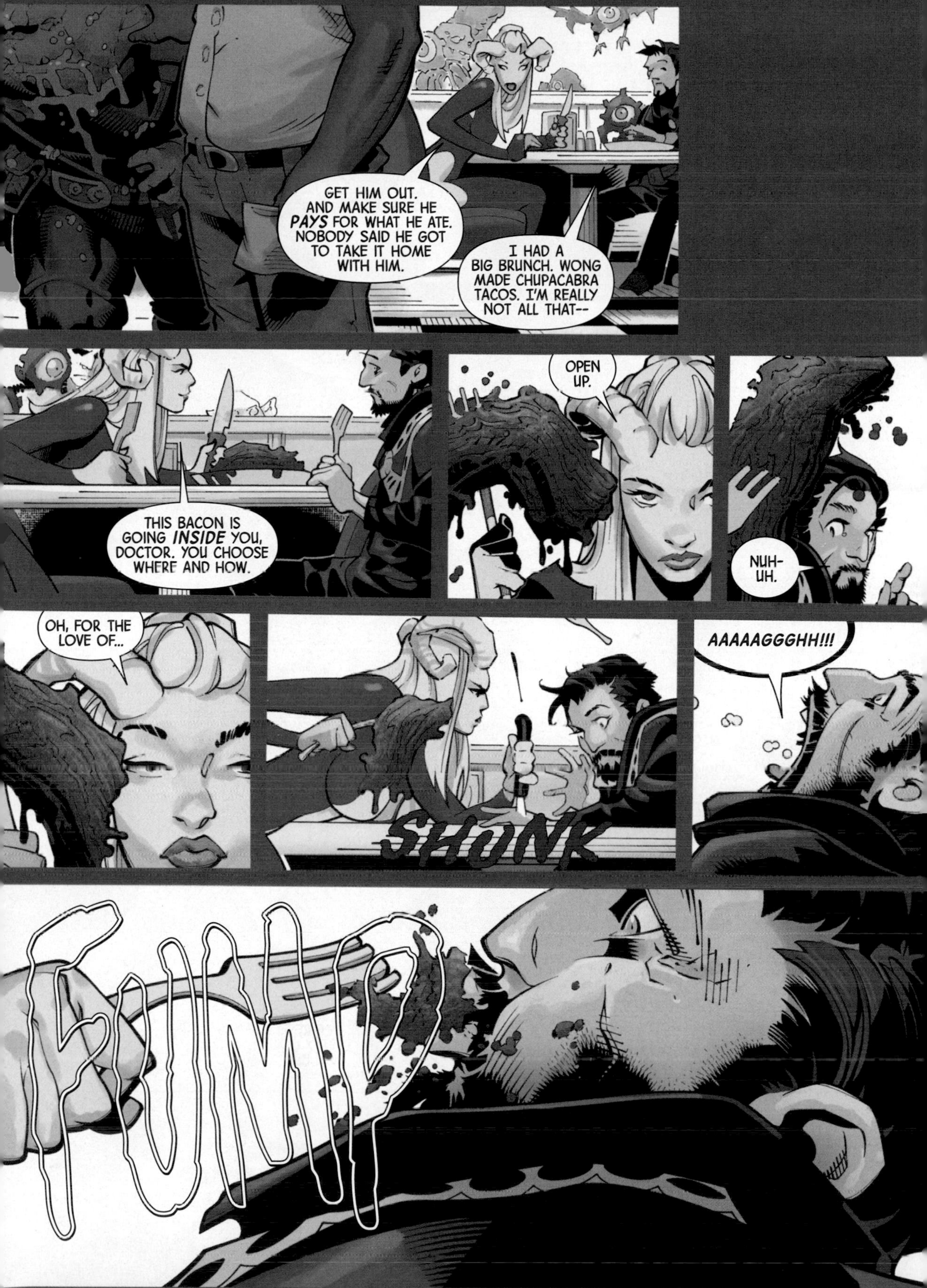
GET HIM OUT. AND MAKE SURE HE PAYS FOR WHAT HE ATE. NOBODY SAID HE GOT TO TAKE IT HOME WITH HIM.
I HAD A BIG BRUNCH. WONG MADE CHUPACABRA TACOS. I'M REALLY NOT ALL THAT--
THIS BACON IS GOING INSIDE YOU, DOCTOR. YOU CHOOSE WHERE AND HOW.
OPEN UP.
NUH-UH.
OH, FOR THE LOVE OF...
SHUNK
AAAAAGGGHH!!!
FOMP

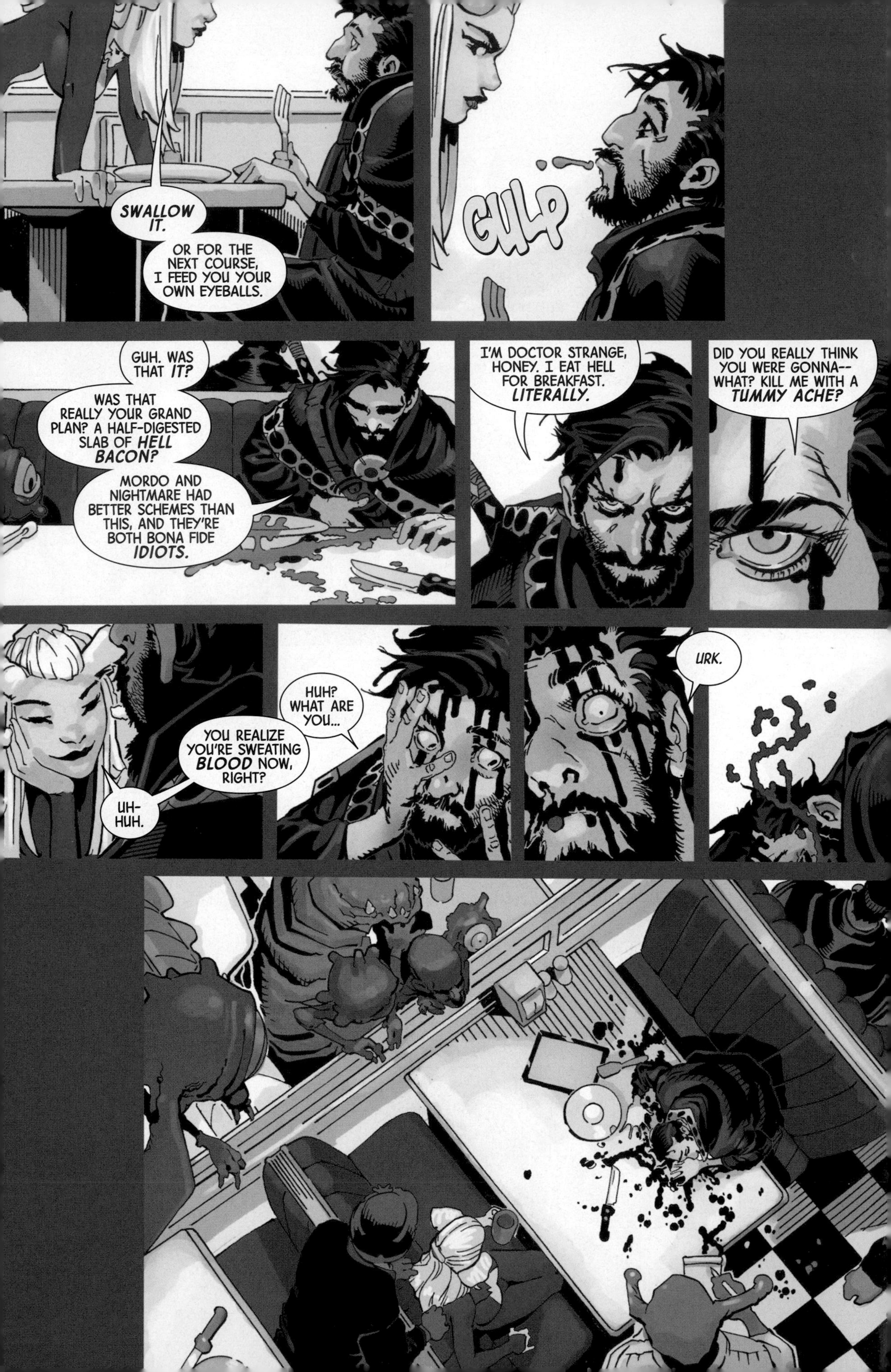
SWALLOW IT.
OR FOR THE NEXT COURSE, I FEED YOU YOUR OWN EYEBALLS.
GULP
GUH. WAS THAT IT?
WAS THAT REALLY YOUR GRAND PLAN? A HALF-DIGESTED SLAB OF HELL BACON?
MORDO AND NIGHTMARE HAD BETTER SCHEMES THAN THIS, AND THEY'RE BOTH BONA FIDE IDIOTS.
I'M DOCTOR STRANGE, HONEY. I EAT HELL FOR BREAKFAST. LITERALLY.
DID YOU REALLY THINK YOU WERE GONNA-- WHAT? KILL ME WITH A TUMMY ACHE?
YOU REALIZE YOU'RE SWEATING BLOOD NOW, RIGHT?
UH-HUH.
HUH? WHAT ARE YOU...
URK.

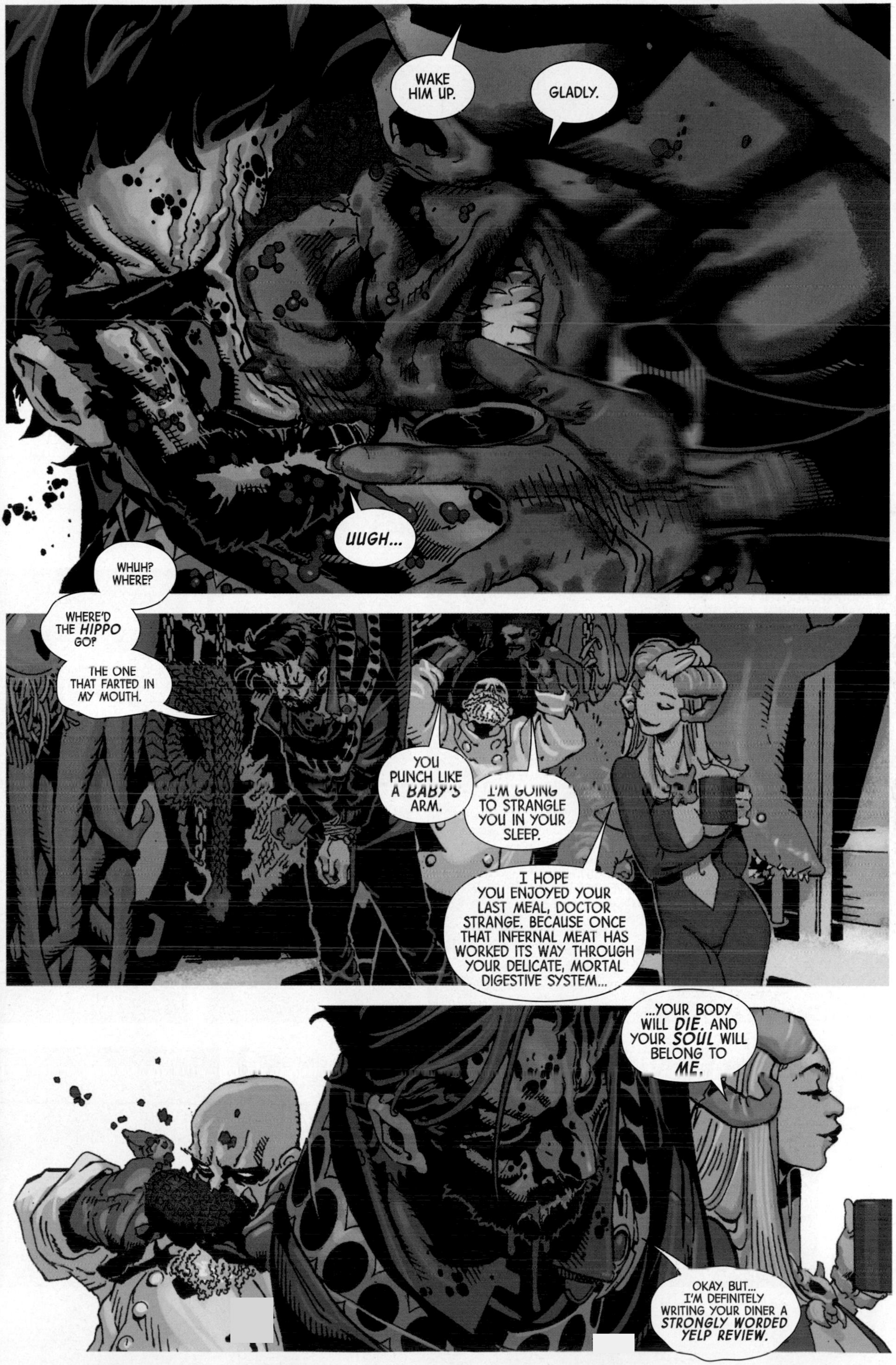
WAKE HIM UP.
GLADLY.
UUGH...
WHUH? WHERE?
WHERE'D THE HIPPO GO?
THE ONE THAT FARTED IN MY MOUTH.
YOU PUNCH LIKE A BABY'S ARM.
I'M GOING TO STRANGLE YOU IN YOUR SLEEP.
I HOPE YOU ENJOYED YOUR LAST MEAL, DOCTOR STRANGE. BECAUSE ONCE THAT INFERNAL MEAT HAS WORKED ITS WAY THROUGH YOUR DELICATE, MORTAL DIGESTIVE SYSTEM...
...YOUR BODY WILL DIE. AND YOUR SOUL WILL BELONG TO ME.
OKAY, BUT... I'M DEFINITELY WRITING YOUR DINER A STRONGLY WORDED YELP REVIEW.

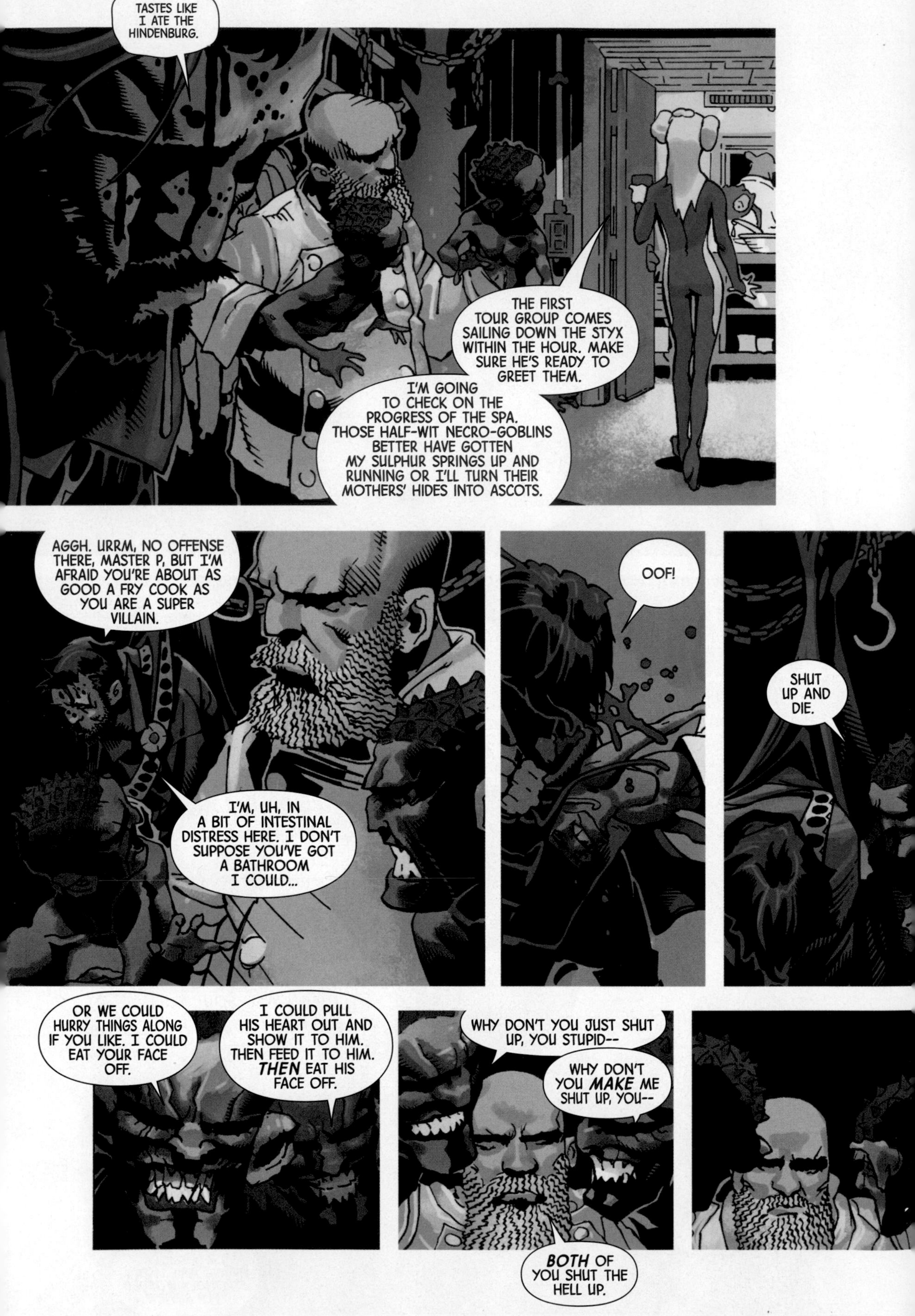
TASTES LIKE I ATE THE HINDENBURG.
THE FIRST TOUR GROUP COMES SAILING DOWN THE STYX WITHIN THE HOUR. MAKE SURE HE'S READY TO GREET THEM.
I'M GOING TO CHECK ON THE PROGRESS OF THE SPA. THOSE HALF-WIT NECRO-GOBLINS BETTER HAVE GOTTEN MY SULPHUR SPRINGS UP AND RUNNING OR I'LL TURN THEIR MOTHERS' HIDES INTO ASCOTS.
AGGH. URRM, NO OFFENSE THERE, MASTER P, BUT I'M AFRAID YOU'RE ABOUT AS GOOD A FRY COOK AS YOU ARE A SUPER VILLAIN.
I'M, UH, IN A BIT OF INTESTINAL DISTRESS HERE. I DON'T SUPPOSE YOU'VE GOT A BATHROOM I COULD...
OOF!
SHUT UP AND DIE.
OR WE COULD HURRY THINGS ALONG IF YOU LIKE. I COULD EAT YOUR FACE OFF.
I COULD PULL HIS HEART OUT AND SHOW IT TO HIM. THEN FEED IT TO HIM. *THEN* EAT HIS FACE OFF.
WHY DON'T YOU JUST SHUT UP, YOU STUPID--
WHY DON'T YOU *MAKE* ME SHUT UP, YOU--
BOTH OF YOU SHUT THE HELL UP.

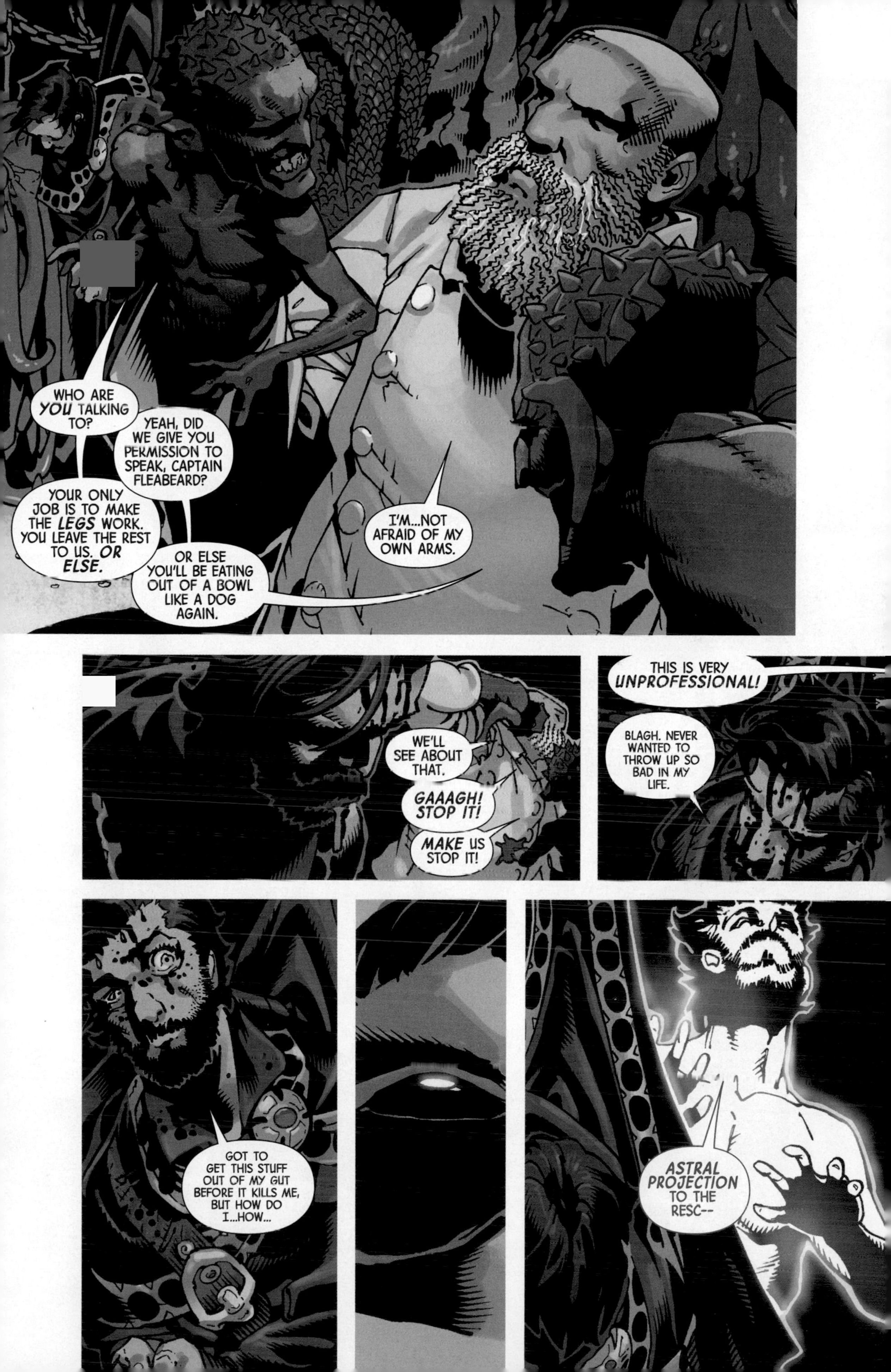
WHO ARE *YOU* TALKING TO?
YEAH, DID WE GIVE YOU PERMISSION TO SPEAK, CAPTAIN FLEABEARD?
YOUR ONLY JOB IS TO MAKE THE *LEGS* WORK. YOU LEAVE THE REST TO US. *OR ELSE.*
OR ELSE YOU'LL BE EATING OUT OF A BOWL LIKE A DOG AGAIN.
I'M...NOT AFRAID OF MY OWN ARMS.
WE'LL SEE ABOUT THAT.
GAAAGH! STOP IT!
MAKE US STOP IT!
THIS IS VERY *UNPROFESSIONAL!*
BLAGH. NEVER WANTED TO THROW UP SO BAD IN MY LIFE.
GOT TO GET THIS STUFF OUT OF MY GUT BEFORE IT KILLS ME, BUT HOW DO I...HOW...
ASTRAL PROJECTION TO THE RESC--

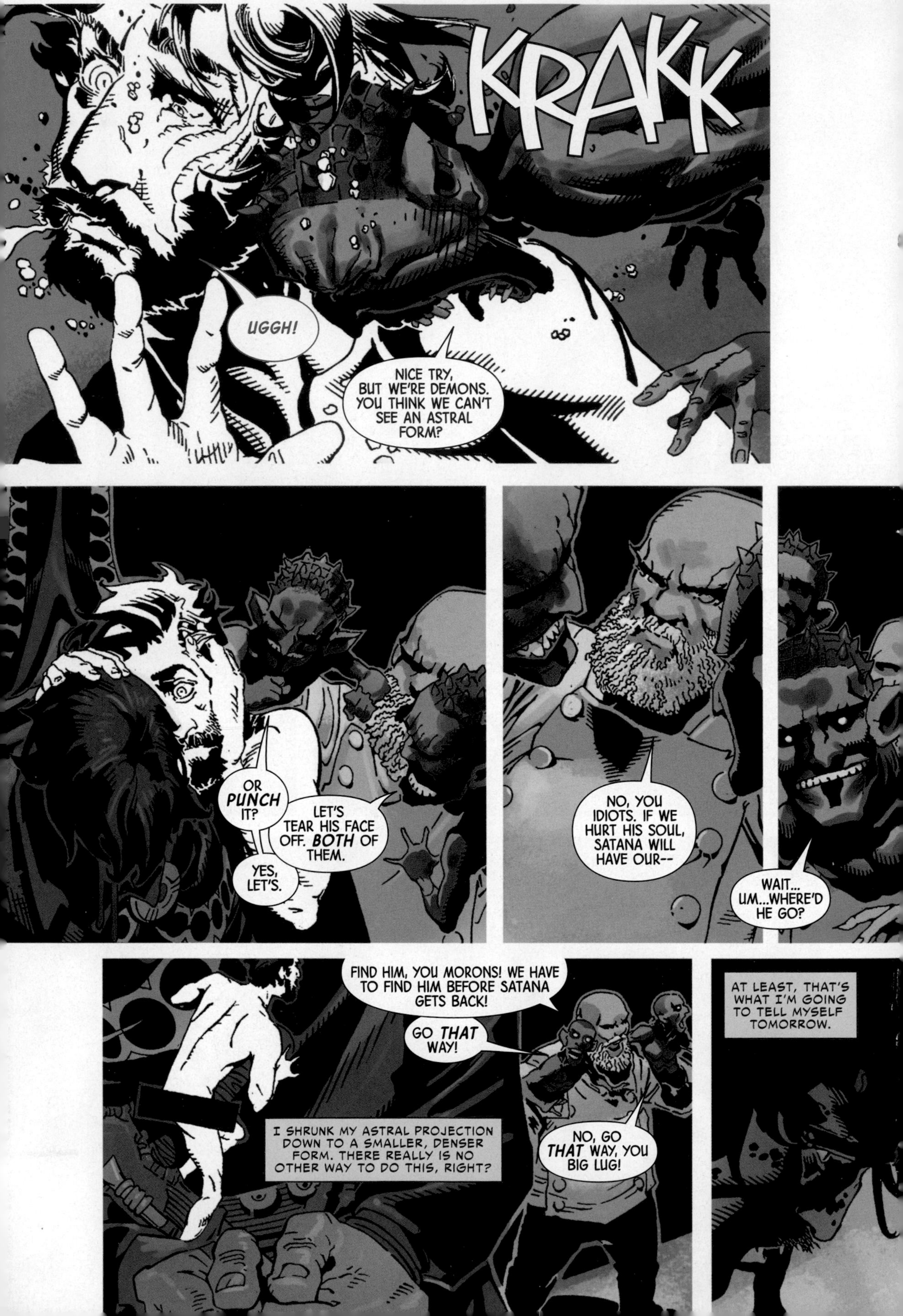
KRAKK
UGGH!
NICE TRY, BUT WE'RE DEMONS. YOU THINK WE CAN'T SEE AN ASTRAL FORM?
OR PUNCH IT?
LET'S TEAR HIS FACE OFF. BOTH OF THEM.
YES, LET'S.
NO, YOU IDIOTS. IF WE HURT HIS SOUL, SATANA WILL HAVE OUR--
WAIT... UM...WHERE'D HE GO?
FIND HIM, YOU MORONS! WE HAVE TO FIND HIM BEFORE SATANA GETS BACK!
GO THAT WAY!
I SHRUNK MY ASTRAL PROJECTION DOWN TO A SMALLER, DENSER FORM. THERE REALLY IS NO OTHER WAY TO DO THIS, RIGHT?
NO, GO THAT WAY, YOU BIG LUG!
AT LEAST, THAT'S WHAT I'M GOING TO TELL MYSELF TOMORROW.

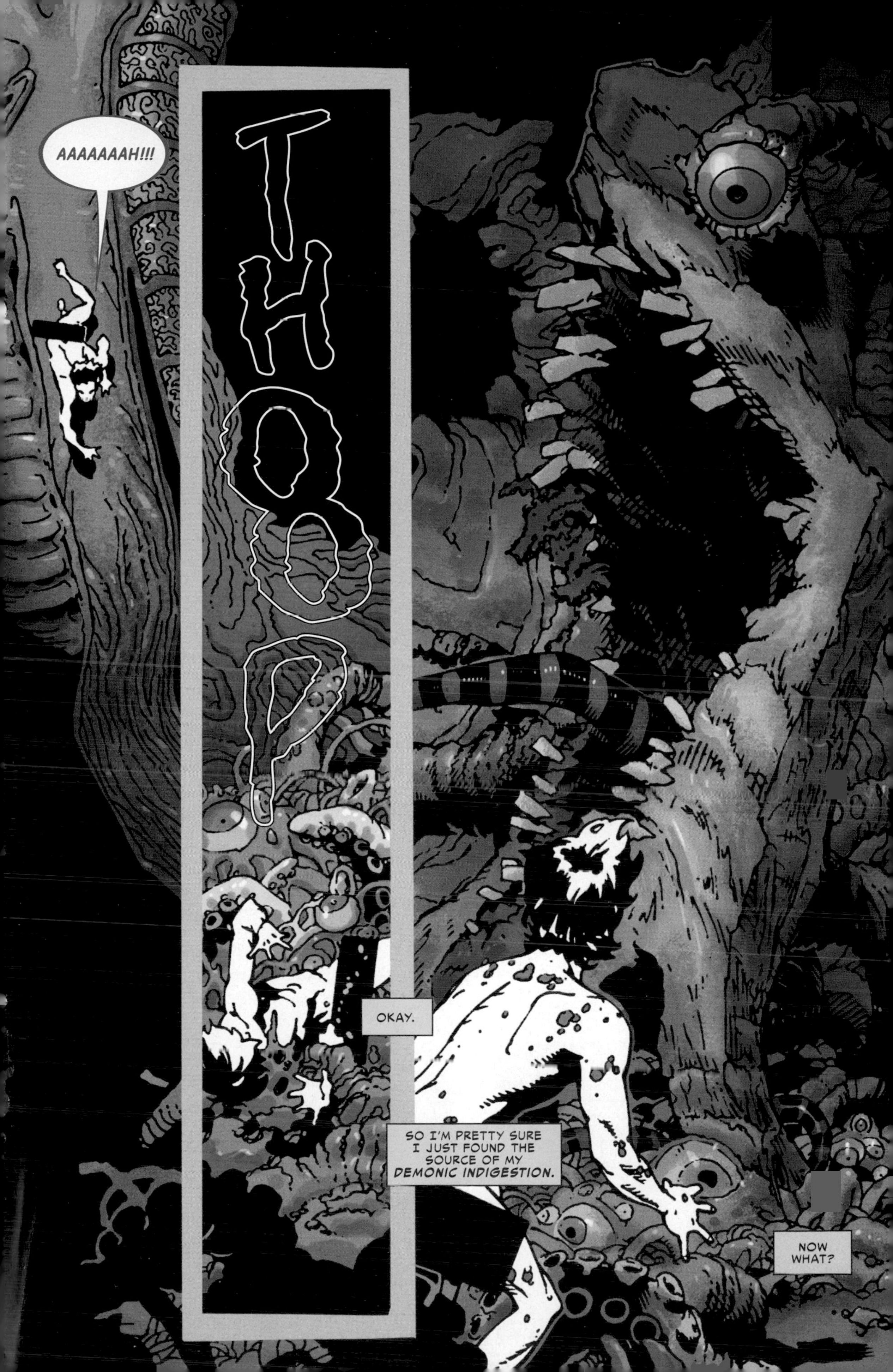
AAAAAAAH!!!
THOOP
OKAY.
SO I'M PRETTY SURE I JUST FOUND THE SOURCE OF MY DEMONIC INDIGESTION.
NOW WHAT?

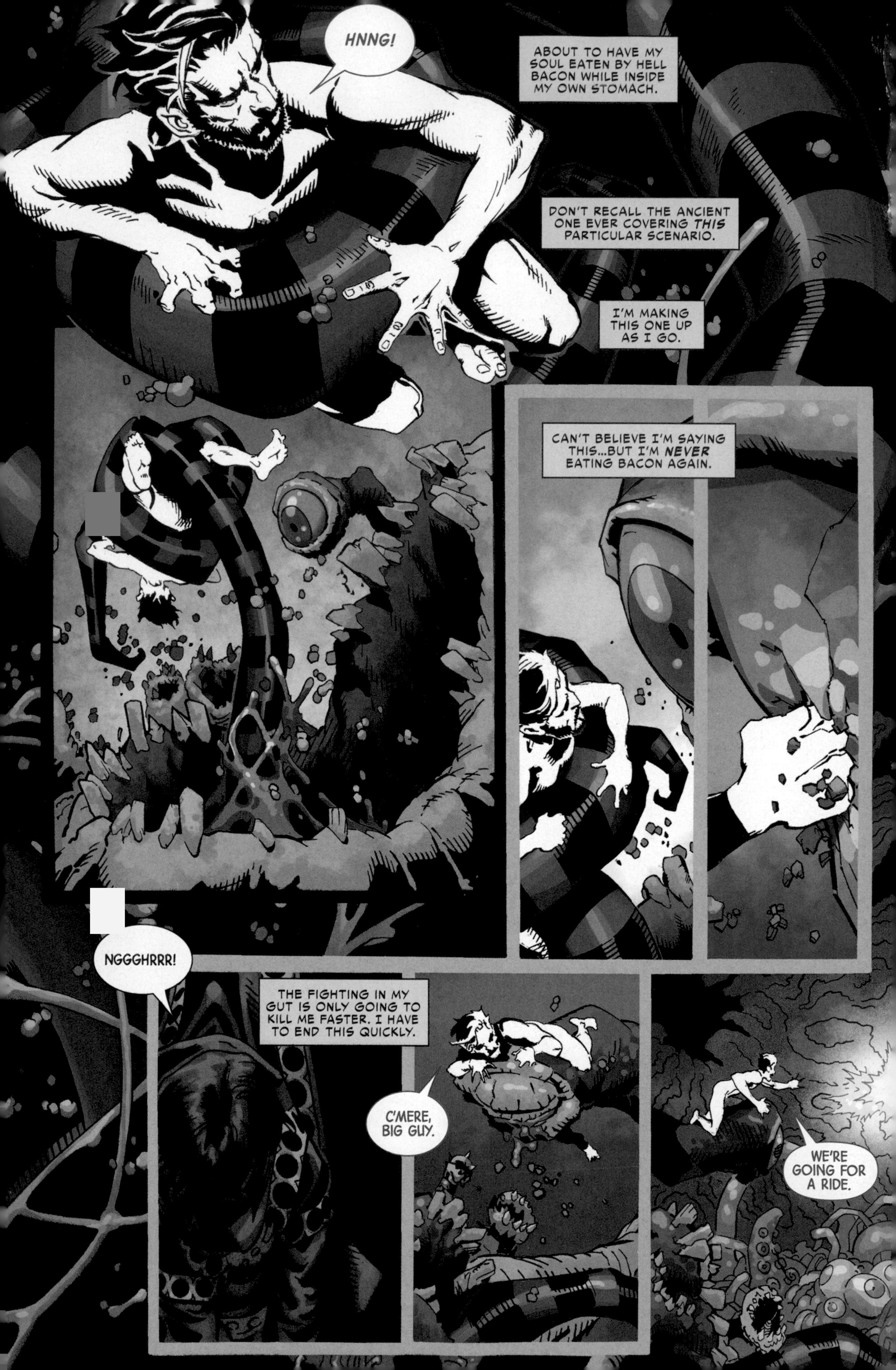
HNNG!
ABOUT TO HAVE MY SOUL EATEN BY HELL BACON WHILE INSIDE MY OWN STOMACH.
DON'T RECALL THE ANCIENT ONE EVER COVERING THIS PARTICULAR SCENARIO.
I'M MAKING THIS ONE UP AS I GO.
CAN'T BELIEVE I'M SAYING THIS...BUT I'M NEVER EATING BACON AGAIN.
NGGGHRRR!
THE FIGHTING IN MY GUT IS ONLY GOING TO KILL ME FASTER. I HAVE TO END THIS QUICKLY.
C'MERE, BIG GUY.
WE'RE GOING FOR A RIDE.

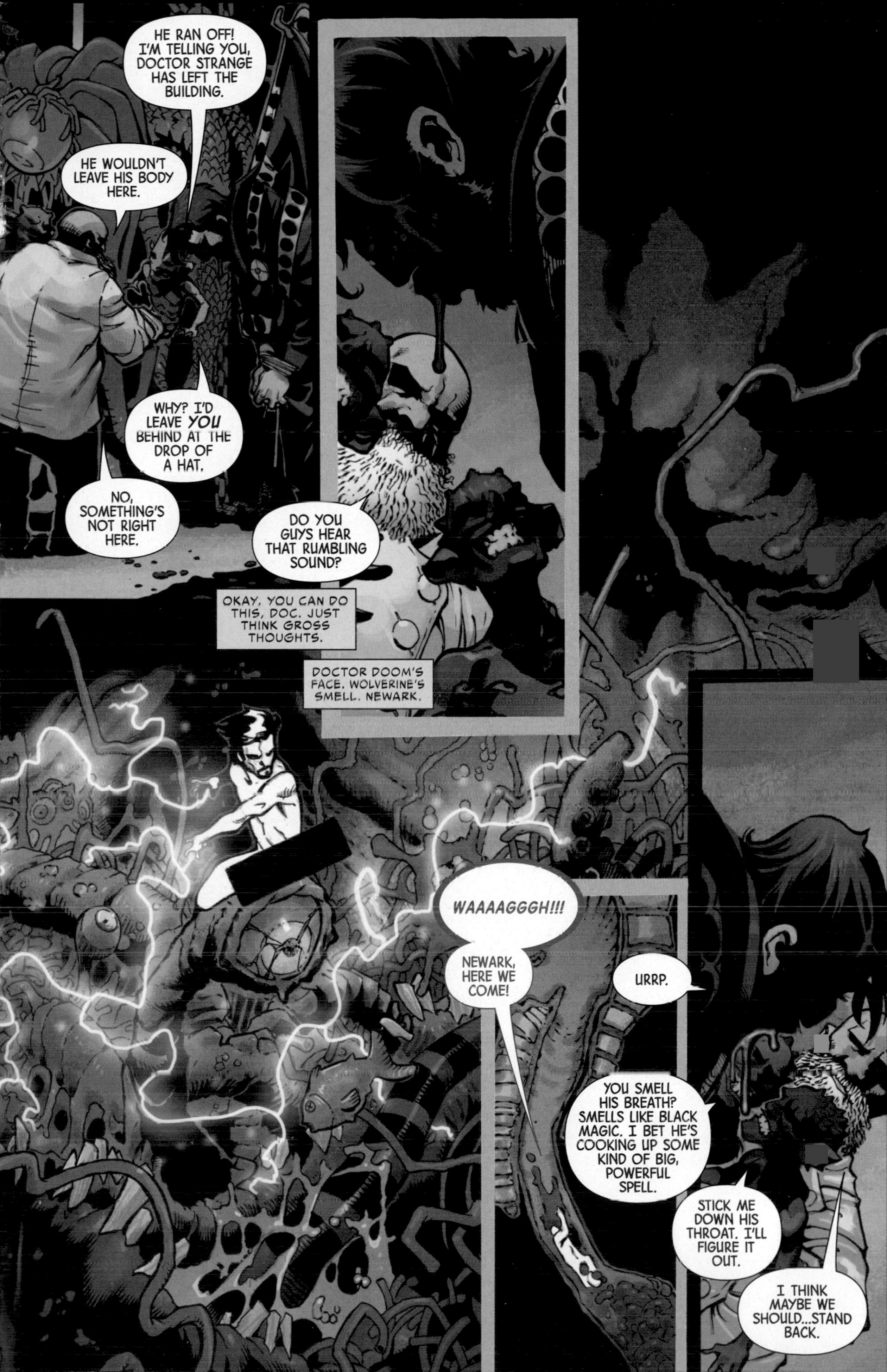
HE RAN OFF! I'M TELLING YOU, DOCTOR STRANGE HAS LEFT THE BUILDING.
HE WOULDN'T LEAVE HIS BODY HERE.
WHY? I'D LEAVE YOU BEHIND AT THE DROP OF A HAT.
NO, SOMETHING'S NOT RIGHT HERE.
DO YOU GUYS HEAR THAT RUMBLING SOUND?
OKAY, YOU CAN DO THIS, DOC. JUST THINK GROSS THOUGHTS.
DOCTOR DOOM'S FACE. WOLVERINE'S SMELL. NEWARK.
WAAAAGGGH!!!
NEWARK, HERE WE COME!
URRP.
YOU SMELL HIS BREATH? SMELLS LIKE BLACK MAGIC. I BET HE'S COOKING UP SOME KIND OF BIG, POWERFUL SPELL.
STICK ME DOWN HIS THROAT. I'LL FIGURE IT OUT.
I THINK MAYBE WE SHOULD...STAND BACK.

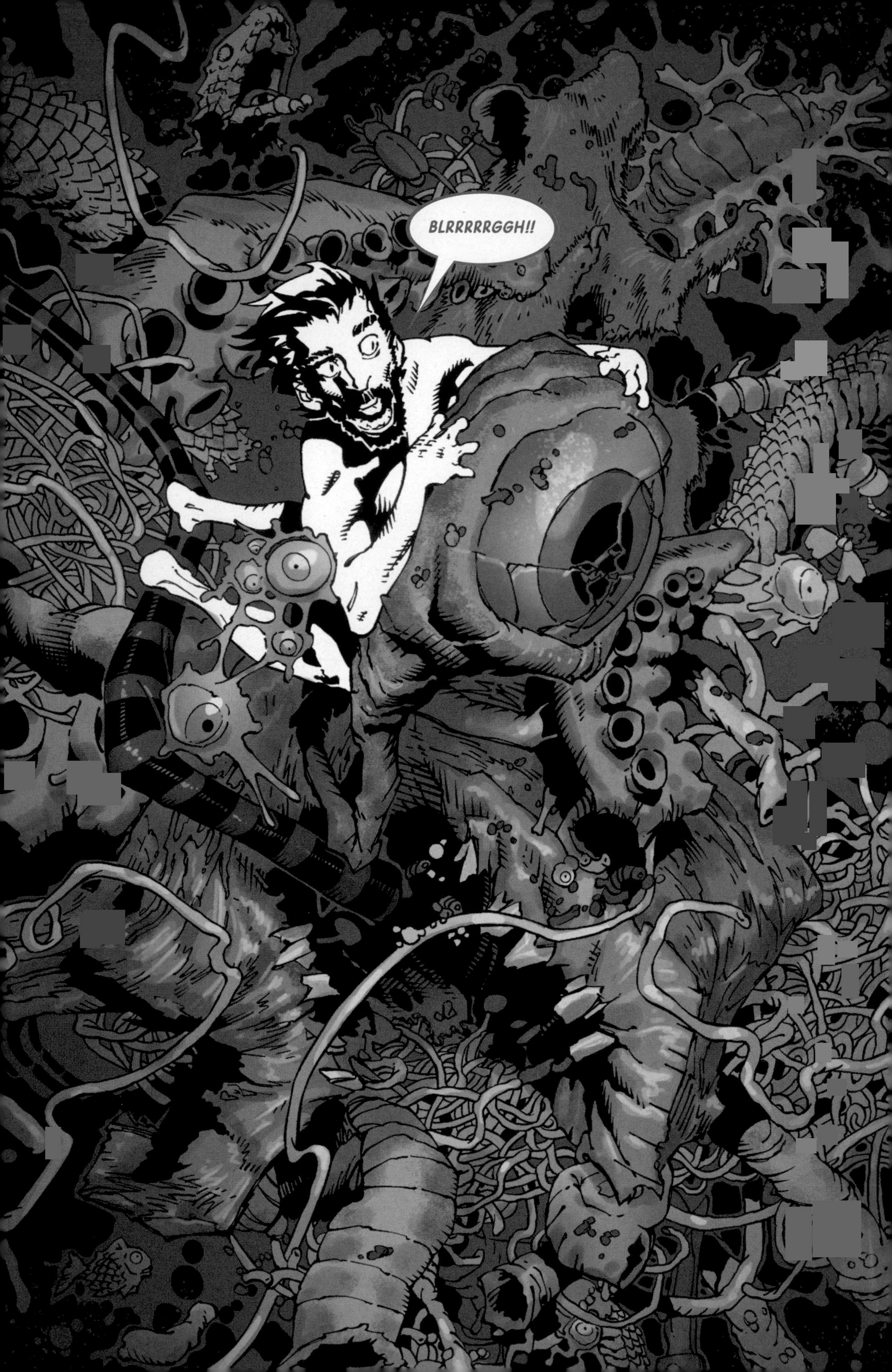
BLRRRRRRGGH!!

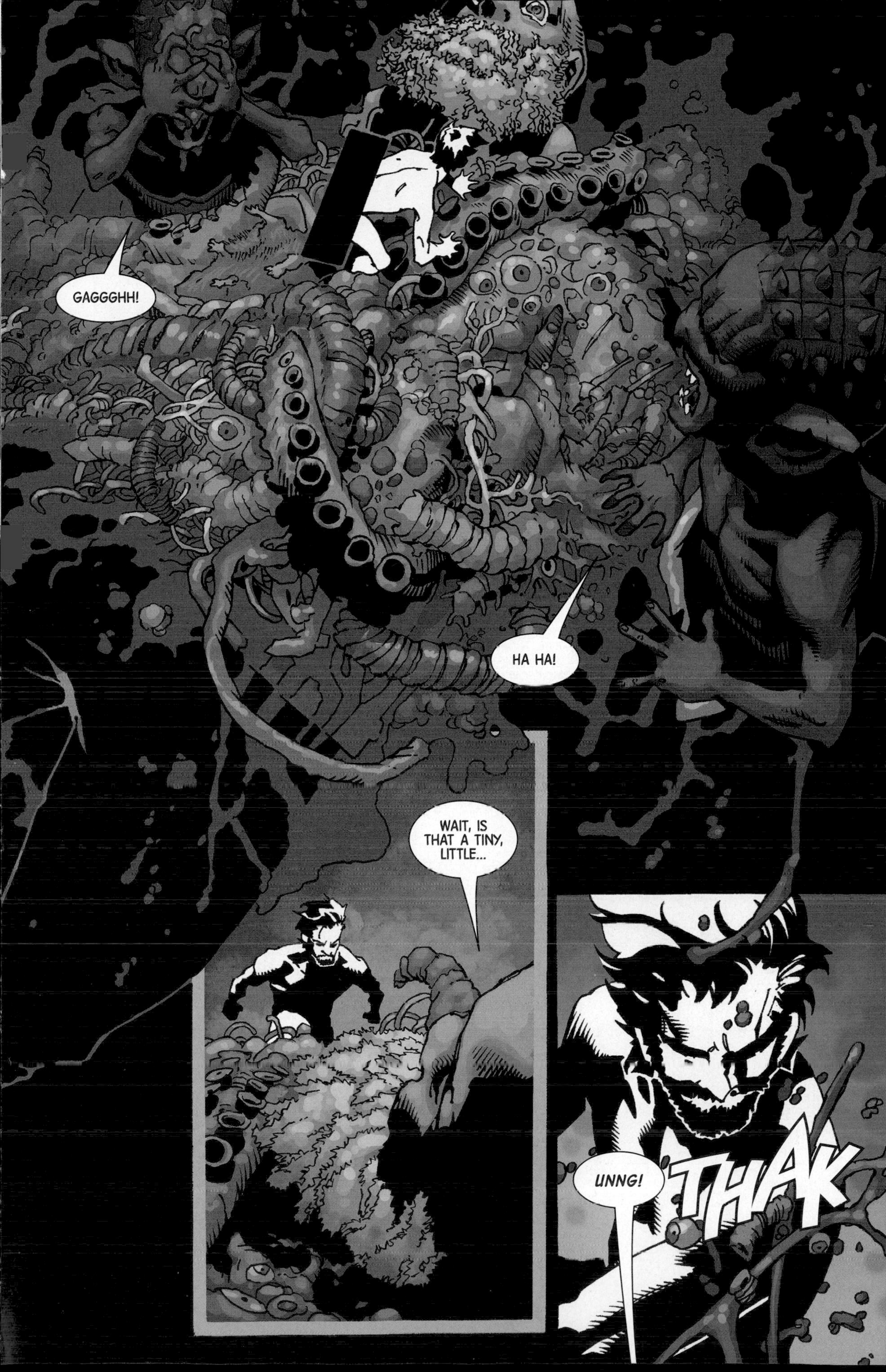
GAGGGHH!
HA HA!
WAIT, IS THAT A TINY, LITTLE...
UNNG!
THAK

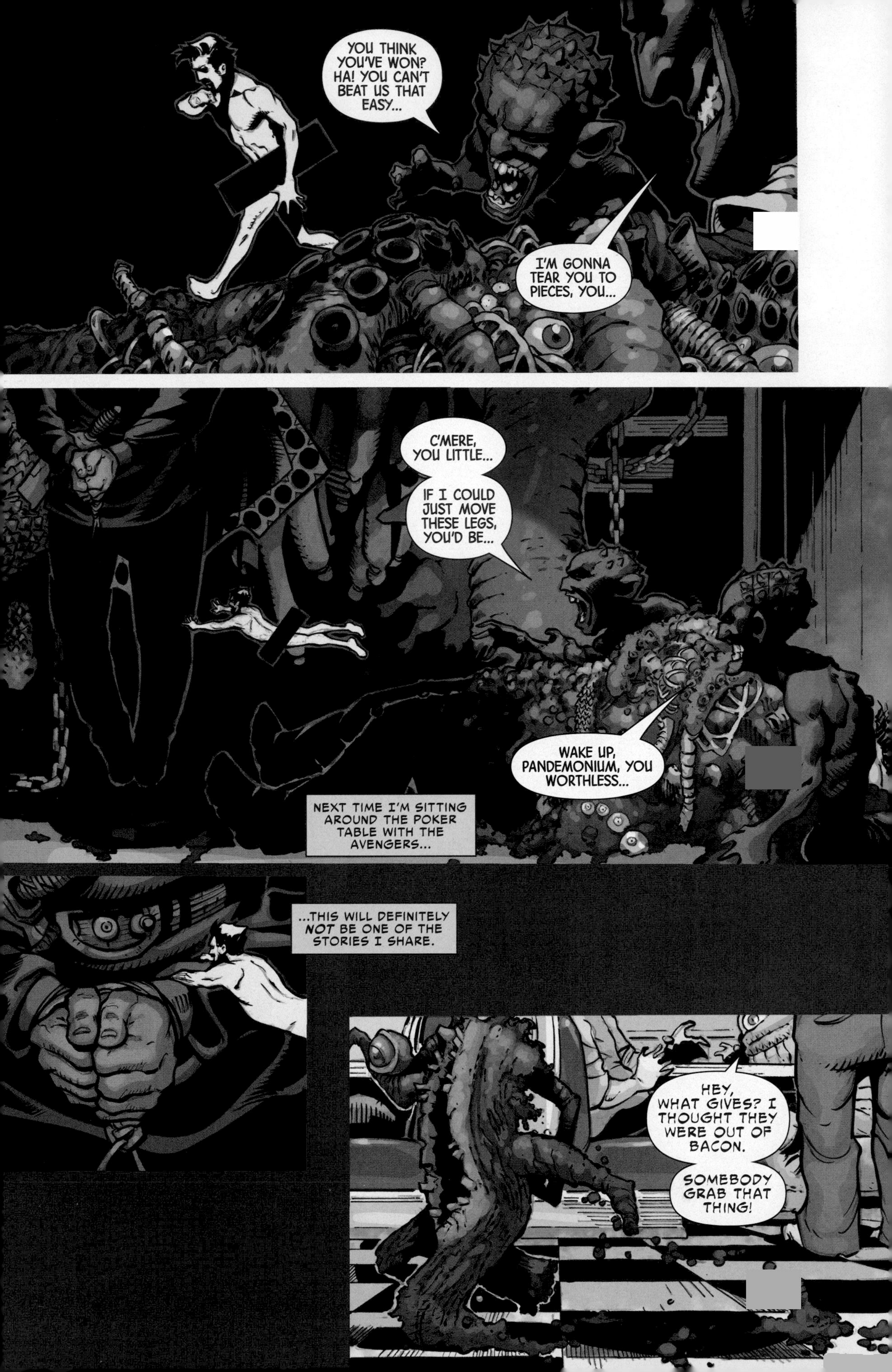
YOU THINK YOU'VE WON? HA! YOU CAN'T BEAT US THAT EASY...
I'M GONNA TEAR YOU TO PIECES, YOU...
C'MERE, YOU LITTLE...
IF I COULD JUST MOVE THESE LEGS, YOU'D BE...
WAKE UP, PANDEMONIUM, YOU WORTHLESS...
NEXT TIME I'M SITTING AROUND THE POKER TABLE WITH THE AVENGERS...
...THIS WILL DEFINITELY *NOT* BE ONE OF THE STORIES I SHARE.
HEY, WHAT GIVES? I THOUGHT THEY WERE OUT OF BACON.
SOMEBODY GRAB THAT THING!

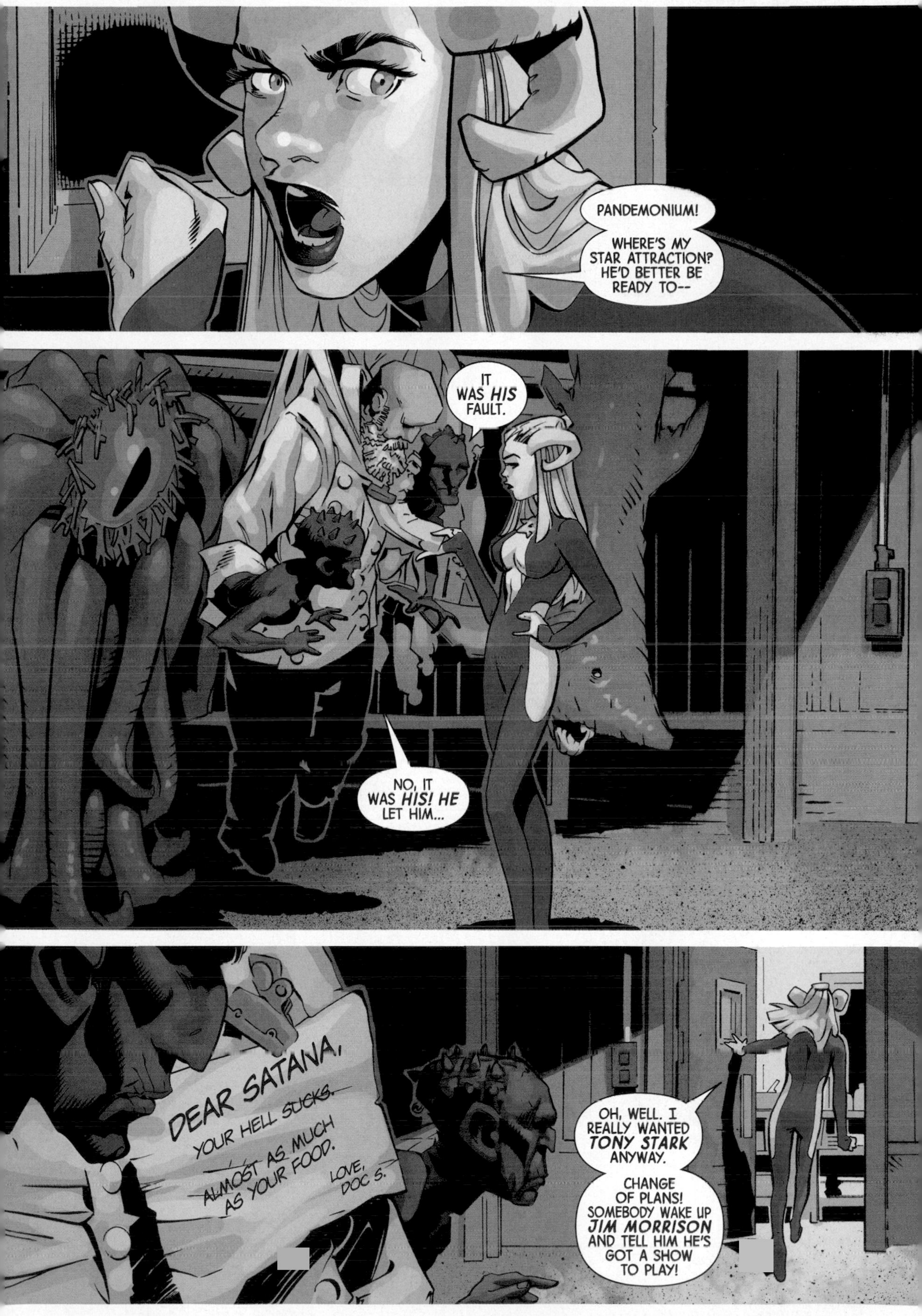
PANDEMONIUM!
WHERE'S MY STAR ATTRACTION? HE'D BETTER BE READY TO--
IT WAS HIS FAULT.
NO, IT WAS HIS! HE LET HIM...
DEAR SATANA, YOUR HELL SUCKS. ALMOST AS MUCH AS YOUR FOOD. LOVE, DOC S.
OH, WELL. I REALLY WANTED TONY STARK ANYWAY.
CHANGE OF PLANS! SOMEBODY WAKE UP JIM MORRISON AND TELL HIM HE'S GOT A SHOW TO PLAY!

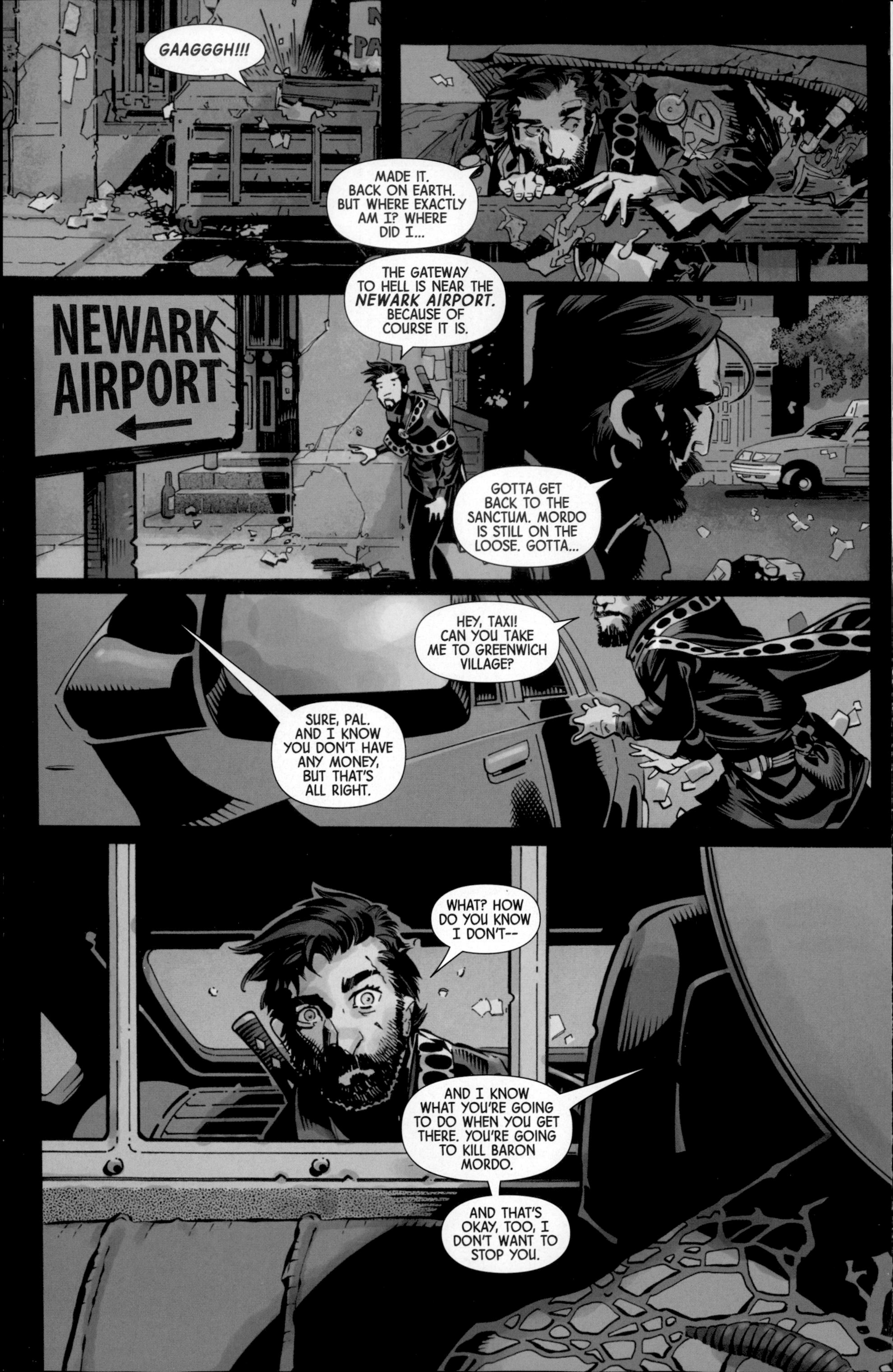
GAAGGGH!!!
MADE IT. BACK ON EARTH. BUT WHERE EXACTLY AM I? WHERE DID I...
THE GATEWAY TO HELL IS NEAR THE NEWARK AIRPORT. BECAUSE OF COURSE IT IS.
NEWARK AIRPORT
GOTTA GET BACK TO THE SANCTUM. MORDO IS STILL ON THE LOOSE. GOTTA...
HEY, TAXI! CAN YOU TAKE ME TO GREENWICH VILLAGE?
SURE, PAL. AND I KNOW YOU DON'T HAVE ANY MONEY, BUT THAT'S ALL RIGHT.
WHAT? HOW DO YOU KNOW I DON'T--
AND I KNOW WHAT YOU'RE GOING TO DO WHEN YOU GET THERE. YOU'RE GOING TO KILL BARON MORDO.
AND THAT'S OKAY, TOO, I DON'T WANT TO STOP YOU.

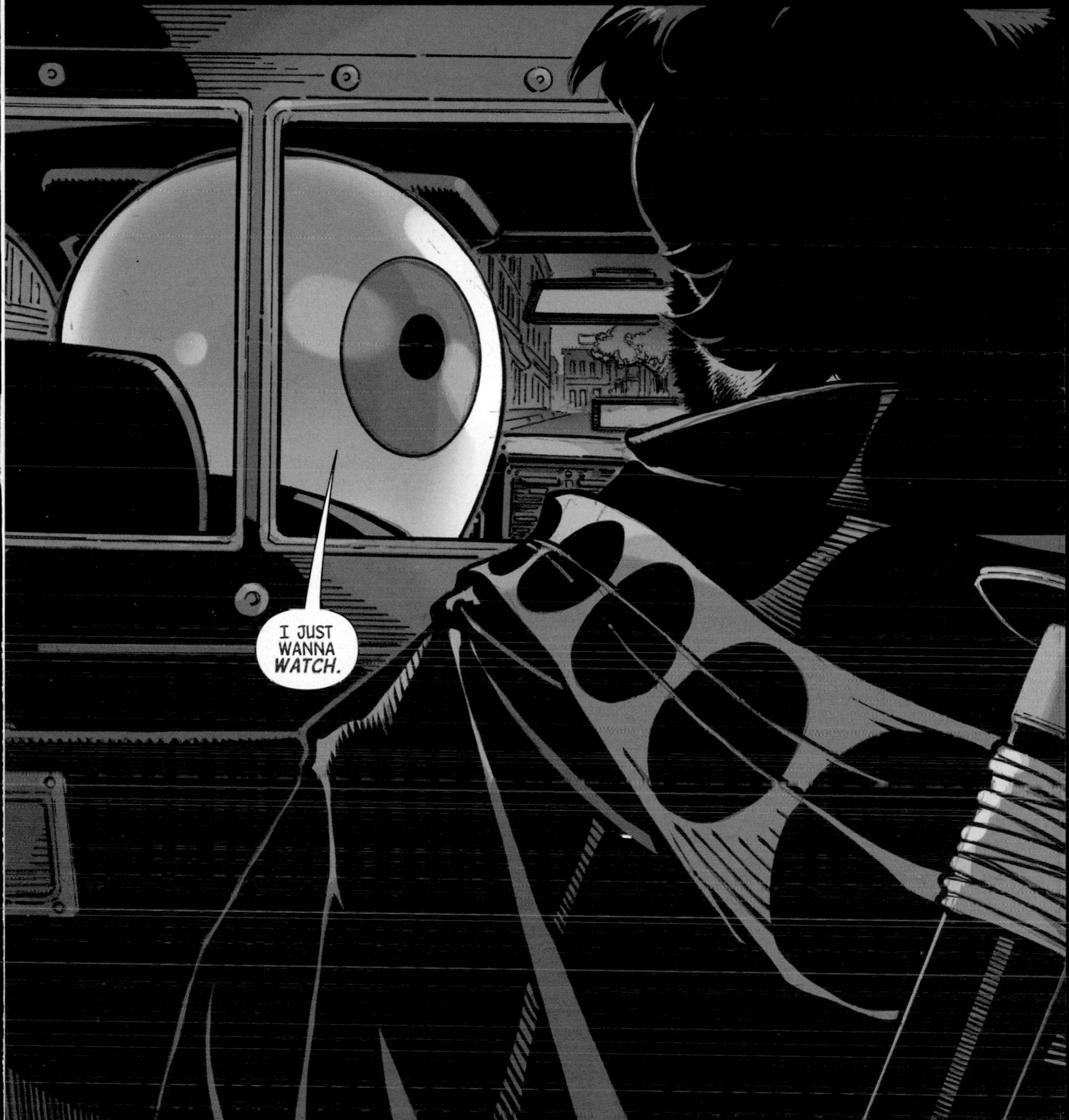
I JUST WANNA WATCH.

I-DON'T-EVEN-KNOW-WHAT-DAY-IT-IS-ANYMORE.
THE ORB.

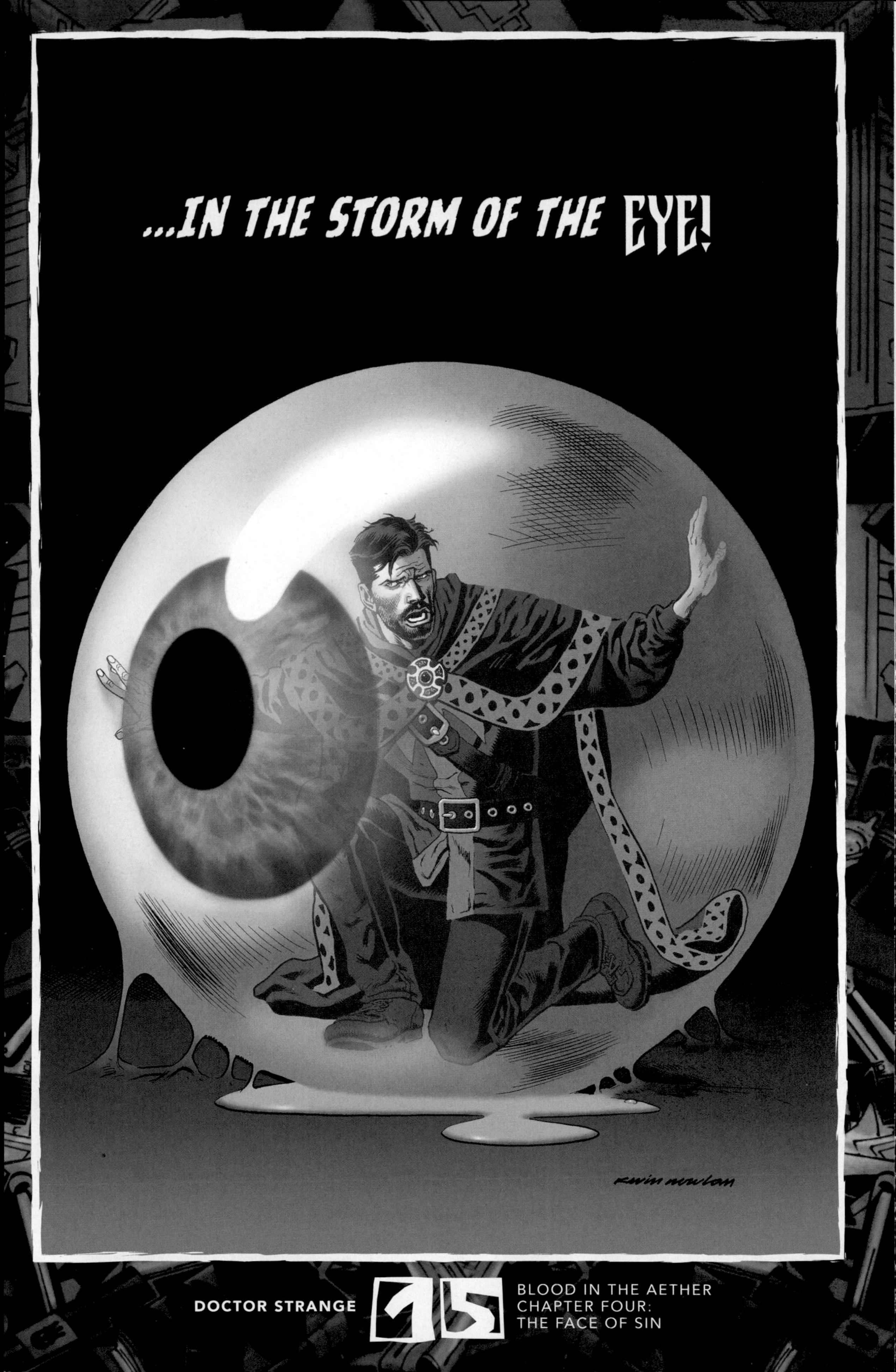
...IN THE STORM OF THE EYE!
DOCTOR STRANGE
15
BLOOD IN THE AETHER
CHAPTER FOUR:
THE FACE OF SIN

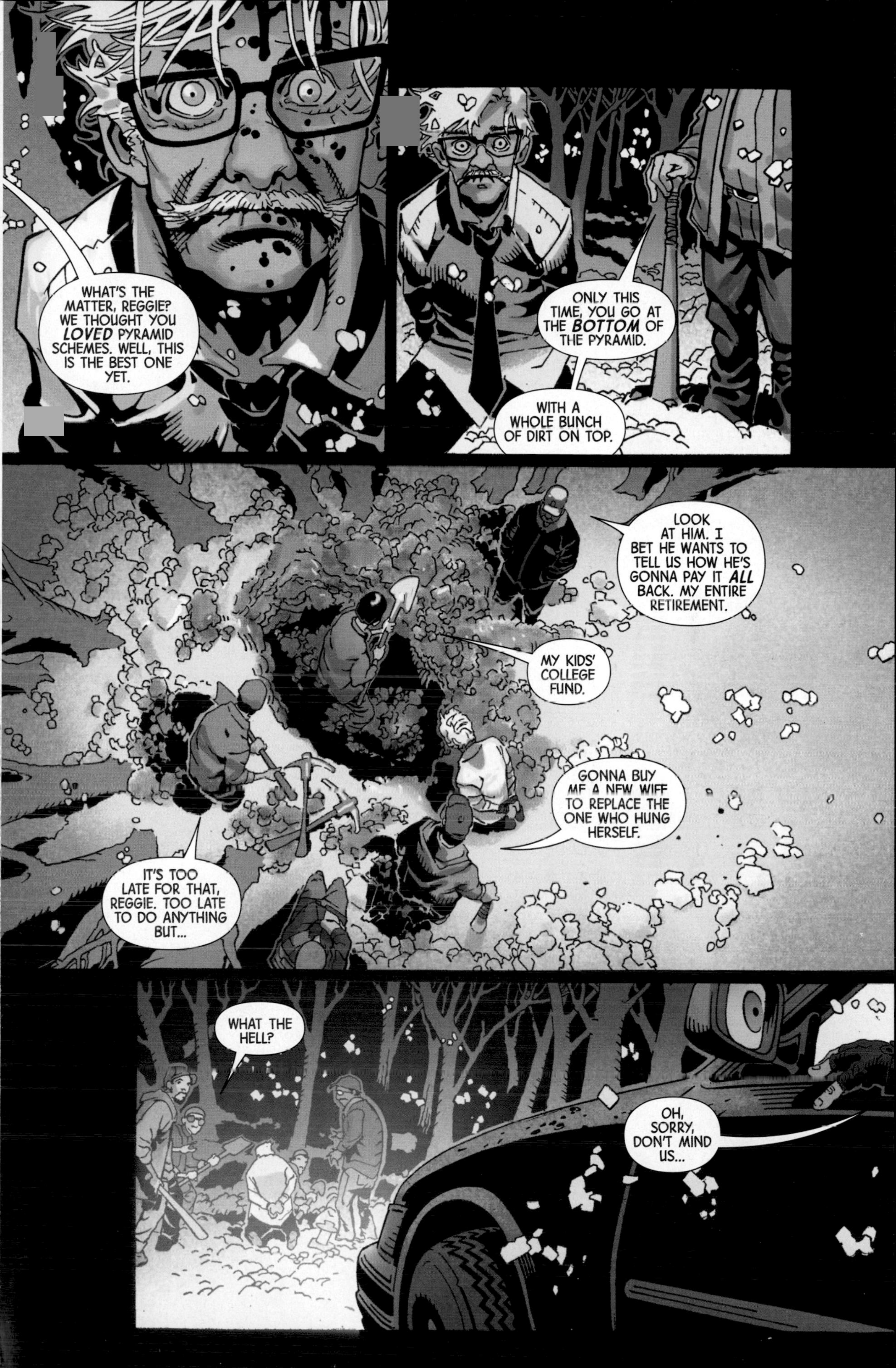
WHAT'S THE MATTER, REGGIE? WE THOUGHT YOU LOVED PYRAMID SCHEMES. WELL, THIS IS THE BEST ONE YET.
ONLY THIS TIME, YOU GO AT THE BOTTOM OF THE PYRAMID.
WITH A WHOLE BUNCH OF DIRT ON TOP.
LOOK AT HIM. I BET HE WANTS TO TELL US HOW HE'S GONNA PAY IT ALL BACK. MY ENTIRE RETIREMENT.
MY KIDS' COLLEGE FUND.
GONNA BUY ME A NEW WIFE TO REPLACE THE ONE WHO HUNG HERSELF.
IT'S TOO LATE FOR THAT, REGGIE. TOO LATE TO DO ANYTHING BUT...
WHAT THE HELL?
OH, SORRY, DON'T MIND US...

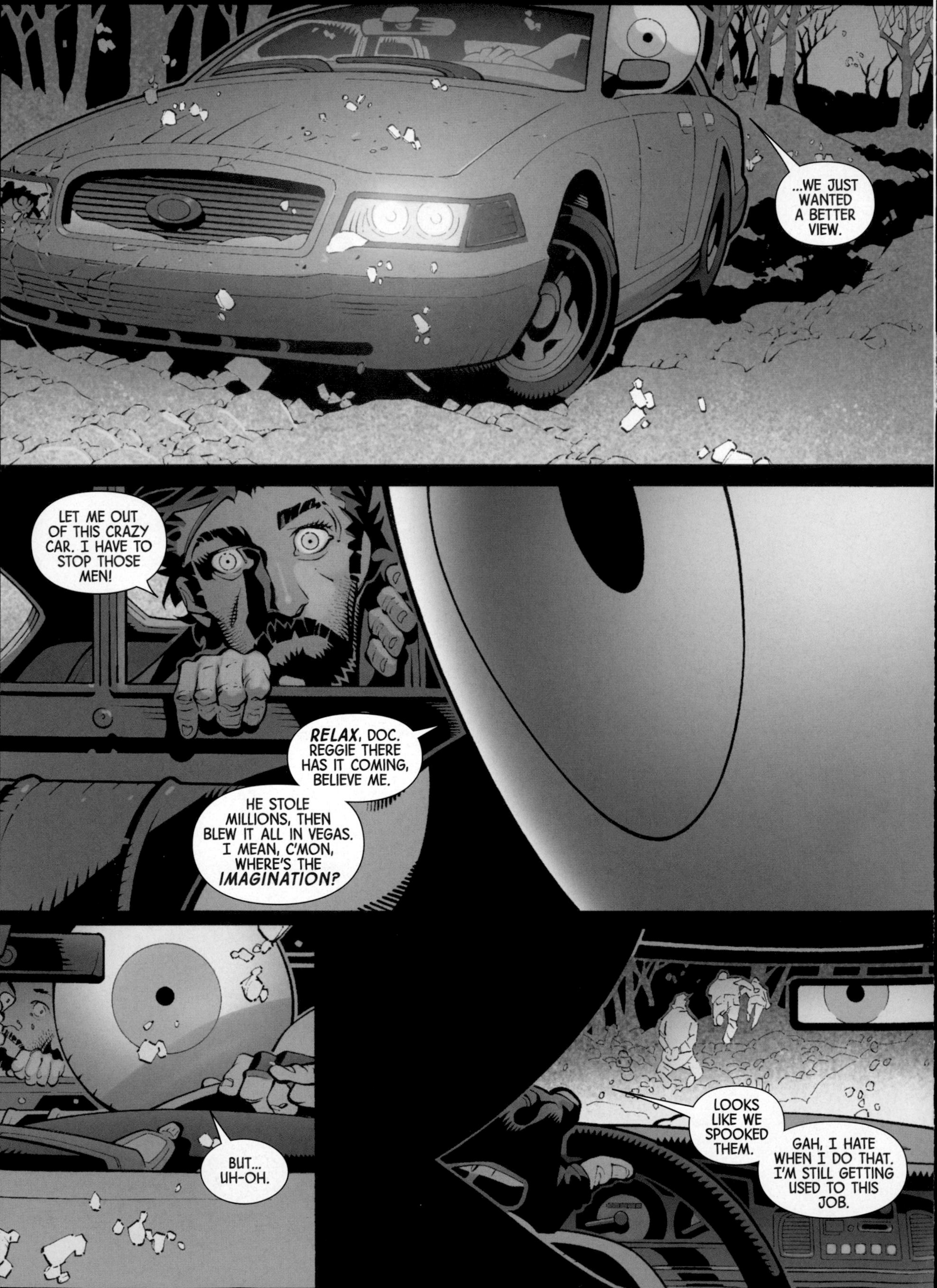
...WE JUST WANTED A BETTER VIEW.
LET ME OUT OF THIS CRAZY CAR. I HAVE TO STOP THOSE MEN!
RELAX, DOC. REGGIE THERE HAS IT COMING, BELIEVE ME.
HE STOLE MILLIONS, THEN BLEW IT ALL IN VEGAS. I MEAN, C'MON, WHERE'S THE IMAGINATION?
BUT... UH-OH.
LOOKS LIKE WE SPOOKED THEM.
GAH, I HATE WHEN I DO THAT. I'M STILL GETTING USED TO THIS JOB.

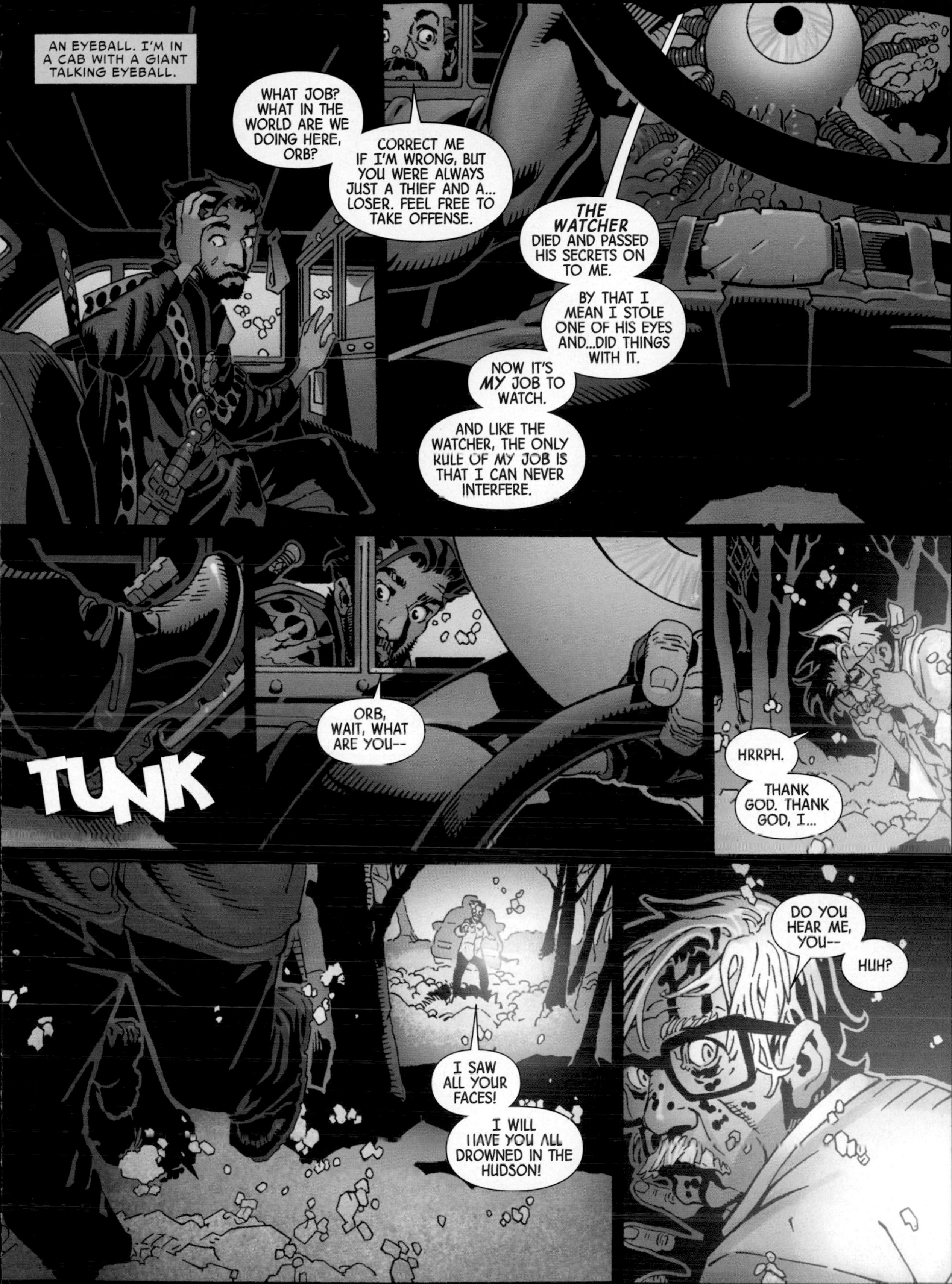
AN EYEBALL. I'M IN A CAB WITH A GIANT TALKING EYEBALL.
WHAT JOB? WHAT IN THE WORLD ARE WE DOING HERE, ORB?
CORRECT ME IF I'M WRONG, BUT YOU WERE ALWAYS JUST A THIEF AND A... LOSER. FEEL FREE TO TAKE OFFENSE.
THE WATCHER DIED AND PASSED HIS SECRETS ON TO ME.
BY THAT I MEAN I STOLE ONE OF HIS EYES AND...DID THINGS WITH IT.
NOW IT'S MY JOB TO WATCH.
AND LIKE THE WATCHER, THE ONLY RULE OF MY JOB IS THAT I CAN NEVER INTERFERE.
ORB, WAIT, WHAT ARE YOU--
TUNK
HRRPH.
THANK GOD. THANK GOD, I...
I SAW ALL YOUR FACES!
I WILL HAVE YOU ALL DROWNED IN THE HUDSON!
DO YOU HEAR ME, YOU--
HUH?

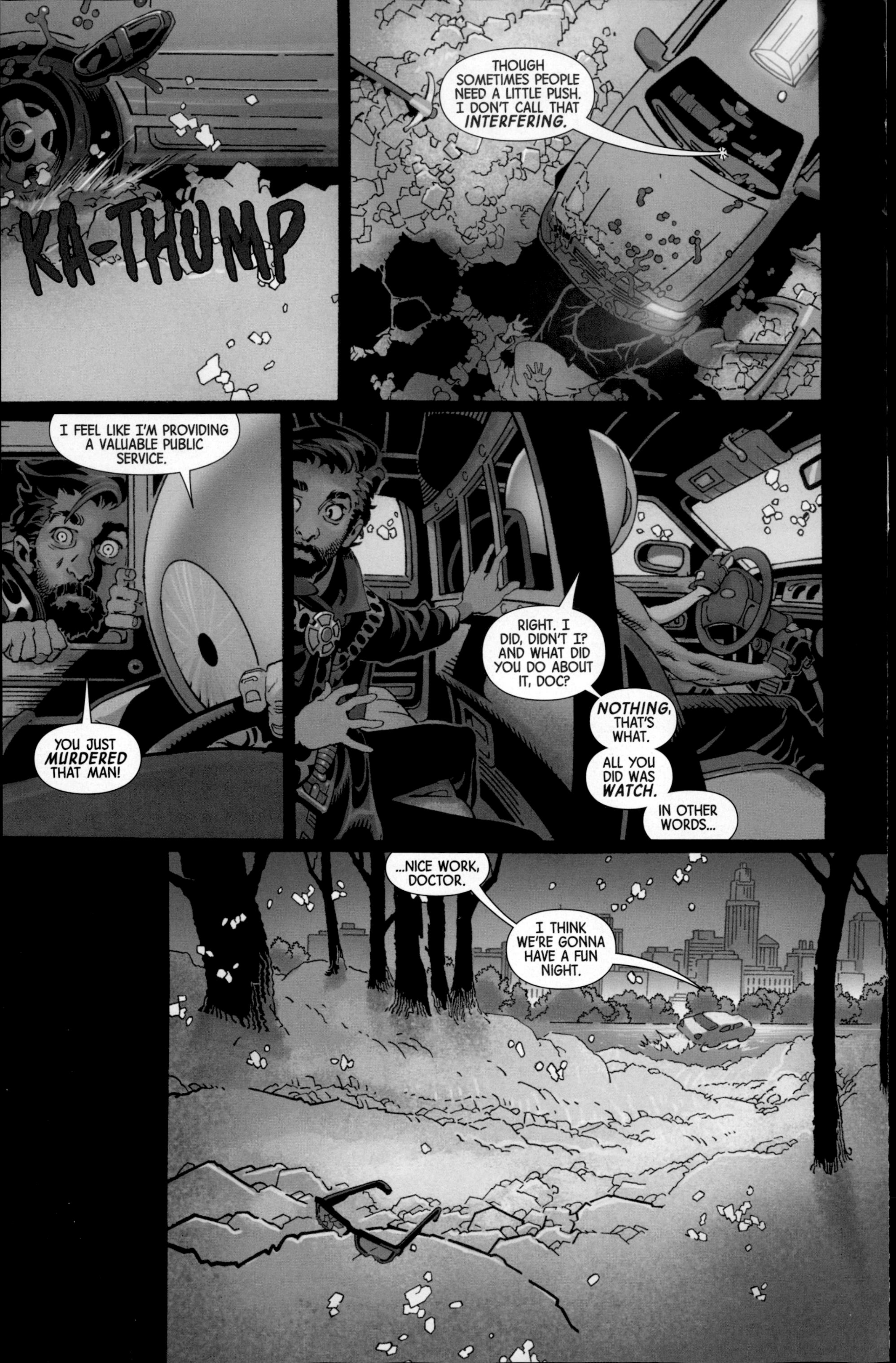
KA-THUMP
THOUGH SOMETIMES PEOPLE NEED A LITTLE PUSH. I DON'T CALL THAT INTERFERING.
I FEEL LIKE I'M PROVIDING A VALUABLE PUBLIC SERVICE.
YOU JUST MURDERED THAT MAN!
RIGHT. I DID, DIDN'T I? AND WHAT DID YOU DO ABOUT IT, DOC?
NOTHING, THAT'S WHAT.
ALL YOU DID WAS WATCH.
IN OTHER WORDS...
...NICE WORK, DOCTOR.
I THINK WE'RE GONNA HAVE A FUN NIGHT.

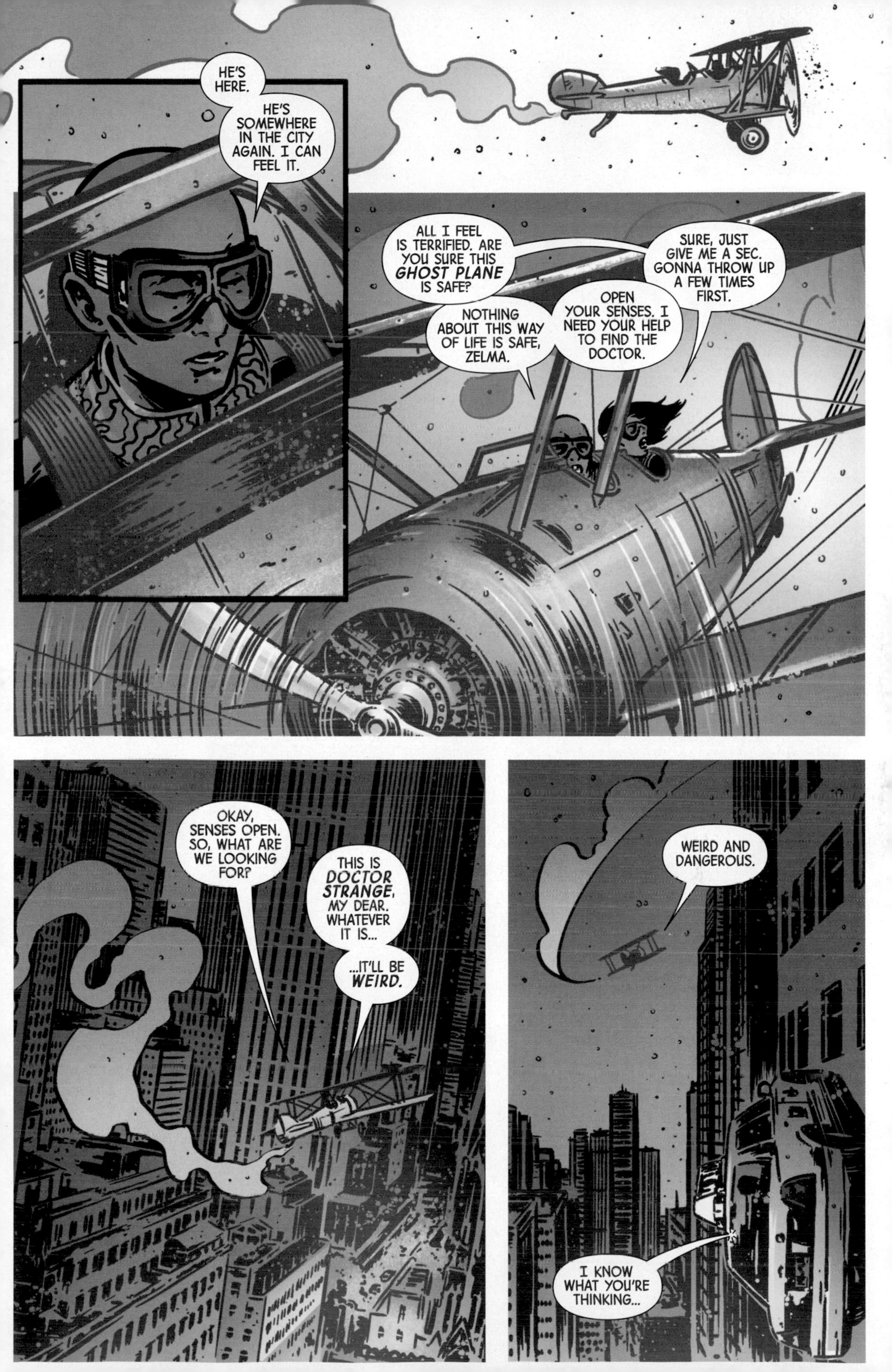
HE'S HERE.
HE'S SOMEWHERE IN THE CITY AGAIN. I CAN FEEL IT.
ALL I FEEL IS TERRIFIED. ARE YOU SURE THIS GHOST PLANE IS SAFE?
NOTHING ABOUT THIS WAY OF LIFE IS SAFE, ZELMA.
OPEN YOUR SENSES. I NEED YOUR HELP TO FIND THE DOCTOR.
SURE, JUST GIVE ME A SEC. GONNA THROW UP A FEW TIMES FIRST.
OKAY, SENSES OPEN. SO, WHAT ARE WE LOOKING FOR?
THIS IS DOCTOR STRANGE, MY DEAR. WHATEVER IT IS...
...IT'LL BE WEIRD.
WEIRD AND DANGEROUS.
I KNOW WHAT YOU'RE THINKING...

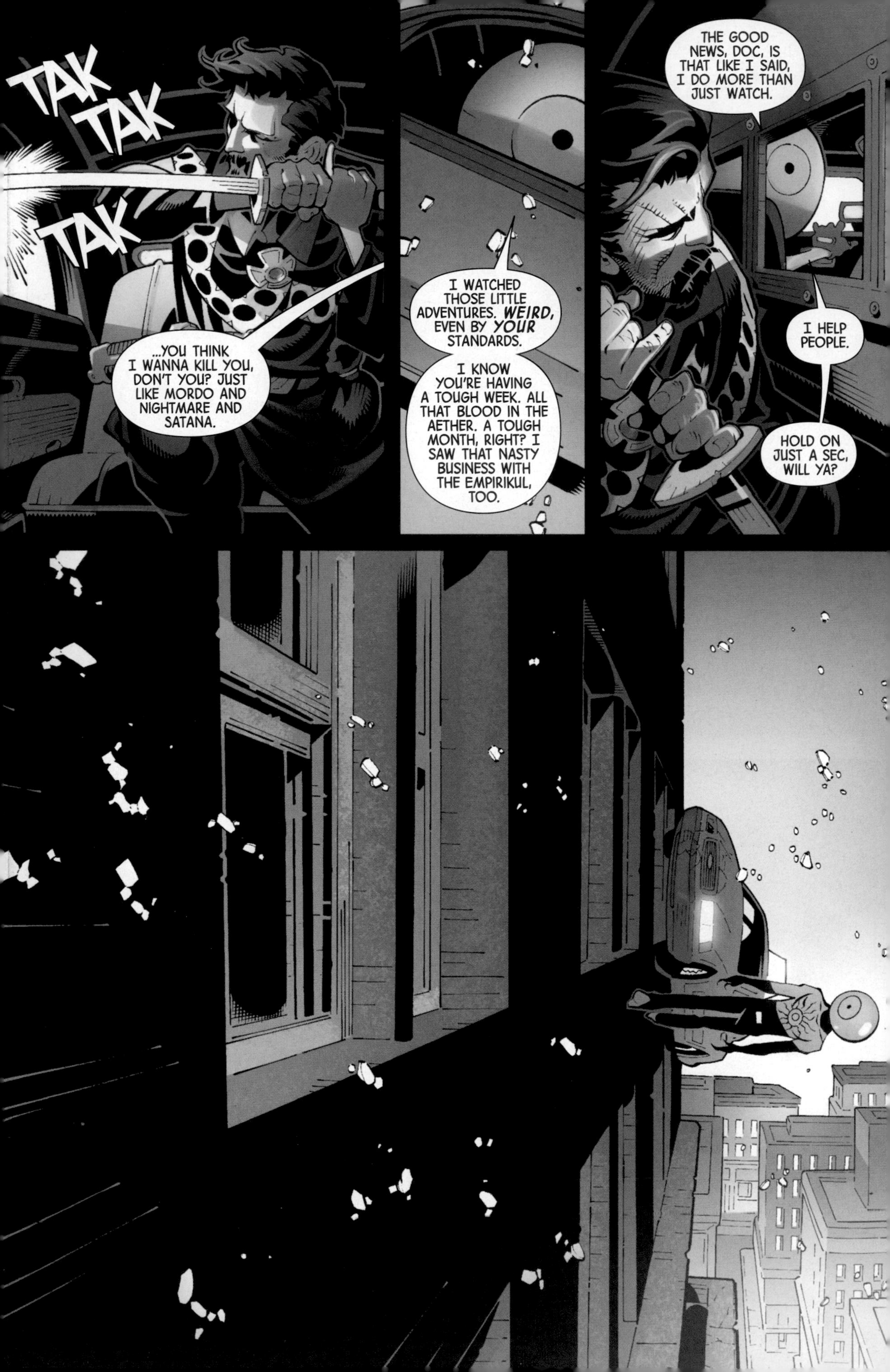
TAK
TAK
TAK
...YOU THINK I WANNA KILL YOU, DON'T YOU? JUST LIKE MORDO AND NIGHTMARE AND SATANA.
I WATCHED THOSE LITTLE ADVENTURES. WEIRD, EVEN BY YOUR STANDARDS.
I KNOW YOU'RE HAVING A TOUGH WEEK. ALL THAT BLOOD IN THE AETHER. A TOUGH MONTH, RIGHT? I SAW THAT NASTY BUSINESS WITH THE EMPIRIKUL, TOO.
THE GOOD NEWS, DOC, IS THAT LIKE I SAID, I DO MORE THAN JUST WATCH.
I HELP PEOPLE.
HOLD ON JUST A SEC, WILL YA?

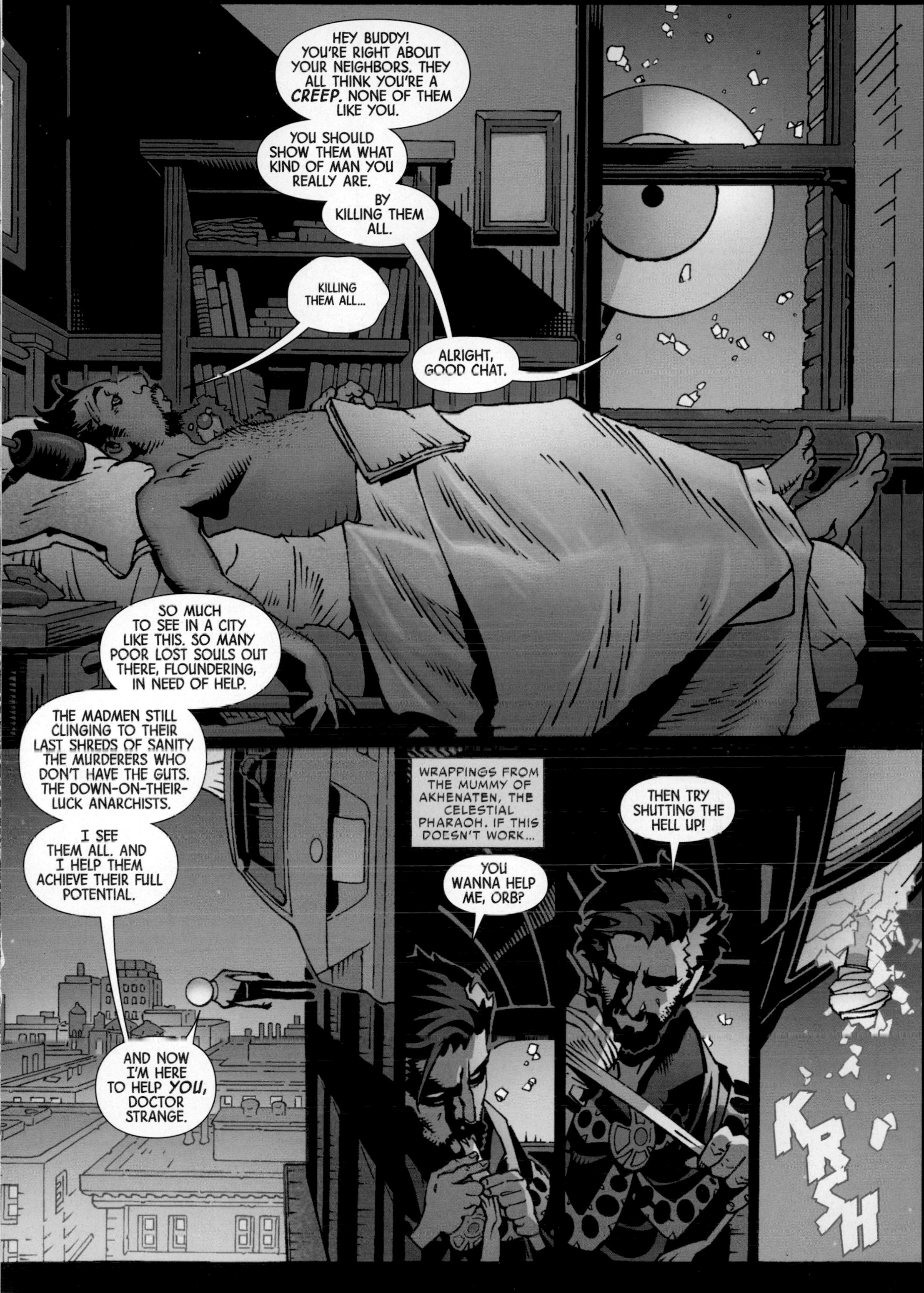
HEY BUDDY! YOU'RE RIGHT ABOUT YOUR NEIGHBORS. THEY ALL THINK YOU'RE A CREEP. NONE OF THEM LIKE YOU.
YOU SHOULD SHOW THEM WHAT KIND OF MAN YOU REALLY ARE.
BY KILLING THEM ALL.
KILLING THEM ALL...
ALRIGHT, GOOD CHAT.
SO MUCH TO SEE IN A CITY LIKE THIS. SO MANY POOR LOST SOULS OUT THERE, FLOUNDERING, IN NEED OF HELP.
THE MADMEN STILL CLINGING TO THEIR LAST SHREDS OF SANITY THE MURDERERS WHO DON'T HAVE THE GUTS. THE DOWN-ON-THEIR-LUCK ANARCHISTS.
I SEE THEM ALL. AND I HELP THEM ACHIEVE THEIR FULL POTENTIAL.
AND NOW I'M HERE TO HELP YOU, DOCTOR STRANGE.
WRAPPINGS FROM THE MUMMY OF AKHENATEN, THE CELESTIAL PHARAOH. IF THIS DOESN'T WORK...
YOU WANNA HELP ME, ORB?
THEN TRY SHUTTING THE HELL UP!
KRSH

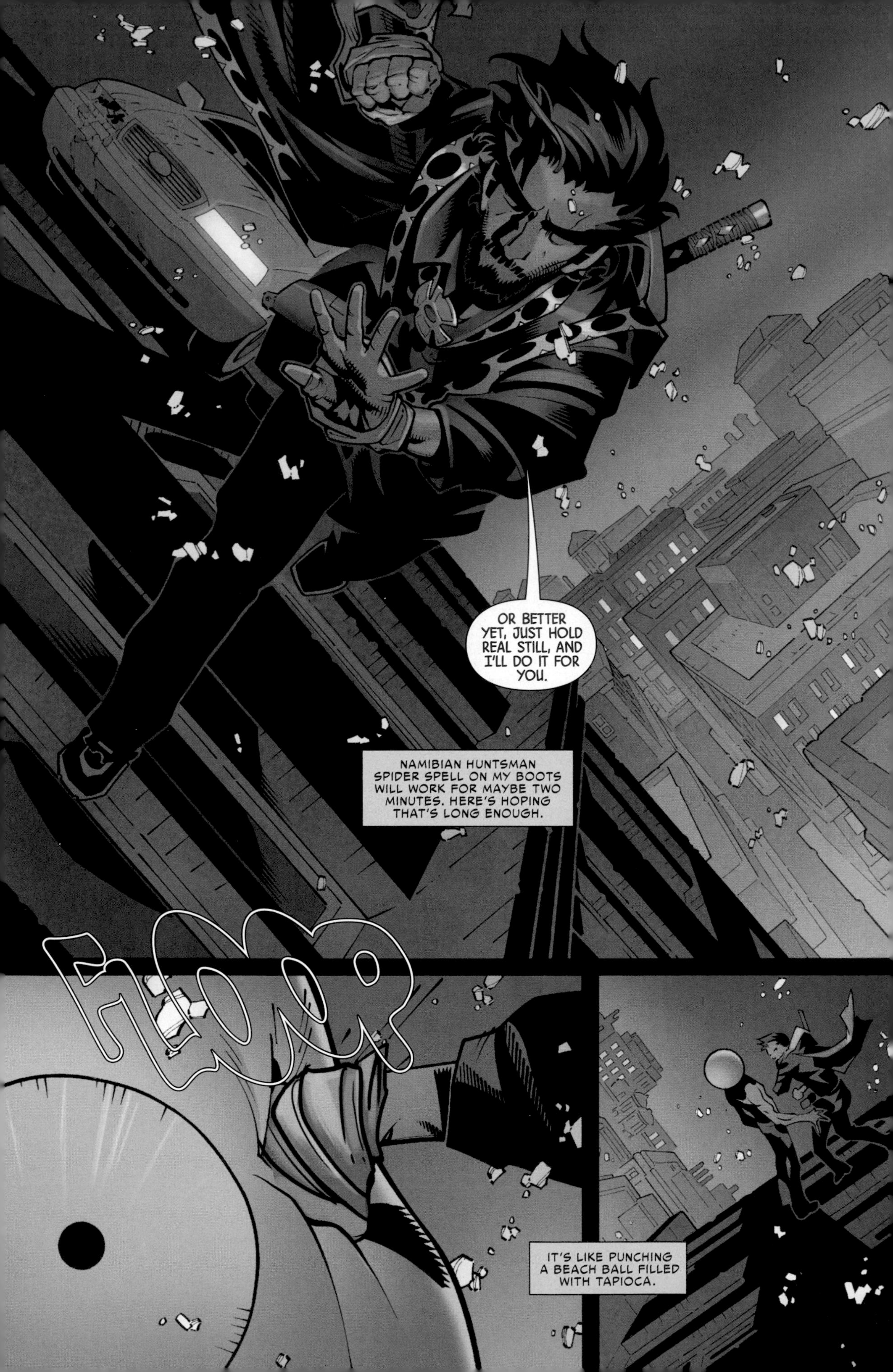
OR BETTER YET, JUST HOLD REAL STILL, AND I'LL DO IT FOR YOU.
NAMIBIAN HUNTSMAN SPIDER SPELL ON MY BOOTS WILL WORK FOR MAYBE TWO MINUTES. HERE'S HOPING THAT'S LONG ENOUGH.
IT'S LIKE PUNCHING A BEACH BALL FILLED WITH TAPIOCA.

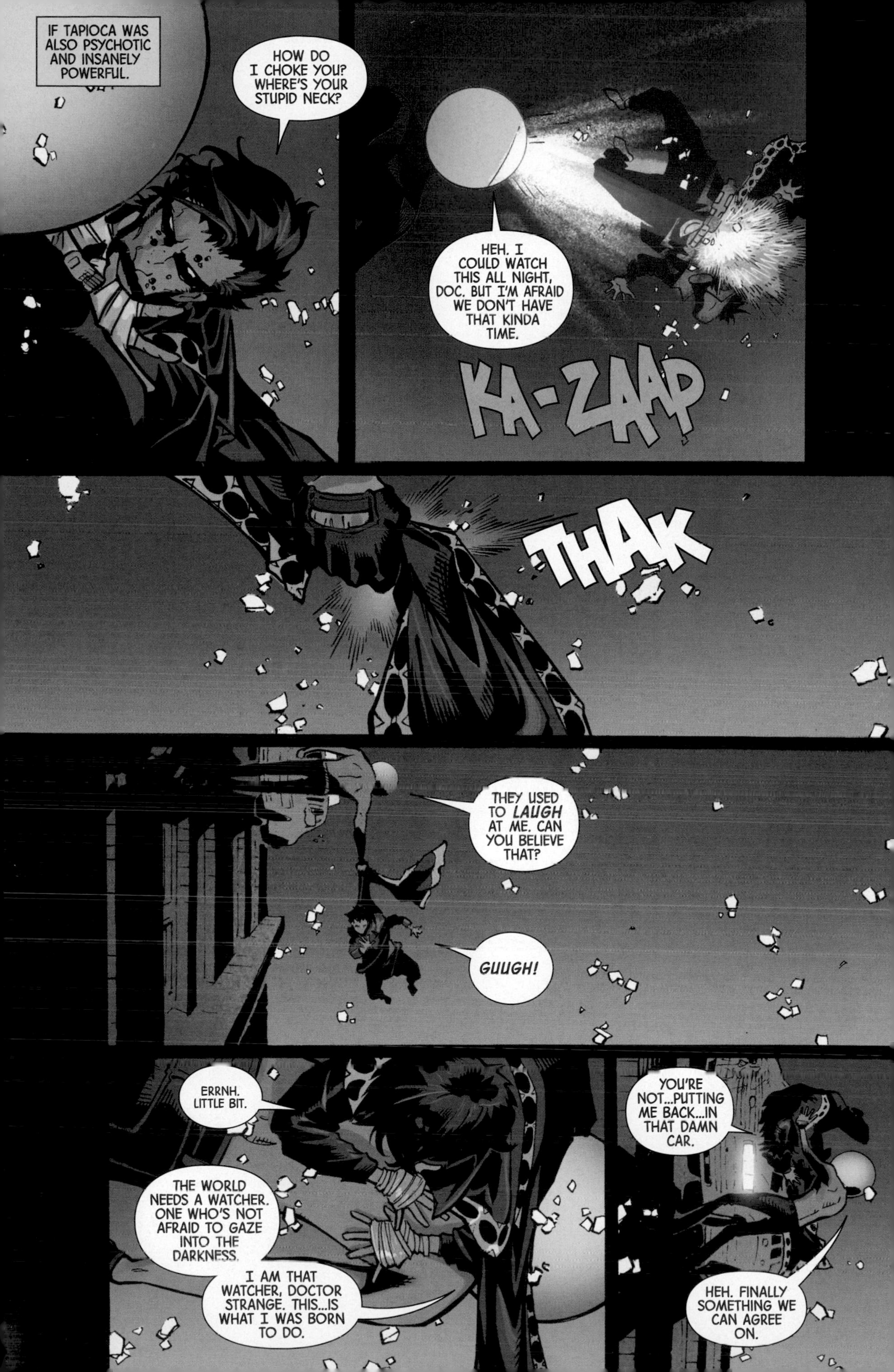
IF TAPIOCA WAS ALSO PSYCHOTIC AND INSANELY POWERFUL.
HOW DO I CHOKE YOU? WHERE'S YOUR STUPID NECK?
HEH. I COULD WATCH THIS ALL NIGHT, DOC. BUT I'M AFRAID WE DON'T HAVE THAT KINDA TIME.
KA-ZAAP
THAK
THEY USED TO LAUGH AT ME. CAN YOU BELIEVE THAT?
GUUGH!
ERRNH. LITTLE BIT.
THE WORLD NEEDS A WATCHER. ONE WHO'S NOT AFRAID TO GAZE INTO THE DARKNESS.
I AM THAT WATCHER, DOCTOR STRANGE. THIS...IS WHAT I WAS BORN TO DO.
YOU'RE NOT...PUTTING ME BACK...IN THAT DAMN CAR.
HEH. FINALLY SOMETHING WE CAN AGREE ON.

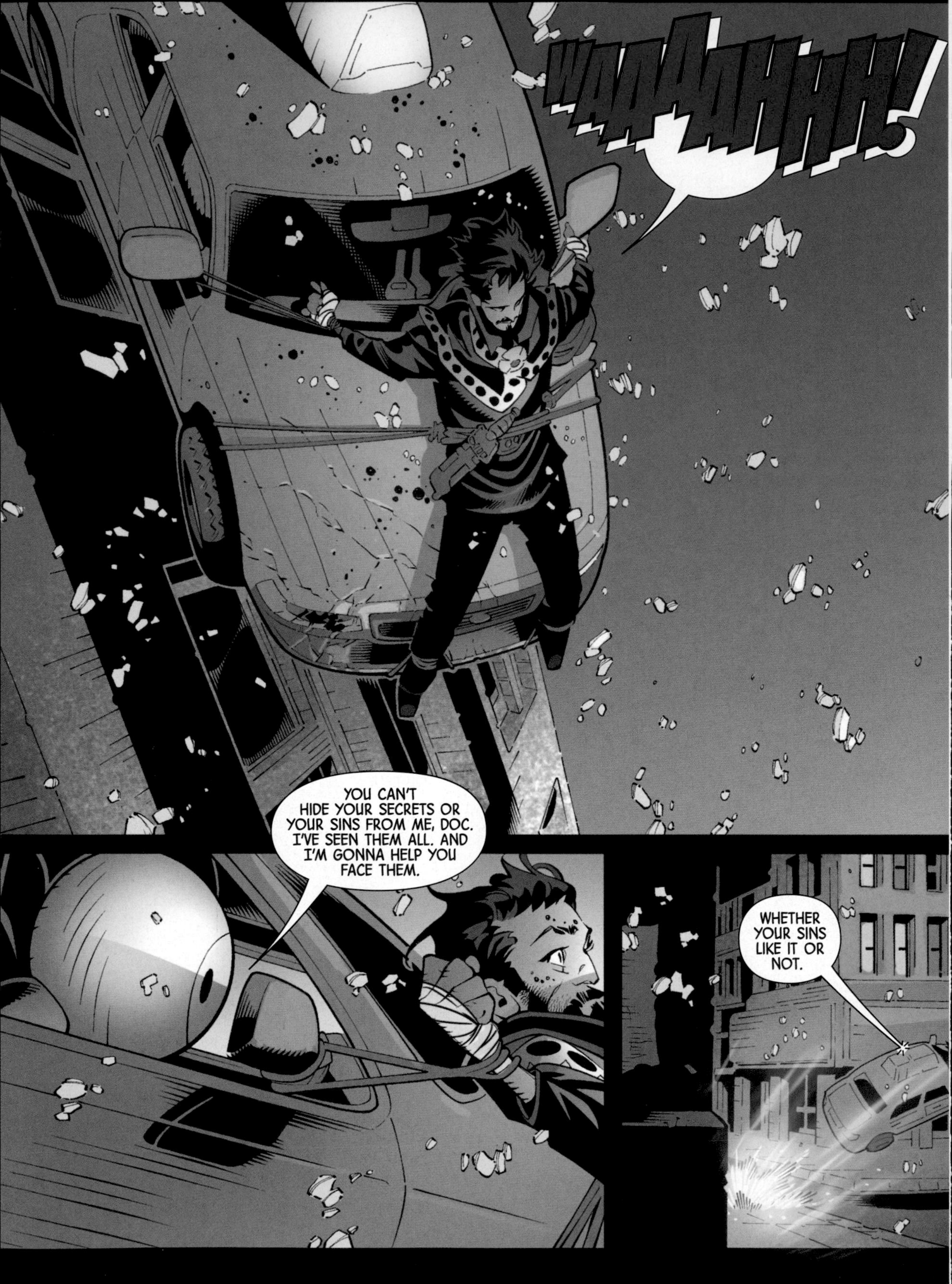
WAAAAHHHH!
YOU CAN'T HIDE YOUR SECRETS OR YOUR SINS FROM ME, DOC. I'VE SEEN THEM ALL. AND I'M GONNA HELP YOU FACE THEM.
WHETHER YOUR SINS LIKE IT OR NOT.

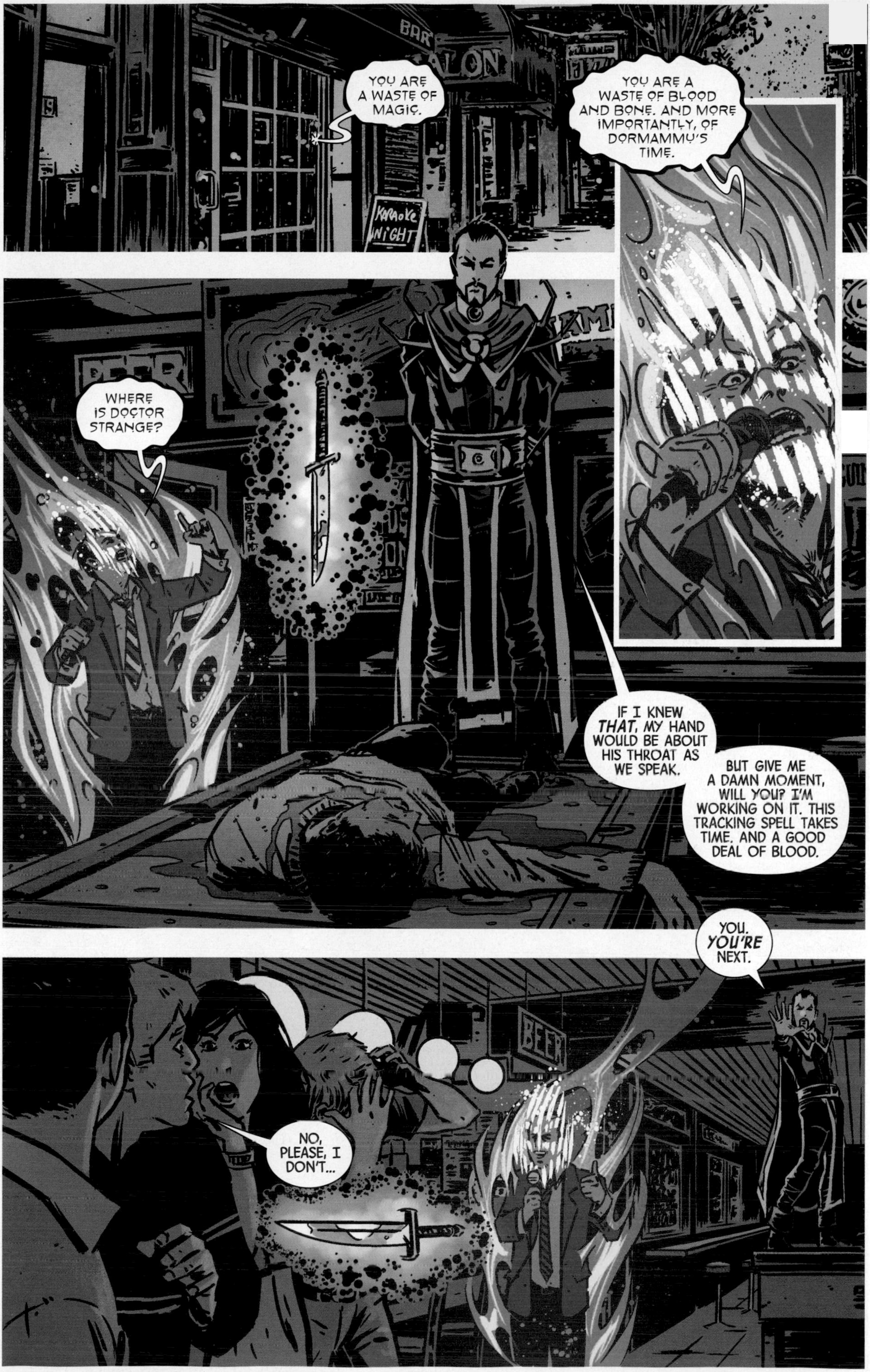
BAR
SALON
KARAOKE NIGHT
YOU ARE A WASTE OF MAGIC.
YOU ARE A WASTE OF BLOOD AND BONE. AND MORE IMPORTANTLY, OF DORMAMMU'S TIME.
BEER
WHERE IS DOCTOR STRANGE?
IF I KNEW *THAT*, MY HAND WOULD BE ABOUT HIS THROAT AS WE SPEAK.
BUT GIVE ME A DAMN MOMENT, WILL YOU? I'M WORKING ON IT. THIS TRACKING SPELL TAKES TIME. AND A GOOD DEAL OF BLOOD.
YOU. *YOU'RE* NEXT.
BEER
NO, PLEASE, I DON'T...

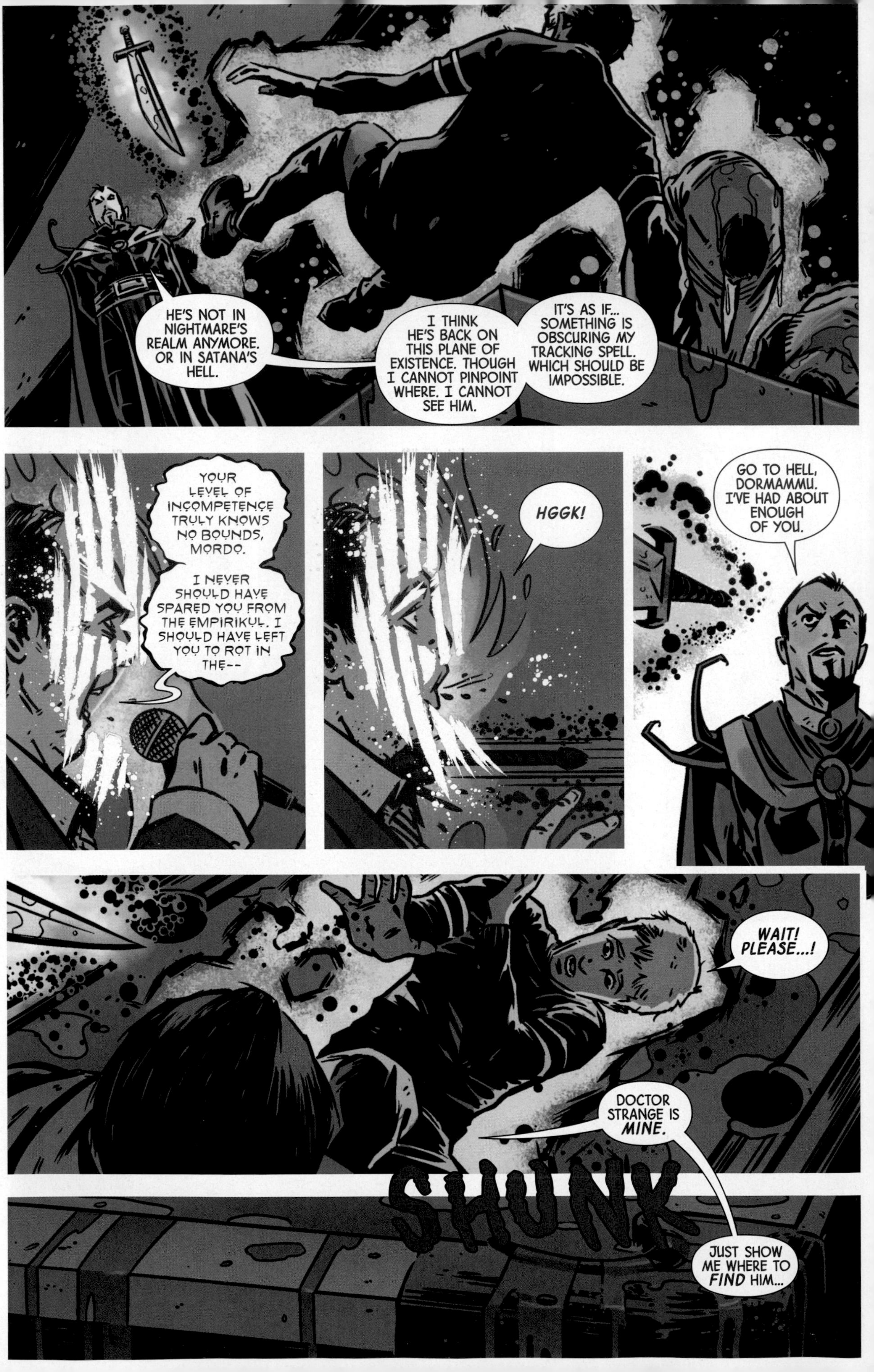
HE'S NOT IN NIGHTMARE'S REALM ANYMORE. OR IN SATANA'S HELL.
I THINK HE'S BACK ON THIS PLANE OF EXISTENCE. THOUGH I CANNOT PINPOINT WHERE. I CANNOT SEE HIM.
IT'S AS IF... SOMETHING IS OBSCURING MY TRACKING SPELL. WHICH SHOULD BE IMPOSSIBLE.
YOUR LEVEL OF INCOMPETENCE TRULY KNOWS NO BOUNDS, MORDO.
I NEVER SHOULD HAVE SPARED YOU FROM THE EMPIRIKUL. I SHOULD HAVE LEFT YOU TO ROT IN THE--
HGGK!
GO TO HELL, DORMAMMU. I'VE HAD ABOUT ENOUGH OF YOU.
WAIT! PLEASE...!
DOCTOR STRANGE IS MINE.
SHUNK
JUST SHOW ME WHERE TO FIND HIM...

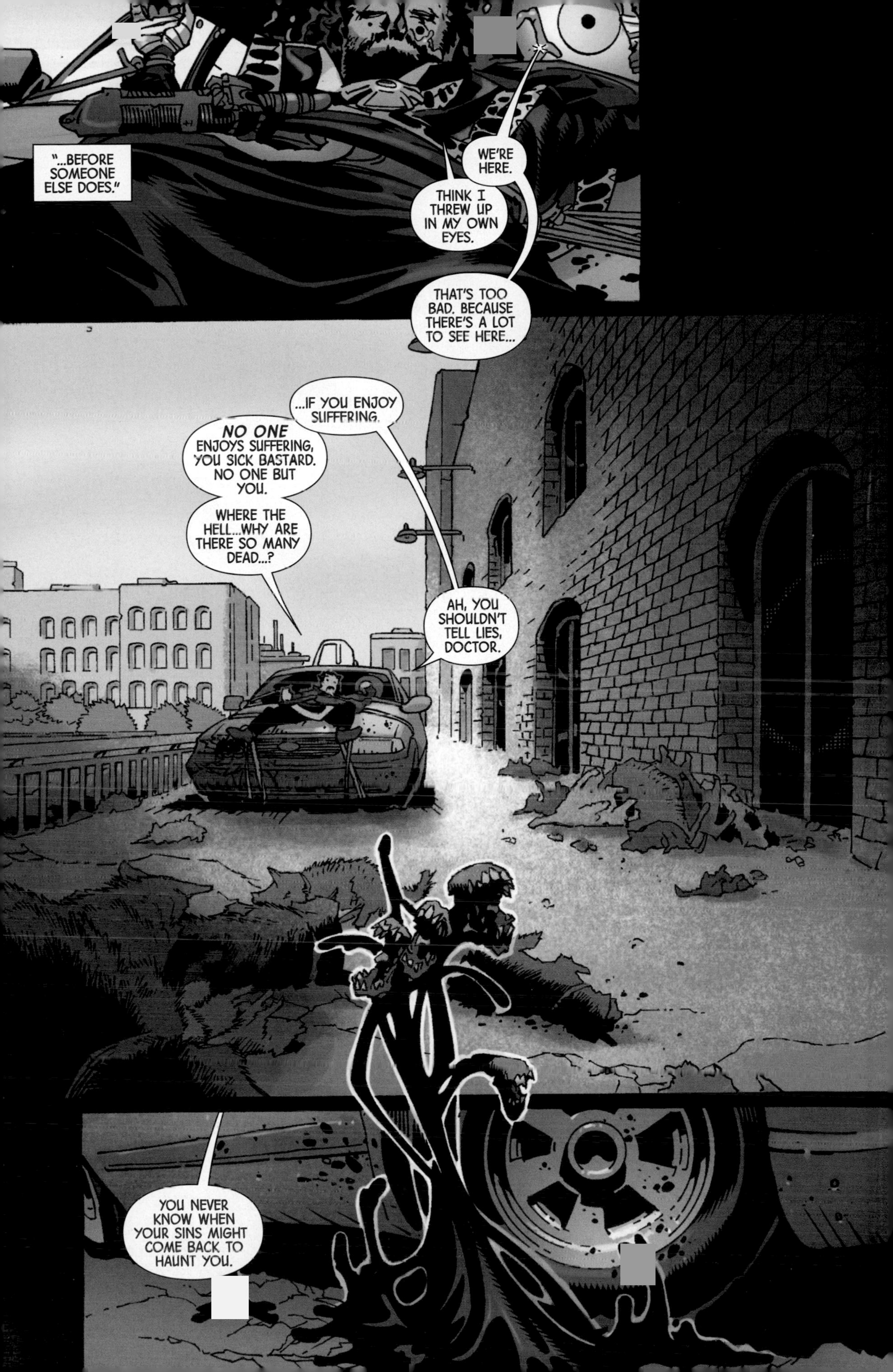
"...BEFORE SOMEONE ELSE DOES."
WE'RE HERE.
THINK I THREW UP IN MY OWN EYES.
THAT'S TOO BAD. BECAUSE THERE'S A LOT TO SEE HERE...
...IF YOU ENJOY SUFFERING.
NO ONE ENJOYS SUFFERING, YOU SICK BASTARD. NO ONE BUT YOU.
WHERE THE HELL...WHY ARE THERE SO MANY DEAD...?
AH, YOU SHOULDN'T TELL LIES, DOCTOR.
YOU NEVER KNOW WHEN YOUR SINS MIGHT COME BACK TO HAUNT YOU.

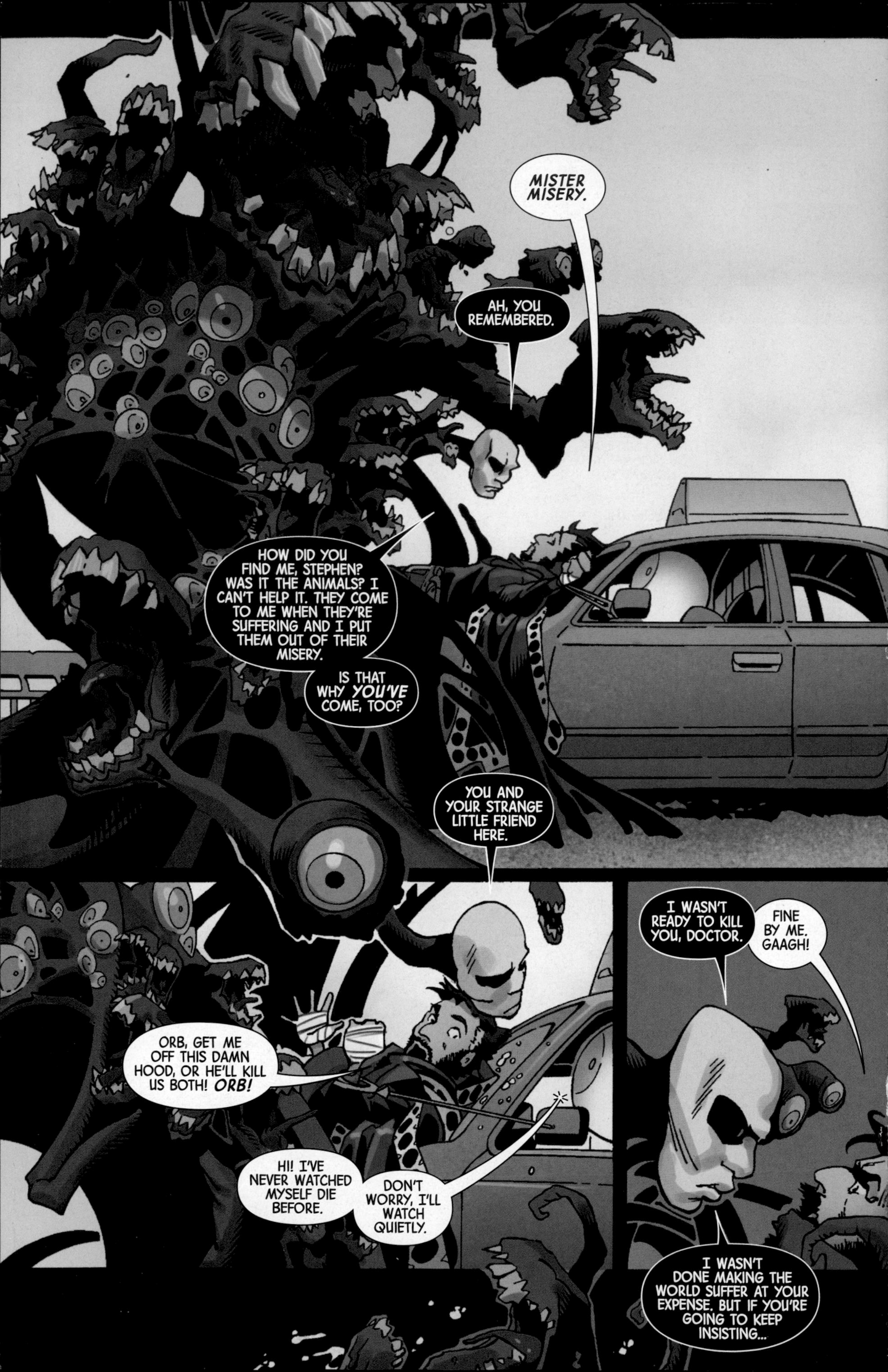

MISTER MISERY.
AH, YOU REMEMBERED.
HOW DID YOU FIND ME, STEPHEN? WAS IT THE ANIMALS? I CAN'T HELP IT. THEY COME TO ME WHEN THEY'RE SUFFERING AND I PUT THEM OUT OF THEIR MISERY.
IS THAT WHY *YOU'VE* COME, TOO?
YOU AND YOUR STRANGE LITTLE FRIEND HERE.
ORB, GET ME OFF THIS DAMN HOOD, OR HE'LL KILL US BOTH! *ORB!*
HI! I'VE NEVER WATCHED MYSELF DIE BEFORE.
DON'T WORRY, I'LL WATCH QUIETLY.
I WASN'T READY TO KILL YOU, DOCTOR.
FINE BY ME. GAAGH!
I WASN'T DONE MAKING THE WORLD SUFFER AT YOUR EXPENSE. BUT IF YOU'RE GOING TO KEEP INSISTING...

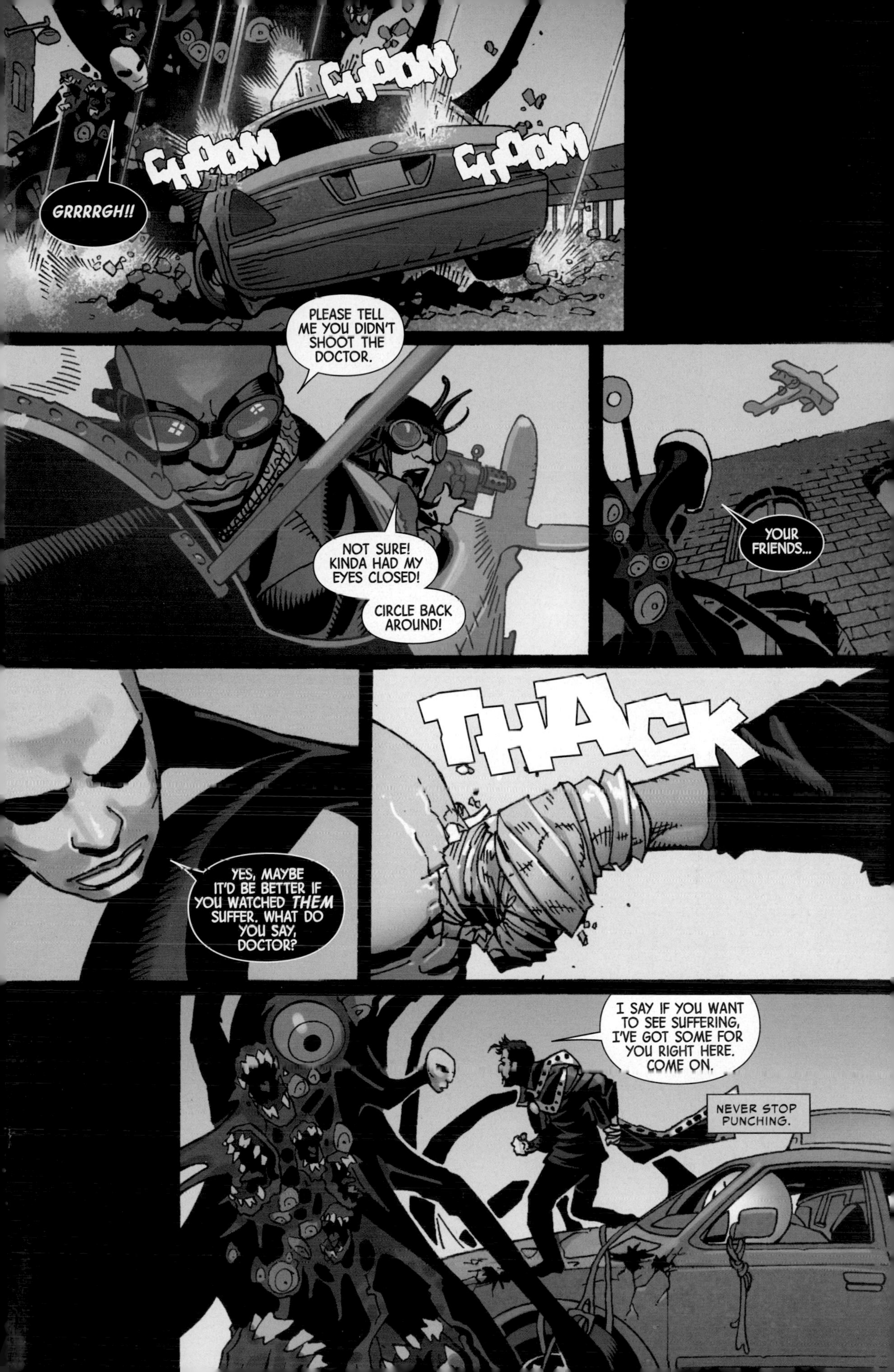
CHOOM
CHOOM
CHOOM
GRRRRGH!!
CHOOM
PLEASE TELL ME YOU DIDN'T SHOOT THE DOCTOR.
NOT SURE! KINDA HAD MY EYES CLOSED!
CIRCLE BACK AROUND!
YOUR FRIENDS...
THACK
YES, MAYBE IT'D BE BETTER IF YOU WATCHED *THEM* SUFFER. WHAT DO YOU SAY, DOCTOR?
I SAY IF YOU WANT TO SEE SUFFERING, I'VE GOT SOME FOR YOU RIGHT HERE. COME ON.
NEVER STOP PUNCHING.

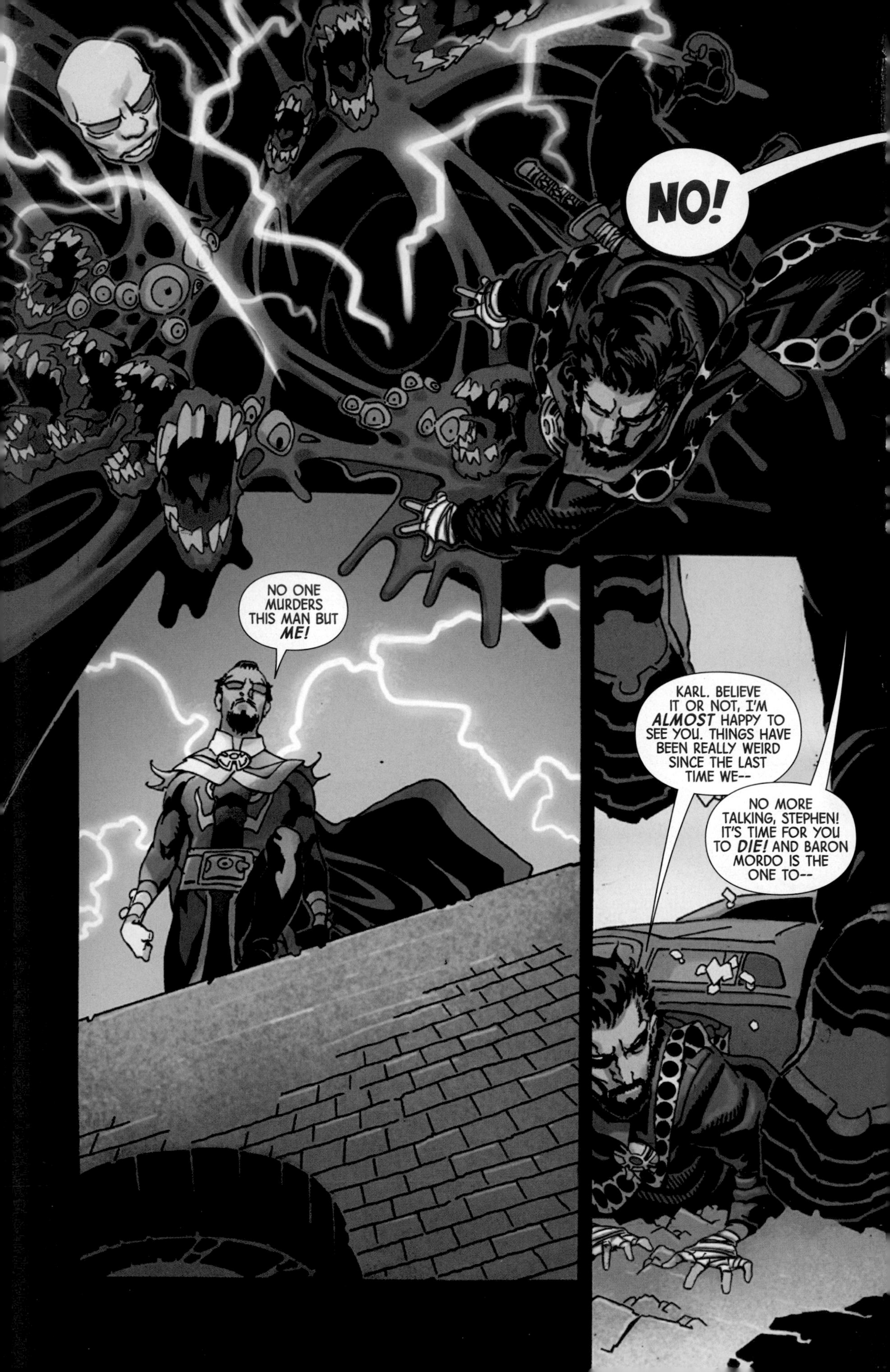
NO!
NO ONE MURDERS THIS MAN BUT ME!
KARL. BELIEVE IT OR NOT, I'M ALMOST HAPPY TO SEE YOU. THINGS HAVE BEEN REALLY WEIRD SINCE THE LAST TIME WE--
NO MORE TALKING, STEPHEN! IT'S TIME FOR YOU TO DIE! AND BARON MORDO IS THE ONE TO--

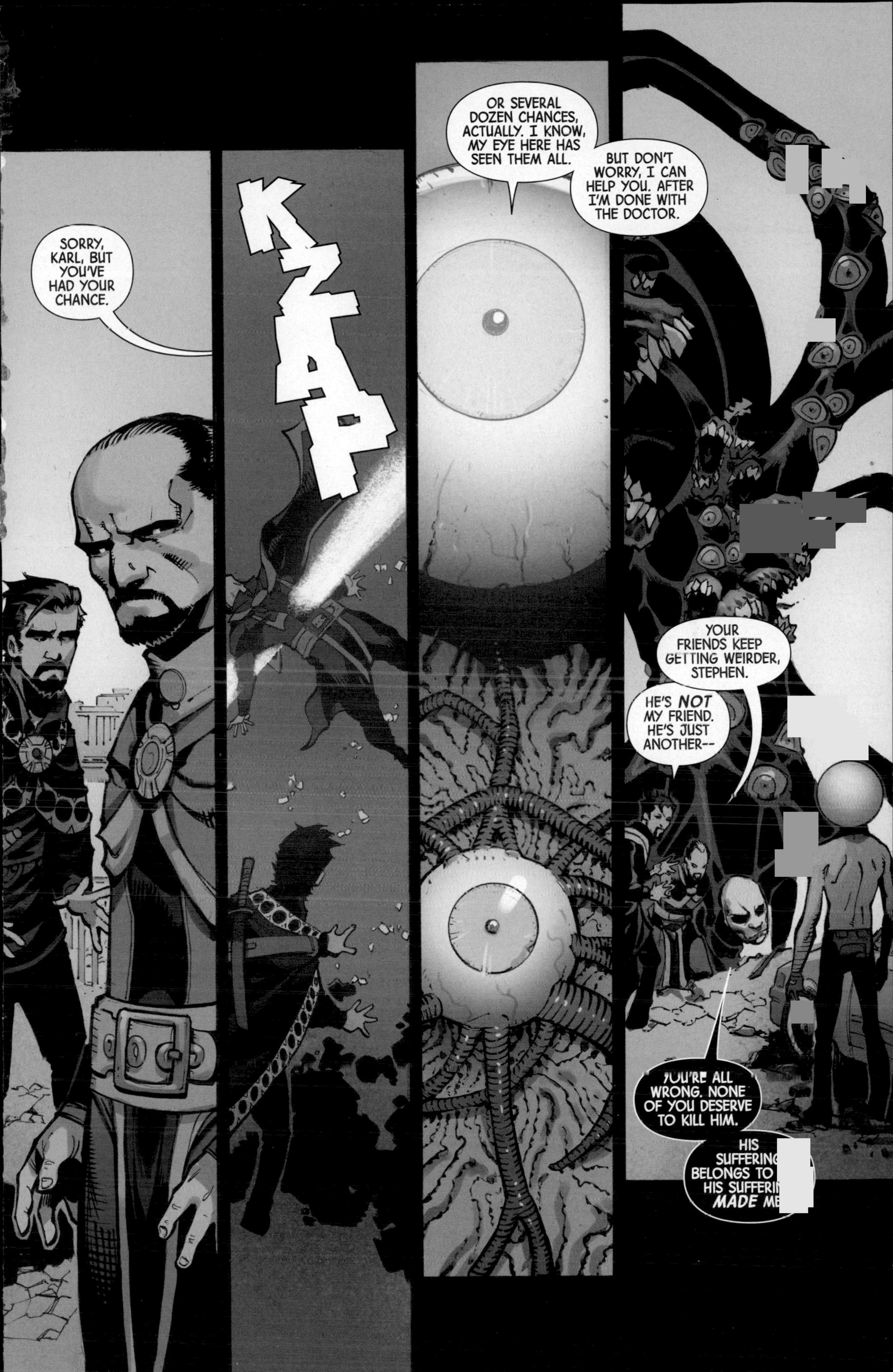
SORRY, KARL, BUT YOU'VE HAD YOUR CHANCE.
KZZAP
OR SEVERAL DOZEN CHANCES, ACTUALLY. I KNOW, MY EYE HERE HAS SEEN THEM ALL.
BUT DON'T WORRY, I CAN HELP YOU. AFTER I'M DONE WITH THE DOCTOR.
YOUR FRIENDS KEEP GETTING WEIRDER, STEPHEN.
HE'S *NOT* MY FRIEND. HE'S JUST ANOTHER--
YOU'RE ALL WRONG. NONE OF YOU DESERVE TO KILL HIM.
HIS SUFFERING BELONGS TO HIS SUFFERING *MADE* ME

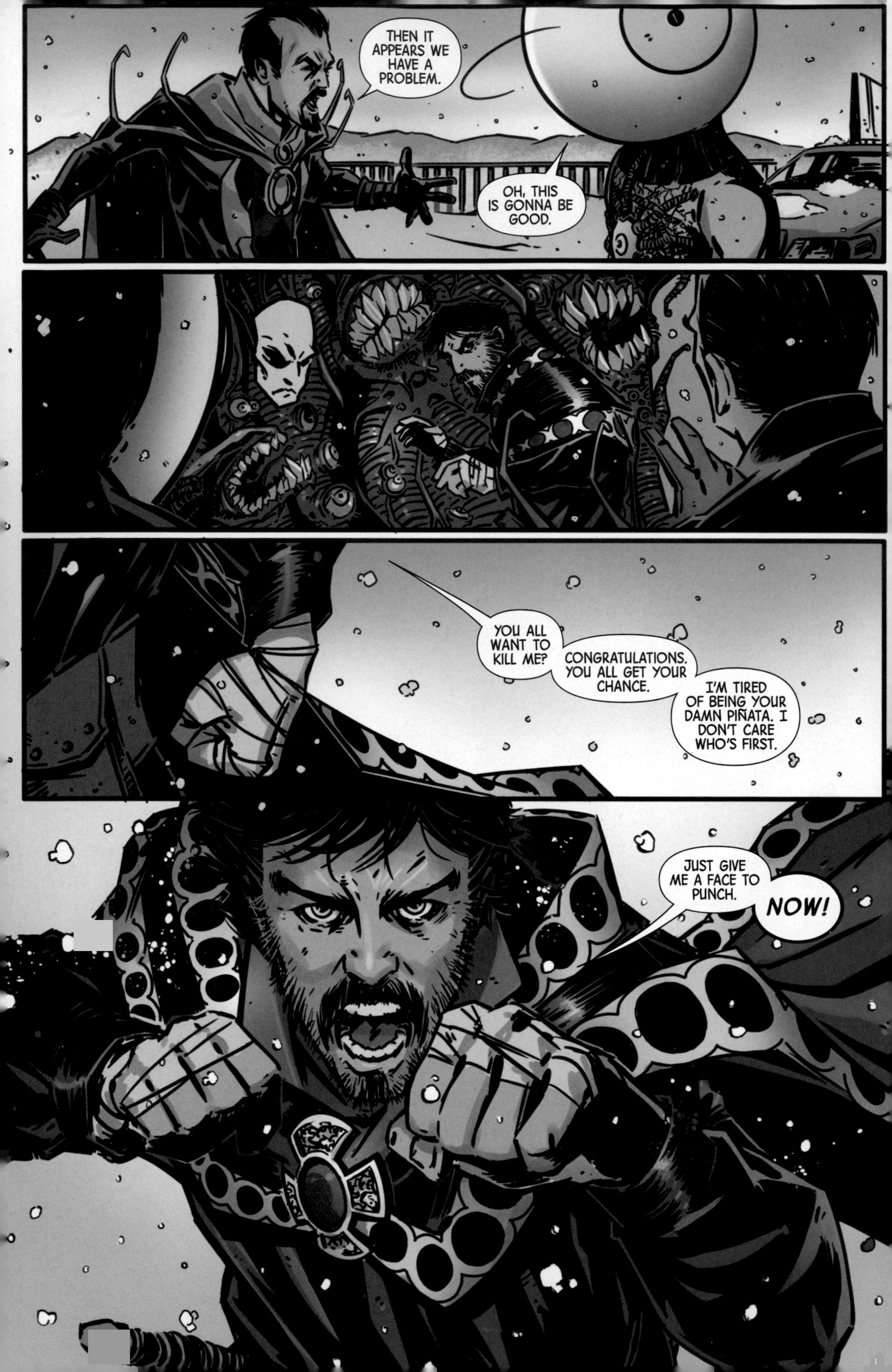
THEN IT APPEARS WE HAVE A PROBLEM.
OH, THIS IS GONNA BE GOOD.
YOU ALL WANT TO KILL ME?
CONGRATULATIONS. YOU ALL GET YOUR CHANCE.
I'M TIRED OF BEING YOUR DAMN PIÑATA. I DON'T CARE WHO'S FIRST.
JUST GIVE ME A FACE TO PUNCH.
NOW!

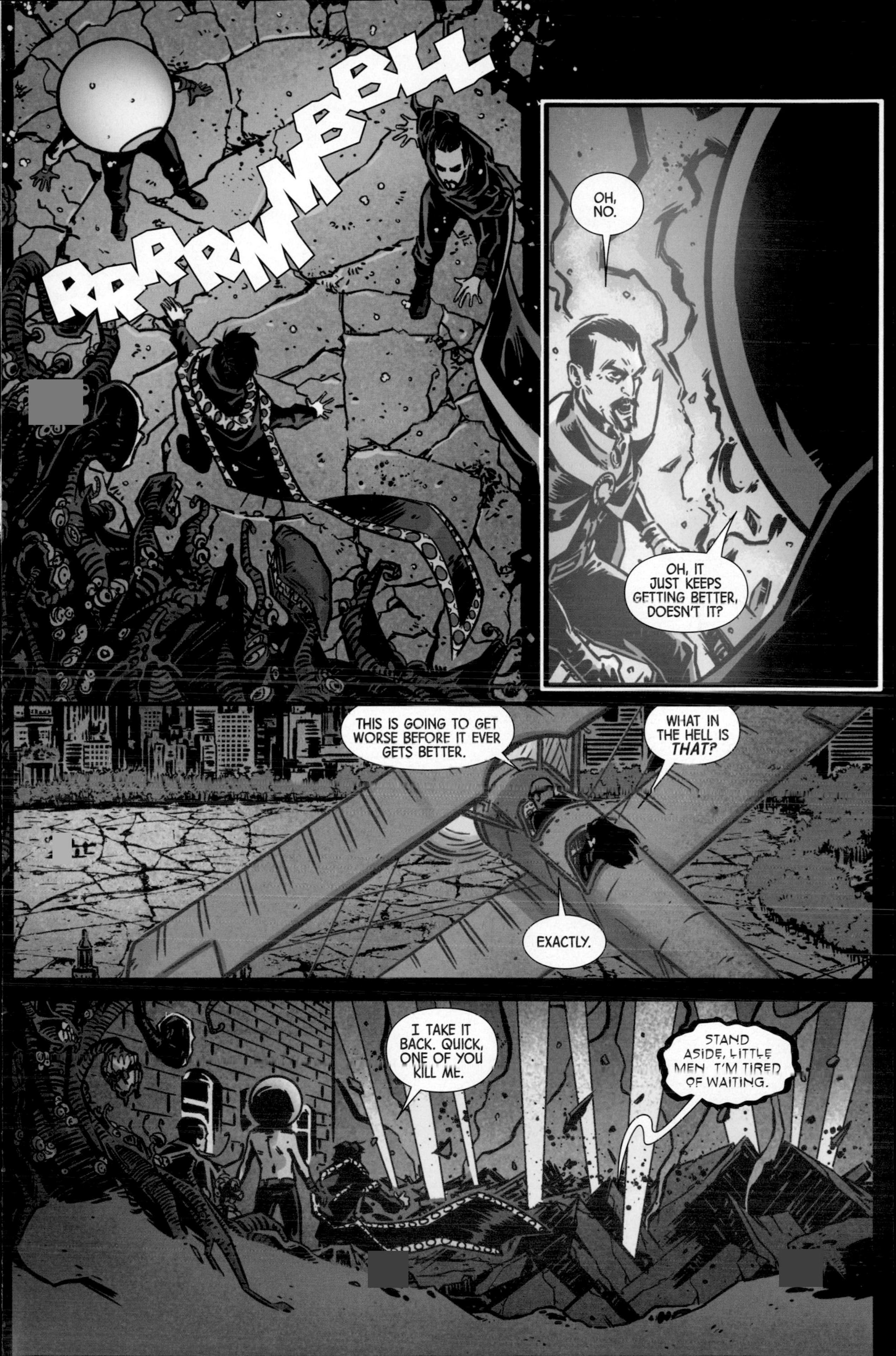
RRRRMMBBLL
OH, NO.
OH, IT JUST KEEPS GETTING BETTER, DOESN'T IT?
THIS IS GOING TO GET WORSE BEFORE IT EVER GETS BETTER.
WHAT IN THE HELL IS *THAT?*
EXACTLY.
I TAKE IT BACK. QUICK, ONE OF YOU KILL ME.
STAND ASIDE, LITTLE MEN I'M TIRED OF WAITING.

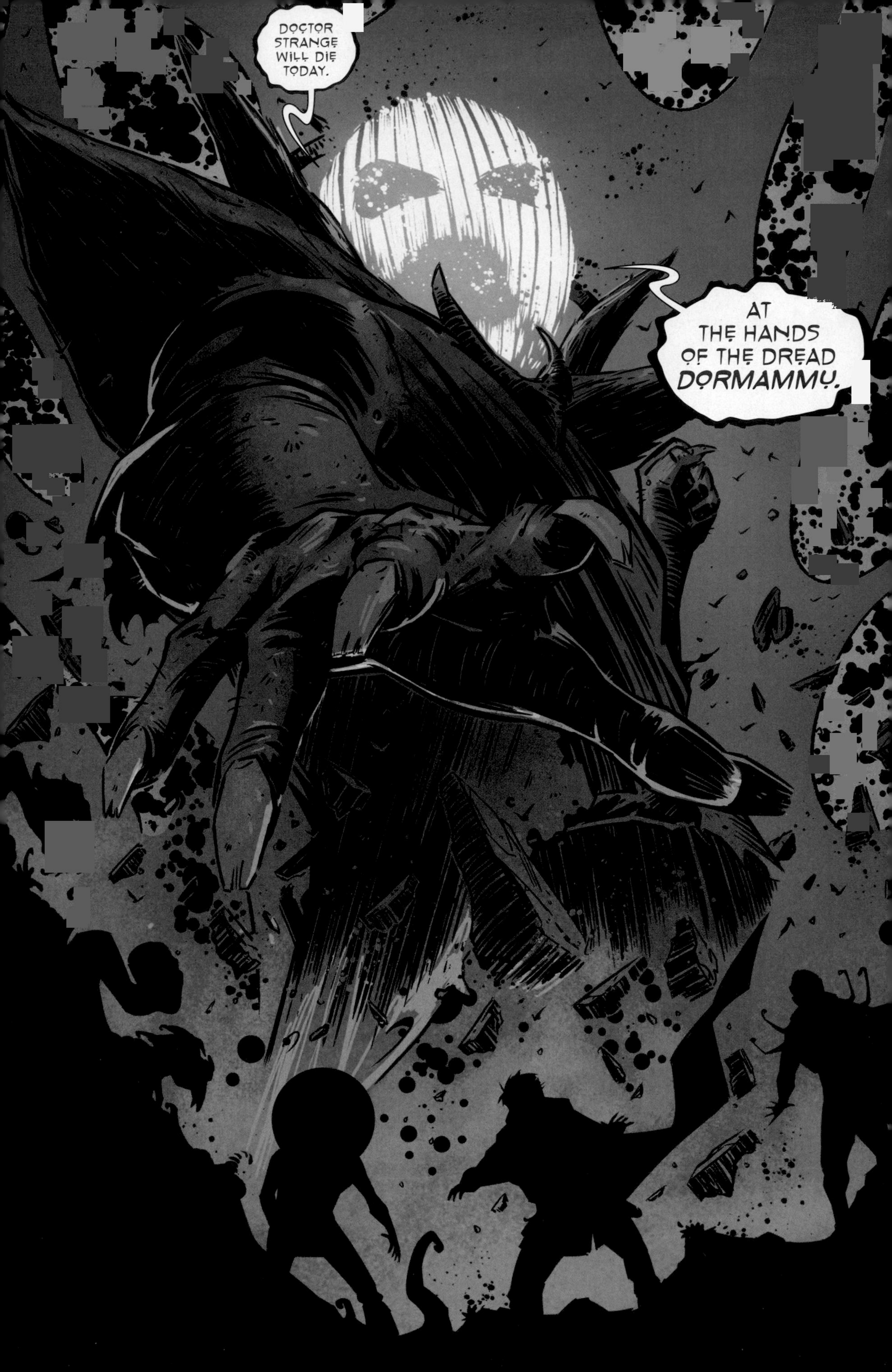
DOCTOR STRANGE WILL DIE TODAY.
AT THE HANDS OF THE DREAD *DORMAMMU*.

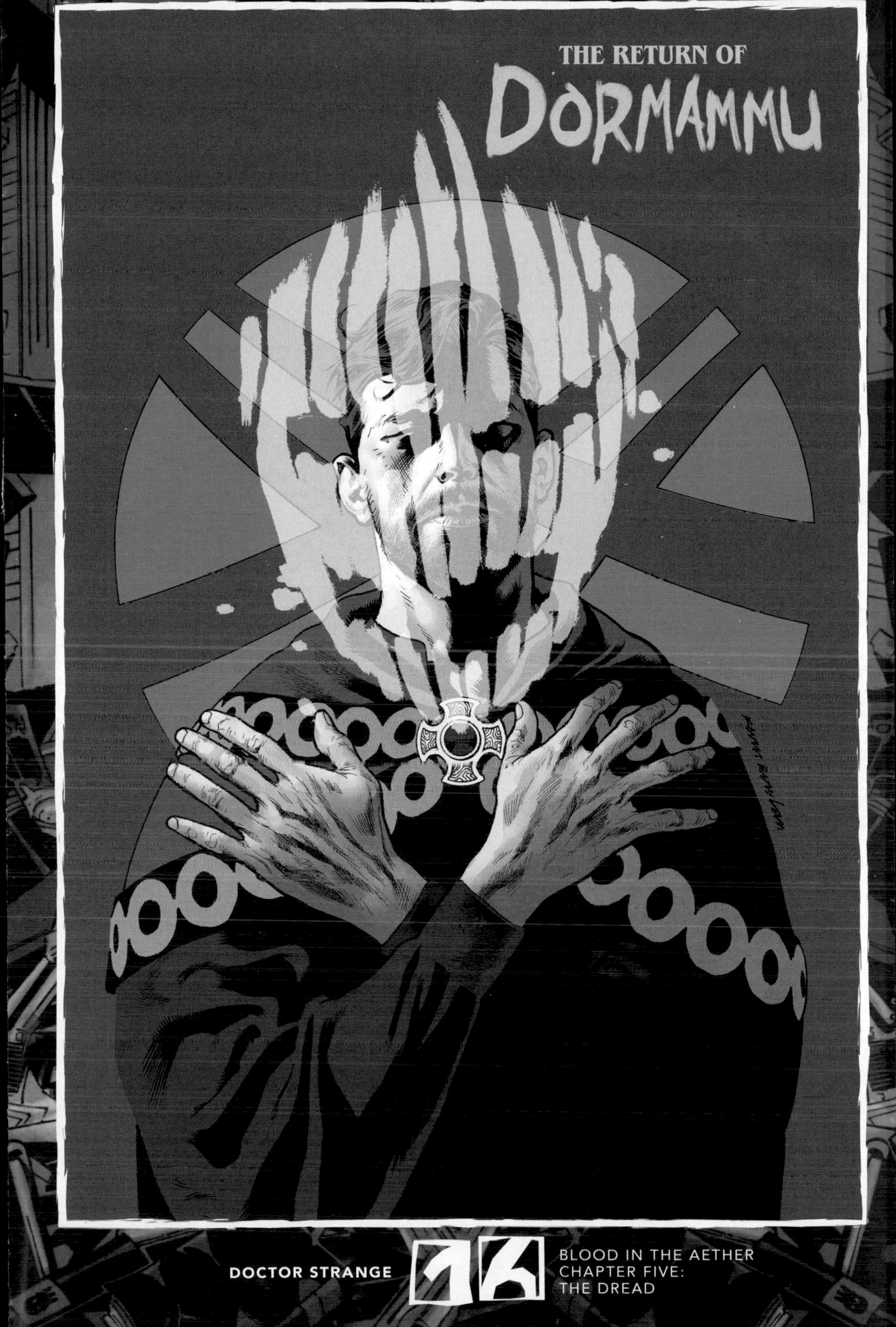
THE RETURN OF
DORMAMMU
DOCTOR STRANGE
16
BLOOD IN THE AETHER
CHAPTER FIVE:
THE DREAD

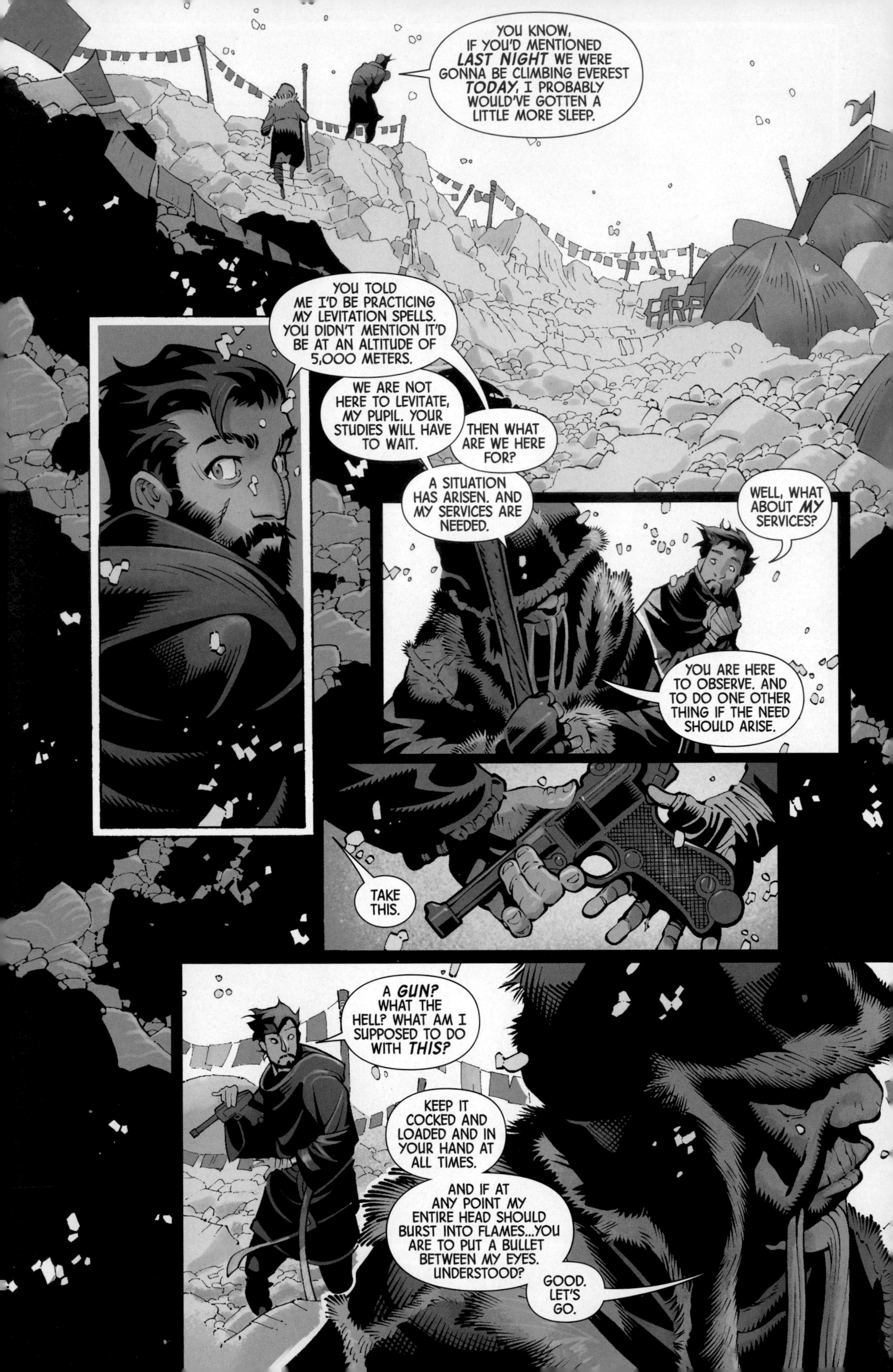
YOU KNOW, IF YOU'D MENTIONED LAST NIGHT WE WERE GONNA BE CLIMBING EVEREST TODAY, I PROBABLY WOULD'VE GOTTEN A LITTLE MORE SLEEP.
YOU TOLD ME I'D BE PRACTICING MY LEVITATION SPELLS. YOU DIDN'T MENTION IT'D BE AT AN ALTITUDE OF 5,000 METERS.
WE ARE NOT HERE TO LEVITATE, MY PUPIL. YOUR STUDIES WILL HAVE TO WAIT.
THEN WHAT ARE WE HERE FOR?
A SITUATION HAS ARISEN. AND MY SERVICES ARE NEEDED.
WELL, WHAT ABOUT MY SERVICES?
YOU ARE HERE TO OBSERVE. AND TO DO ONE OTHER THING IF THE NEED SHOULD ARISE.
TAKE THIS.
A GUN? WHAT THE HELL? WHAT AM I SUPPOSED TO DO WITH THIS?
KEEP IT COCKED AND LOADED AND IN YOUR HAND AT ALL TIMES.
AND IF AT ANY POINT MY ENTIRE HEAD SHOULD BURST INTO FLAMES...YOU ARE TO PUT A BULLET BETWEEN MY EYES. UNDERSTOOD?
GOOD. LET'S GO.

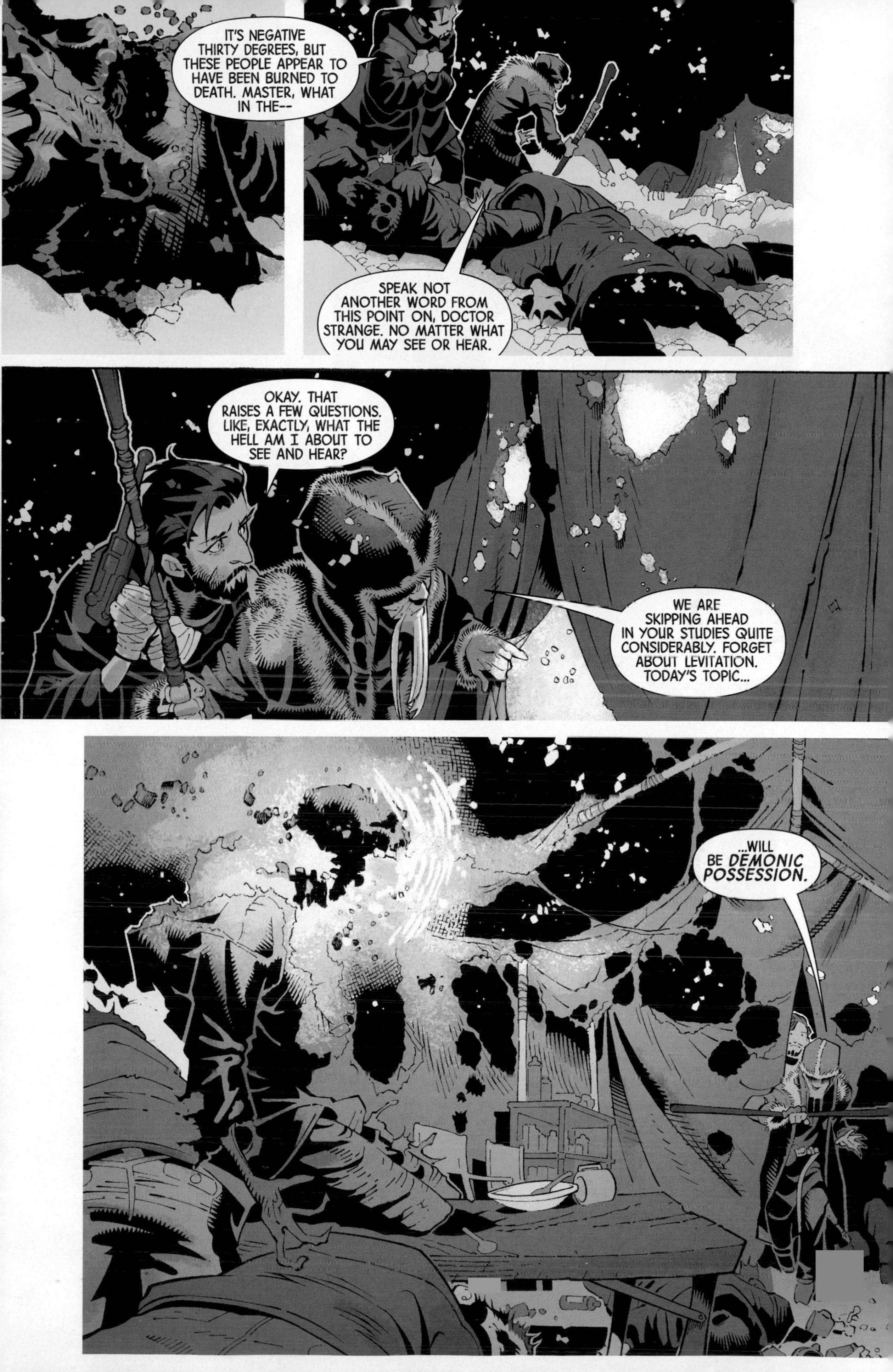
IT'S NEGATIVE THIRTY DEGREES, BUT THESE PEOPLE APPEAR TO HAVE BEEN BURNED TO DEATH. MASTER, WHAT IN THE--
SPEAK NOT ANOTHER WORD FROM THIS POINT ON, DOCTOR STRANGE. NO MATTER WHAT YOU MAY SEE OR HEAR.
OKAY. THAT RAISES A FEW QUESTIONS. LIKE, EXACTLY, WHAT THE HELL AM I ABOUT TO SEE AND HEAR?
WE ARE SKIPPING AHEAD IN YOUR STUDIES QUITE CONSIDERABLY. FORGET ABOUT LEVITATION. TODAY'S TOPIC...
...WILL BE *DEMONIC POSSESSION.*

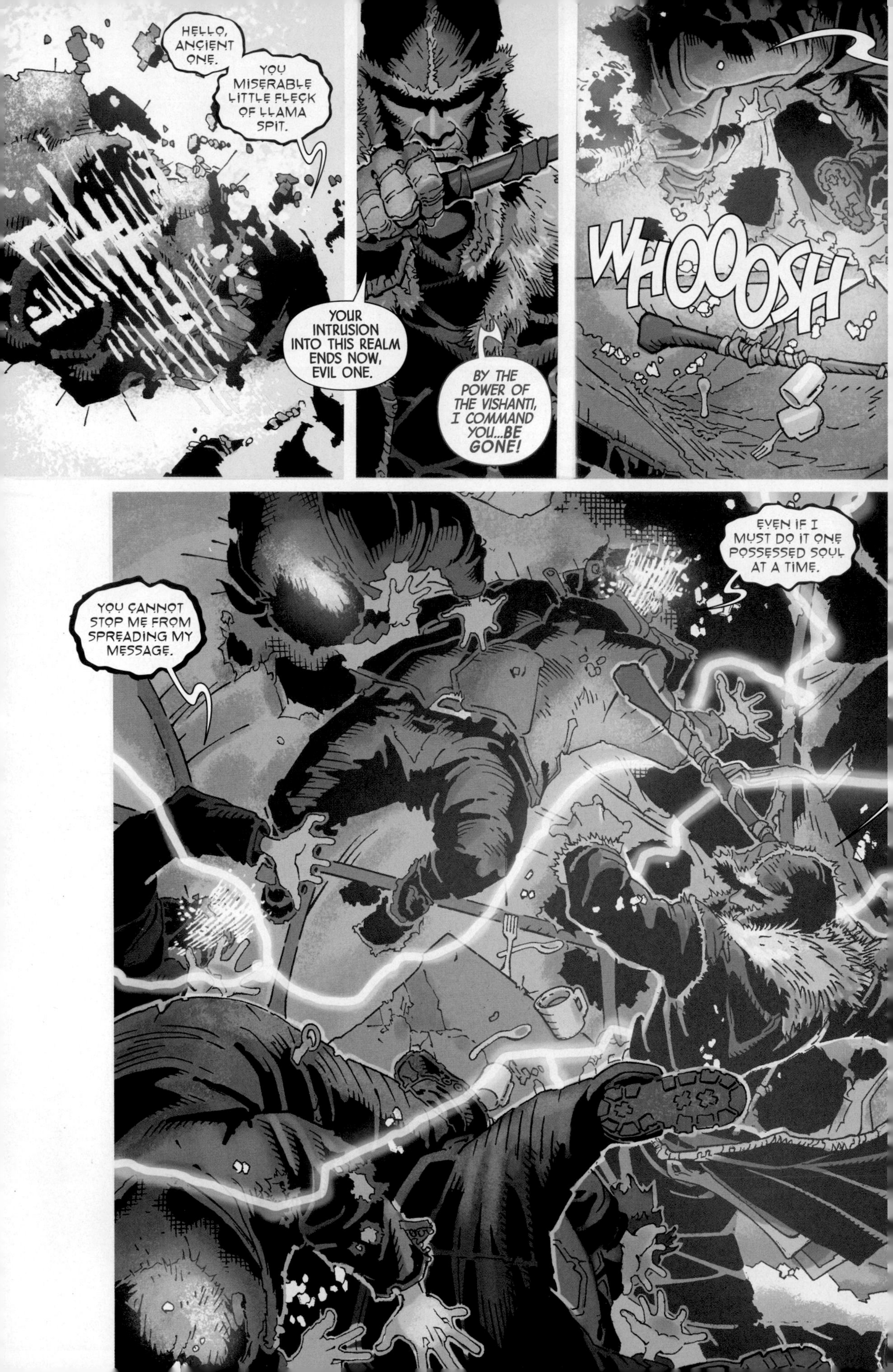
HELLO, ANCIENT ONE.
YOU MISERABLE LITTLE FLECK OF LLAMA SPIT.
YOUR INTRUSION INTO THIS REALM ENDS NOW, EVIL ONE.
BY THE POWER OF THE VISHANTI, I COMMAND YOU...BE GONE!
WHOOOSH
YOU CANNOT STOP ME FROM SPREADING MY MESSAGE.
EVEN IF I MUST DO IT ONE POSSESSED SOUL AT A TIME.

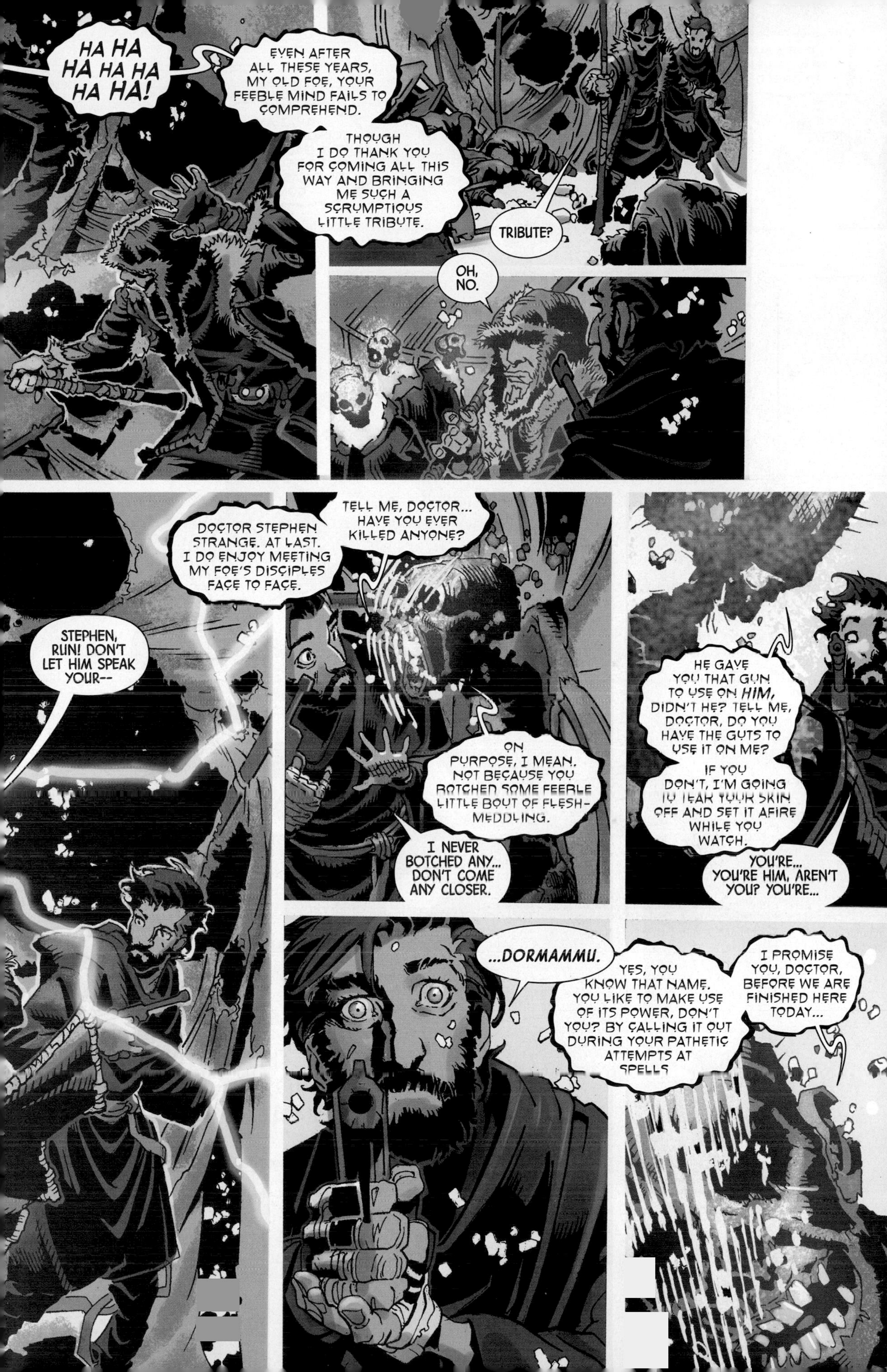
HA HA HA HA HA HA HA!
EVEN AFTER ALL THESE YEARS, MY OLD FOE, YOUR FEEBLE MIND FAILS TO COMPREHEND.
THOUGH I DO THANK YOU FOR COMING ALL THIS WAY AND BRINGING ME SUCH A SCRUMPTIOUS LITTLE TRIBUTE.
TRIBUTE?
OH, NO.
DOCTOR STEPHEN STRANGE. AT LAST. I DO ENJOY MEETING MY FOE'S DISCIPLES FACE TO FACE.
STEPHEN, RUN! DON'T LET HIM SPEAK YOUR--
TELL ME, DOCTOR... HAVE YOU EVER KILLED ANYONE?
ON PURPOSE, I MEAN. NOT BECAUSE YOU BOTCHED SOME FEEBLE LITTLE BOUT OF FLESH-MEDDLING.
I NEVER BOTCHED ANY... DON'T COME ANY CLOSER.
HE GAVE YOU THAT GUN TO USE ON *HIM*, DIDN'T HE? TELL ME, DOCTOR, DO YOU HAVE THE GUTS TO USE IT ON ME?
IF YOU DON'T, I'M GOING TO TEAR YOUR SKIN OFF AND SET IT AFIRE WHILE YOU WATCH.
YOU'RE... YOU'RE HIM, AREN'T YOU? YOU'RE...
...DORMAMMU.
YES, YOU KNOW THAT NAME. YOU LIKE TO MAKE USE OF ITS POWER, DON'T YOU? BY CALLING IT OUT DURING YOUR PATHETIC ATTEMPTS AT SPELLS.
I PROMISE YOU, DOCTOR, BEFORE WE ARE FINISHED HERE TODAY...

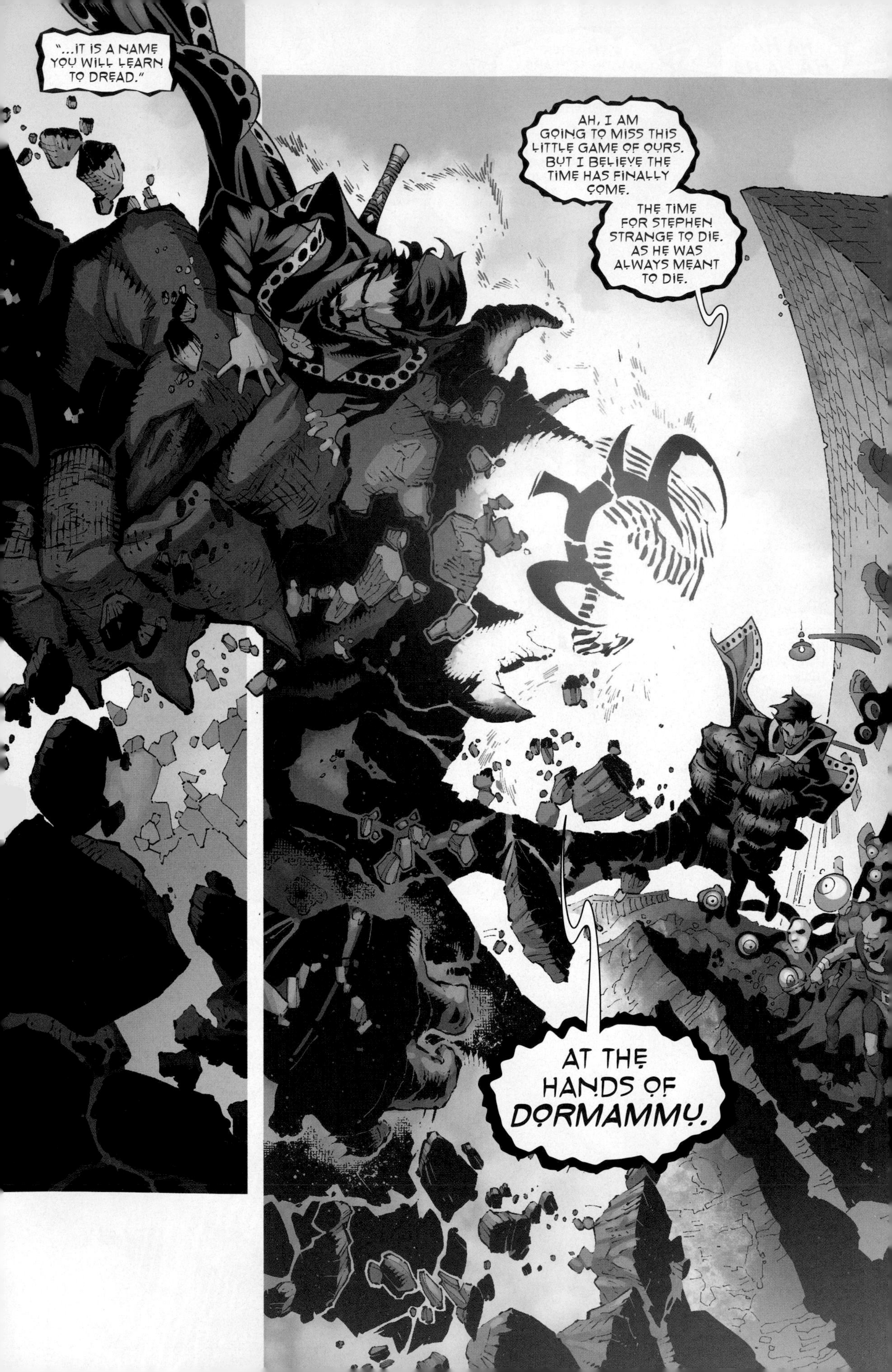
"...IT IS A NAME YOU WILL LEARN TO DREAD."
AH, I AM GOING TO MISS THIS LITTLE GAME OF OURS. BUT I BELIEVE THE TIME HAS FINALLY COME.
THE TIME FOR STEPHEN STRANGE TO DIE. AS HE WAS ALWAYS MEANT TO DIE.
AT THE HANDS OF DORMAMMU.

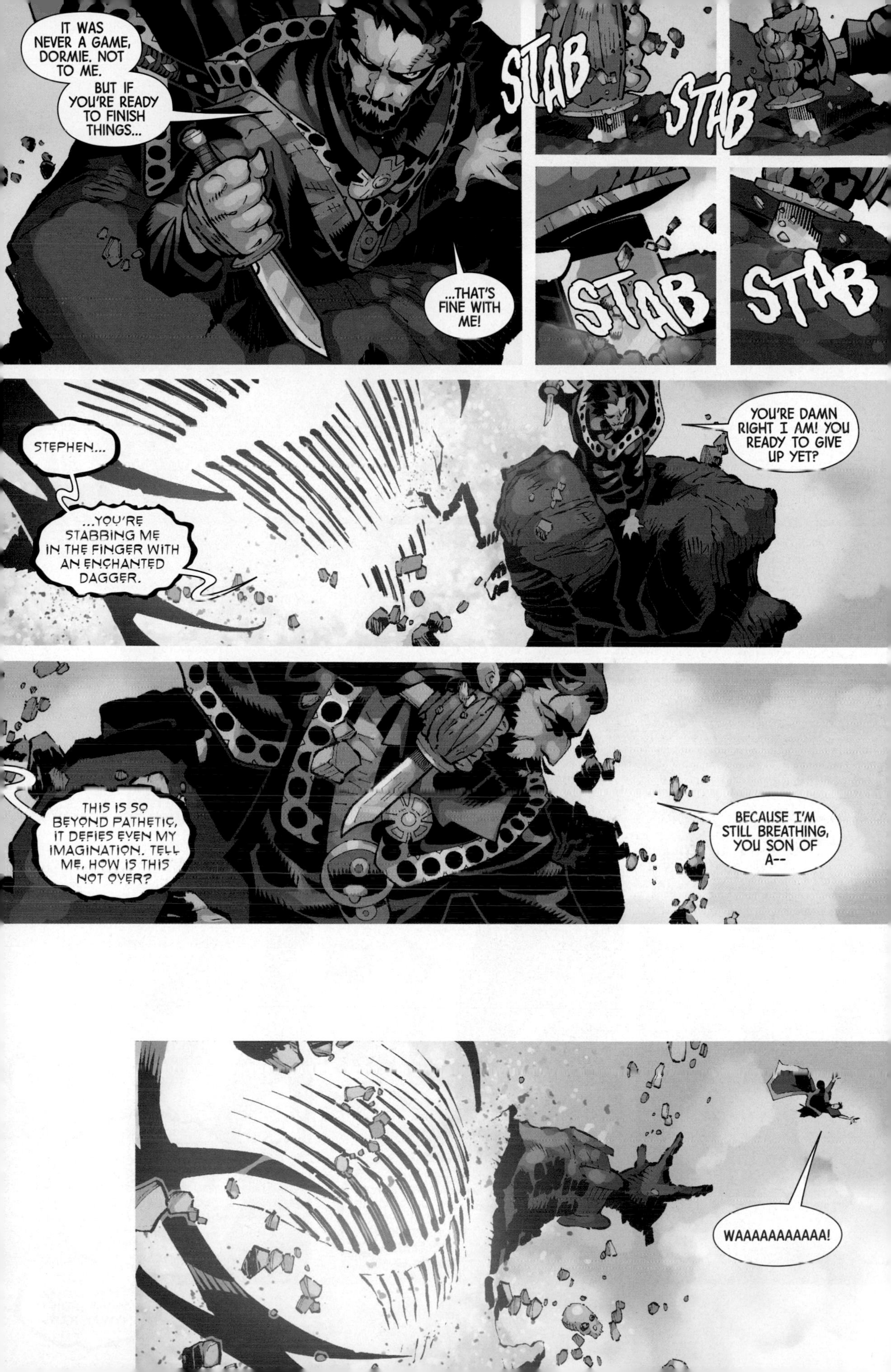
IT WAS NEVER A GAME, DORMIE. NOT TO ME.
BUT IF YOU'RE READY TO FINISH THINGS...
...THAT'S FINE WITH ME!
STAB
STAB
STAB
STAB
STEPHEN...
...YOU'RE STABBING ME IN THE FINGER WITH AN ENCHANTED DAGGER.
YOU'RE DAMN RIGHT I AM! YOU READY TO GIVE UP YET?
THIS IS SO BEYOND PATHETIC, IT DEFIES EVEN MY IMAGINATION. TELL ME, HOW IS THIS NOT OVER?
BECAUSE I'M STILL BREATHING, YOU SON OF A--
WAAAAAAAAAAA!

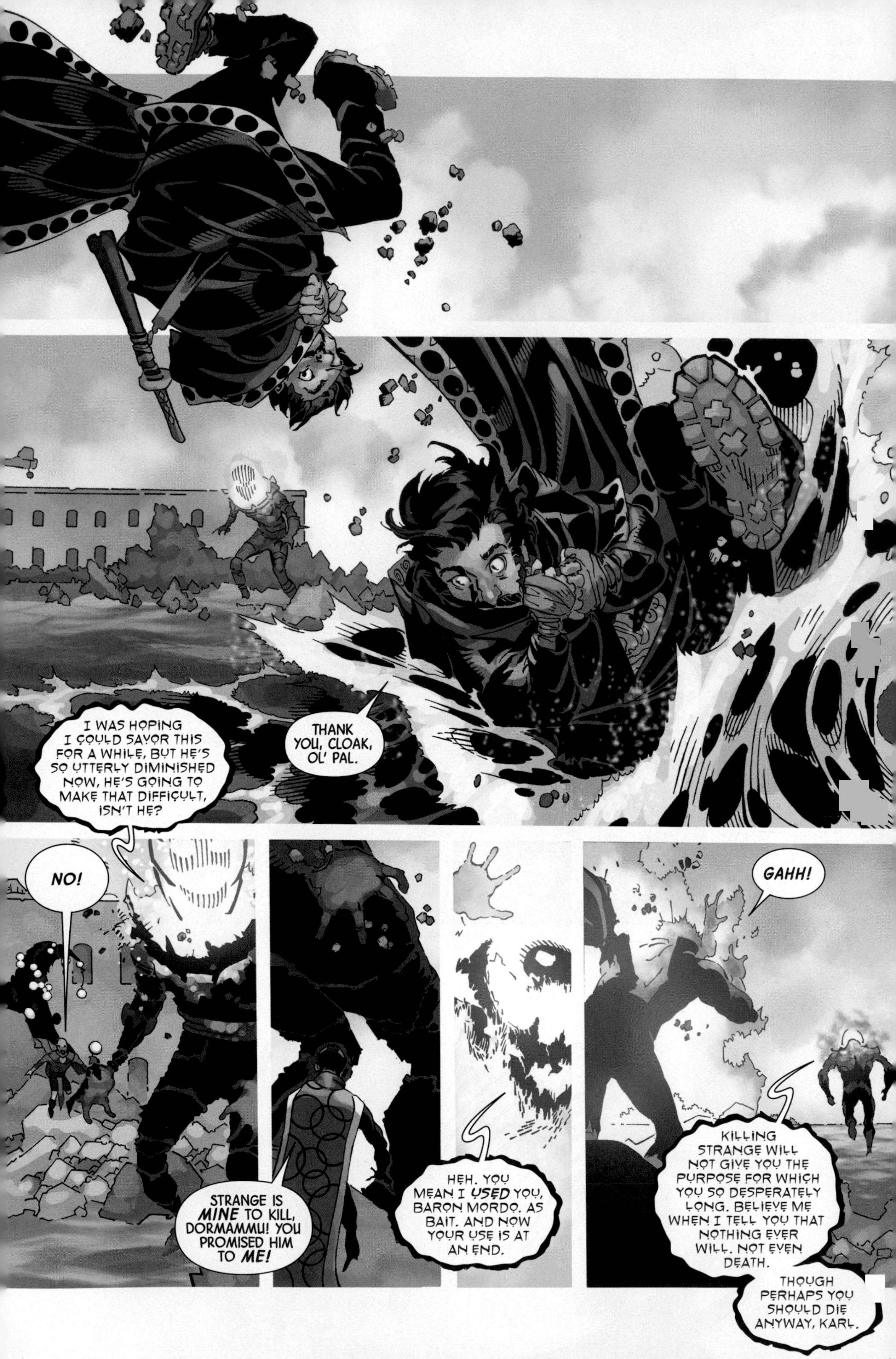
THANK YOU, CLOAK, OL' PAL.
I WAS HOPING I COULD SAVOR THIS FOR A WHILE, BUT HE'S SO UTTERLY DIMINISHED NOW, HE'S GOING TO MAKE THAT DIFFICULT, ISN'T HE?
NO!
STRANGE IS MINE TO KILL, DORMAMMU! YOU PROMISED HIM TO ME!
HEH. YOU MEAN I USED YOU, BARON MORDO. AS BAIT. AND NOW YOUR USE IS AT AN END.
GAHH!
KILLING STRANGE WILL NOT GIVE YOU THE PURPOSE FOR WHICH YOU SO DESPERATELY LONG. BELIEVE ME WHEN I TELL YOU THAT NOTHING EVER WILL. NOT EVEN DEATH.
THOUGH PERHAPS YOU SHOULD DIE ANYWAY, KARL.

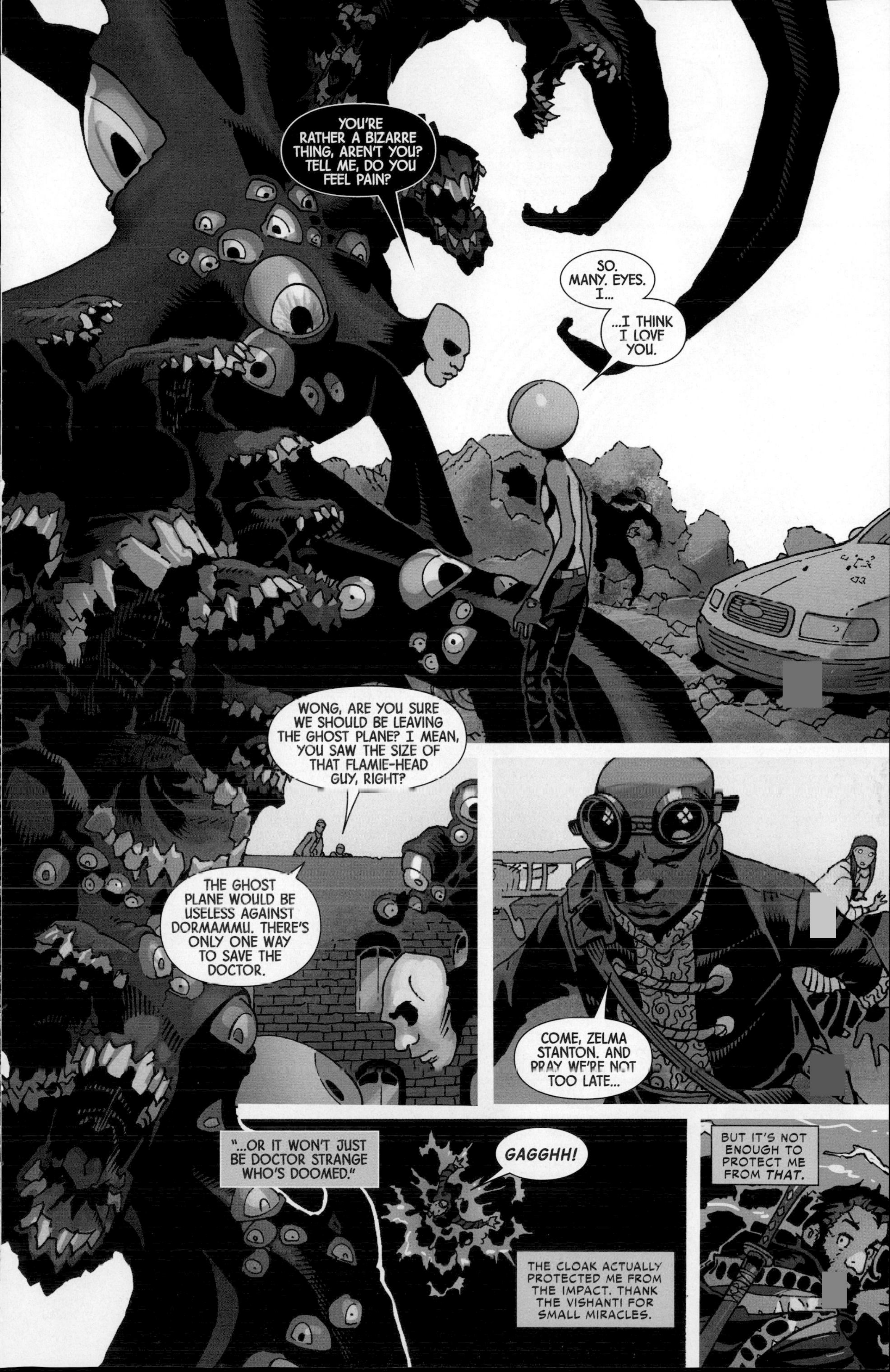
YOU'RE RATHER A BIZARRE THING, AREN'T YOU? TELL ME, DO YOU FEEL PAIN?
SO. MANY. EYES. I...
...I THINK I LOVE YOU.
WONG, ARE YOU SURE WE SHOULD BE LEAVING THE GHOST PLANE? I MEAN, YOU SAW THE SIZE OF THAT FLAMIE-HEAD GUY, RIGHT?
THE GHOST PLANE WOULD BE USELESS AGAINST DORMAMMU. THERE'S ONLY ONE WAY TO SAVE THE DOCTOR.
COME, ZELMA STANTON. AND PRAY WE'RE NOT TOO LATE...
"...OR IT WON'T JUST BE DOCTOR STRANGE WHO'S DOOMED."
GAGGHH!
THE CLOAK ACTUALLY PROTECTED ME FROM THE IMPACT. THANK THE VISHANTI FOR SMALL MIRACLES.
BUT IT'S NOT ENOUGH TO PROTECT ME FROM THAT.

CAN YOU SEE IT, DOCTOR? IN YOUR MIND'S EYE?
I KNOW YOU HAVE A WICKED IMAGINATION. I WANT YOU TO BE ABLE TO SEE IT BEFORE YOU DIE. TRULY SEE IT.
TO SEE WHAT WILL BECOME OF YOUR WORLD, ONCE THE SORCERER SUPREME HAS FALLEN AND I HAVE FLUNG WIDE THE GATES BETWEEN OUR DIMENSIONS.
OPEN YOUR EYES, DOCTOR STRANGE, AND SEE THE FIRES. SEE THE FACES FILLED WITH HORROR.
FLESH WILL BURN. SOULS WILL BE RAVAGED.
MAN WILL CONSUME MAN. MOTHERS WILL MURDER BABIES STILL MEWLING FOR THE TEAT.

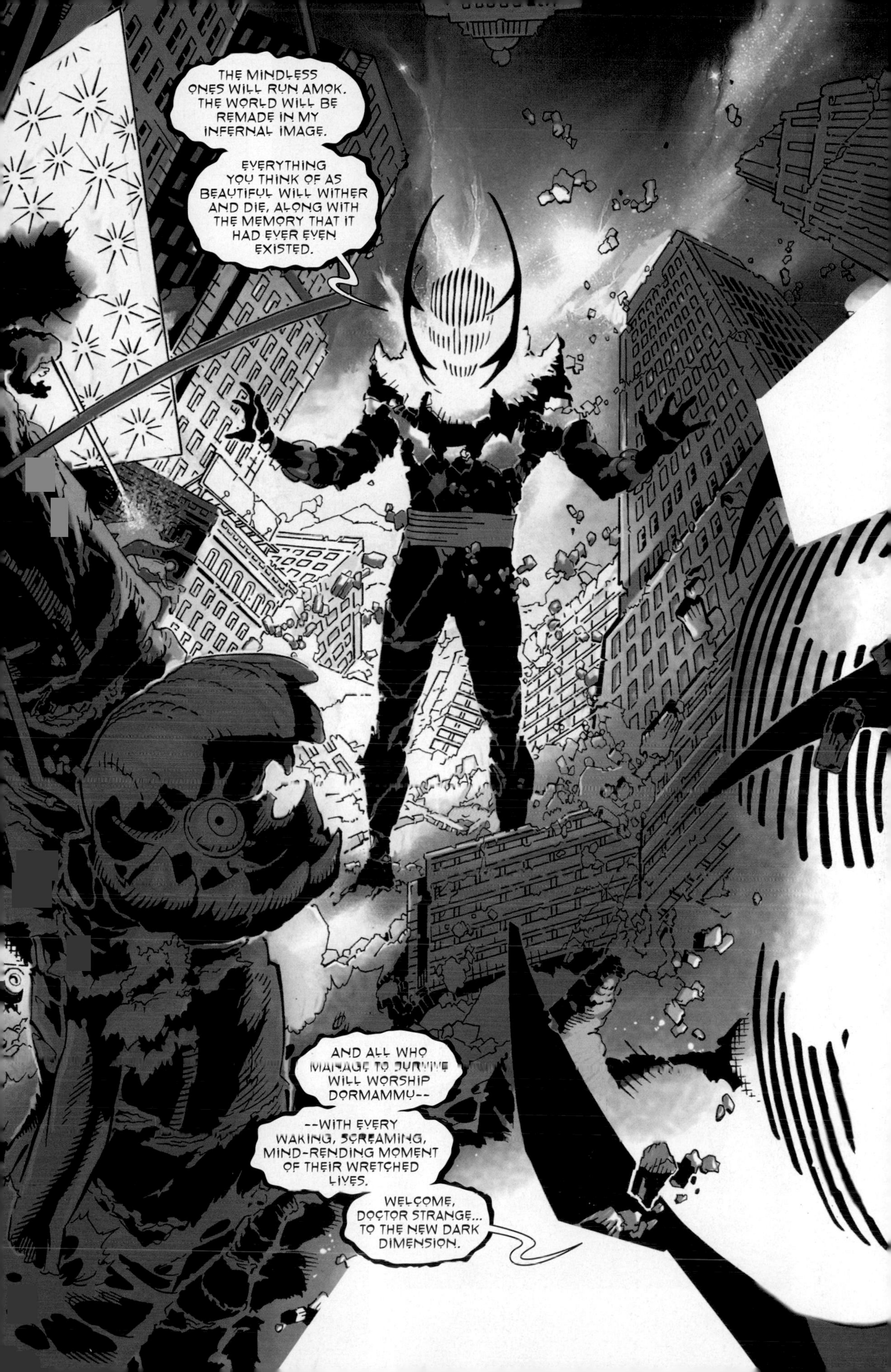
THE MINDLESS ONES WILL RUN AMOK. THE WORLD WILL BE REMADE IN MY INFERNAL IMAGE.
EVERYTHING YOU THINK OF AS BEAUTIFUL WILL WITHER AND DIE, ALONG WITH THE MEMORY THAT IT HAD EVER EVEN EXISTED.
AND ALL WHO MANAGE TO SURVIVE WILL WORSHIP DORMAMMU--
--WITH EVERY WAKING, SCREAMING, MIND-RENDING MOMENT OF THEIR WRETCHED LIVES.
WELCOME, DOCTOR STRANGE... TO THE NEW DARK DIMENSION.

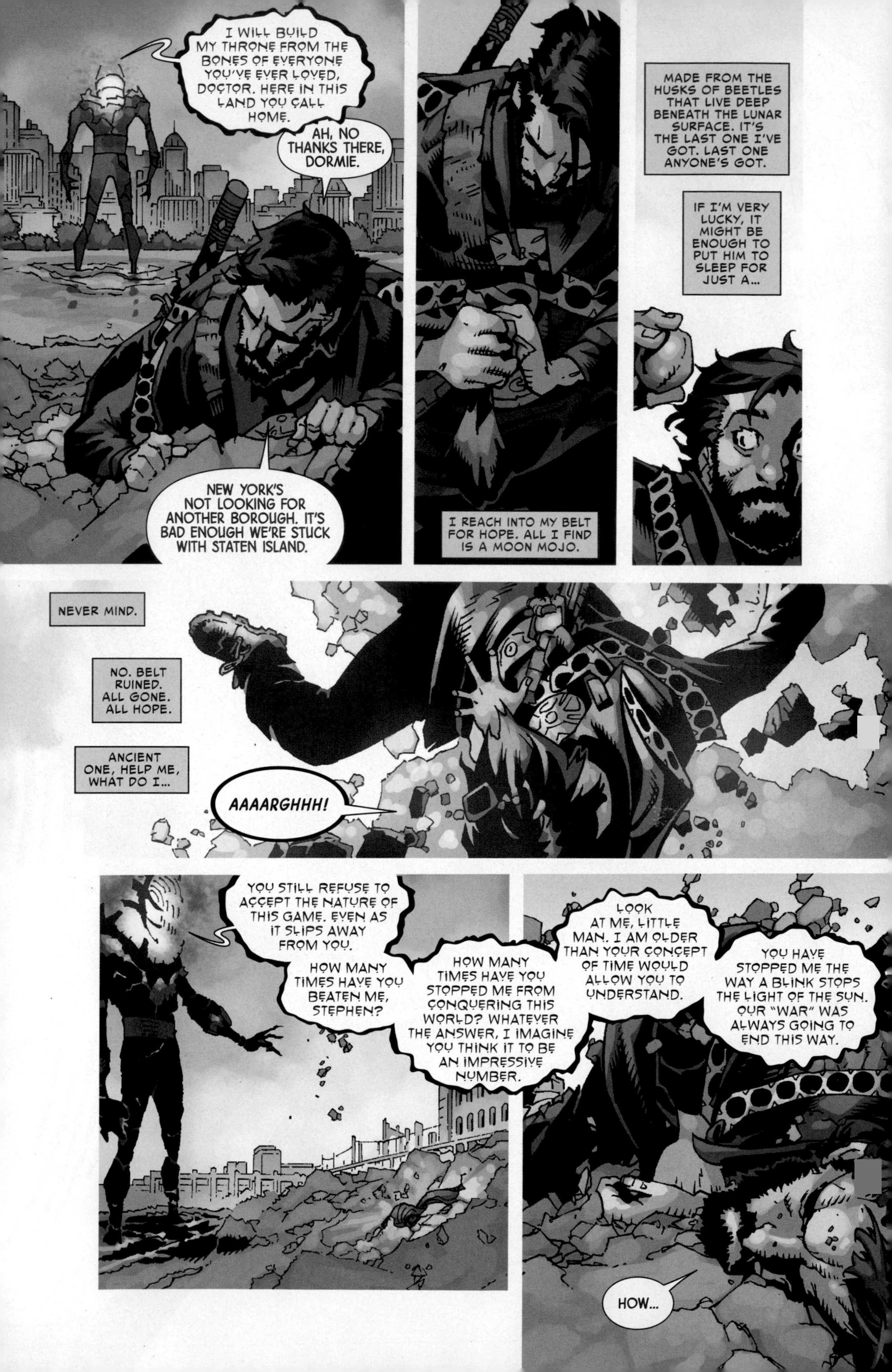
I WILL BUILD MY THRONE FROM THE BONES OF EVERYONE YOU'VE EVER LOVED, DOCTOR. HERE IN THIS LAND YOU CALL HOME.
AH, NO THANKS THERE, DORMIE.
NEW YORK'S NOT LOOKING FOR ANOTHER BOROUGH. IT'S BAD ENOUGH WE'RE STUCK WITH STATEN ISLAND.
I REACH INTO MY BELT FOR HOPE. ALL I FIND IS A MOON MOJO.
MADE FROM THE HUSKS OF BEETLES THAT LIVE DEEP BENEATH THE LUNAR SURFACE. IT'S THE LAST ONE I'VE GOT. LAST ONE ANYONE'S GOT.
IF I'M VERY LUCKY, IT MIGHT BE ENOUGH TO PUT HIM TO SLEEP FOR JUST A...
NEVER MIND.
NO. BELT RUINED. ALL GONE. ALL HOPE.
ANCIENT ONE, HELP ME, WHAT DO I...
AAAARGHHH!
YOU STILL REFUSE TO ACCEPT THE NATURE OF THIS GAME. EVEN AS IT SLIPS AWAY FROM YOU.
HOW MANY TIMES HAVE YOU BEATEN ME, STEPHEN?
HOW MANY TIMES HAVE YOU STOPPED ME FROM CONQUERING THIS WORLD? WHATEVER THE ANSWER, I IMAGINE YOU THINK IT TO BE AN IMPRESSIVE NUMBER.
LOOK AT ME, LITTLE MAN. I AM OLDER THAN YOUR CONCEPT OF TIME WOULD ALLOW YOU TO UNDERSTAND.
YOU HAVE STOPPED ME THE WAY A BLINK STOPS THE LIGHT OF THE SUN. OUR "WAR" WAS ALWAYS GOING TO END THIS WAY.
HOW...

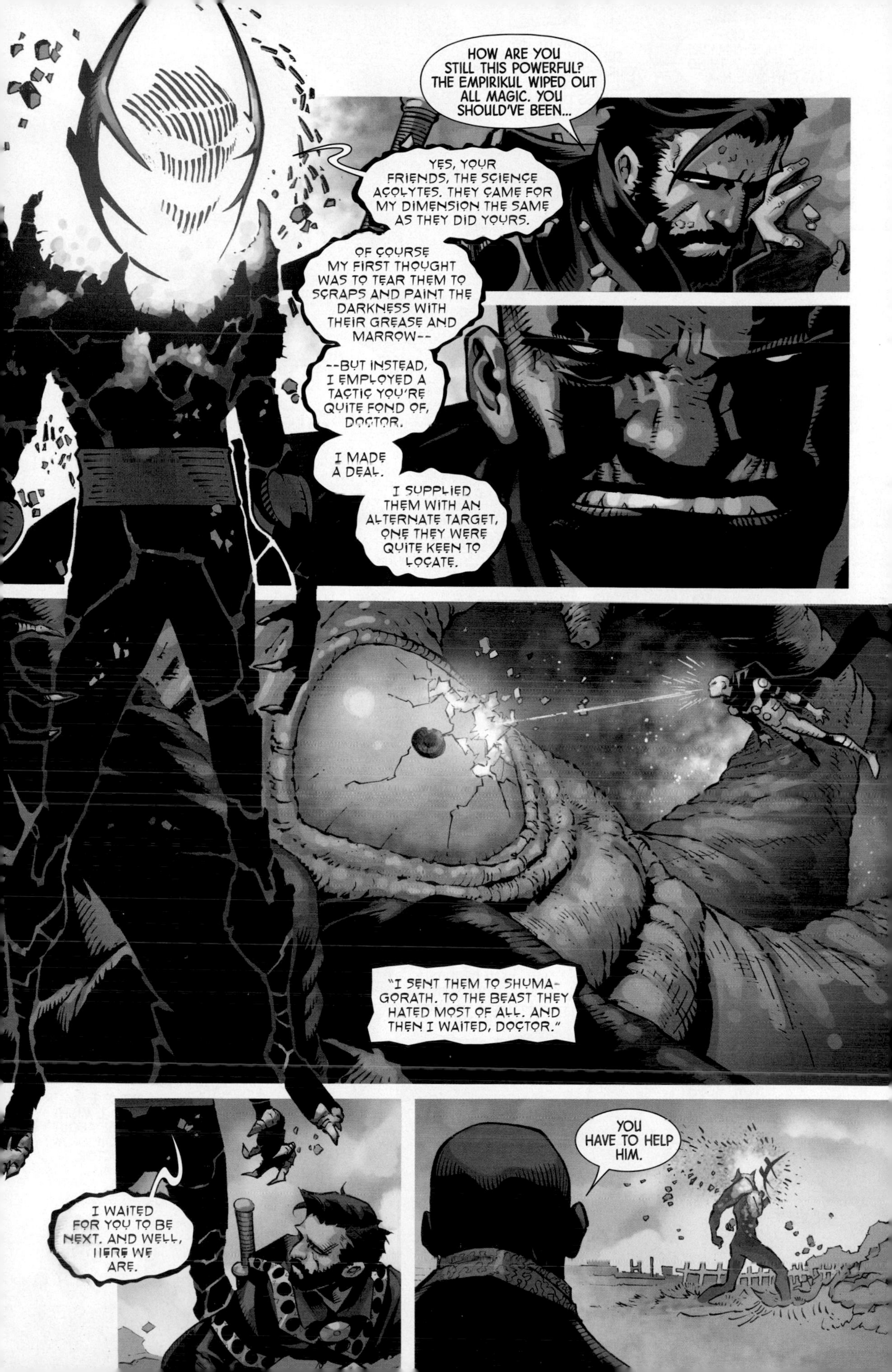
HOW ARE YOU STILL THIS POWERFUL? THE EMPIRIKUL WIPED OUT ALL MAGIC. YOU SHOULD'VE BEEN...
YES, YOUR FRIENDS, THE SCIENCE ACOLYTES. THEY CAME FOR MY DIMENSION THE SAME AS THEY DID YOURS.
OF COURSE MY FIRST THOUGHT WAS TO TEAR THEM TO SCRAPS AND PAINT THE DARKNESS WITH THEIR GREASE AND MARROW--
--BUT INSTEAD, I EMPLOYED A TACTIC YOU'RE QUITE FOND OF, DOCTOR.
I MADE A DEAL.
I SUPPLIED THEM WITH AN ALTERNATE TARGET, ONE THEY WERE QUITE KEEN TO LOCATE.
"I SENT THEM TO SHUMA-GORATH. TO THE BEAST THEY HATED MOST OF ALL. AND THEN I WAITED, DOCTOR."
I WAITED FOR YOU TO BE NEXT. AND WELL, HERE WE ARE.
YOU HAVE TO HELP HIM.

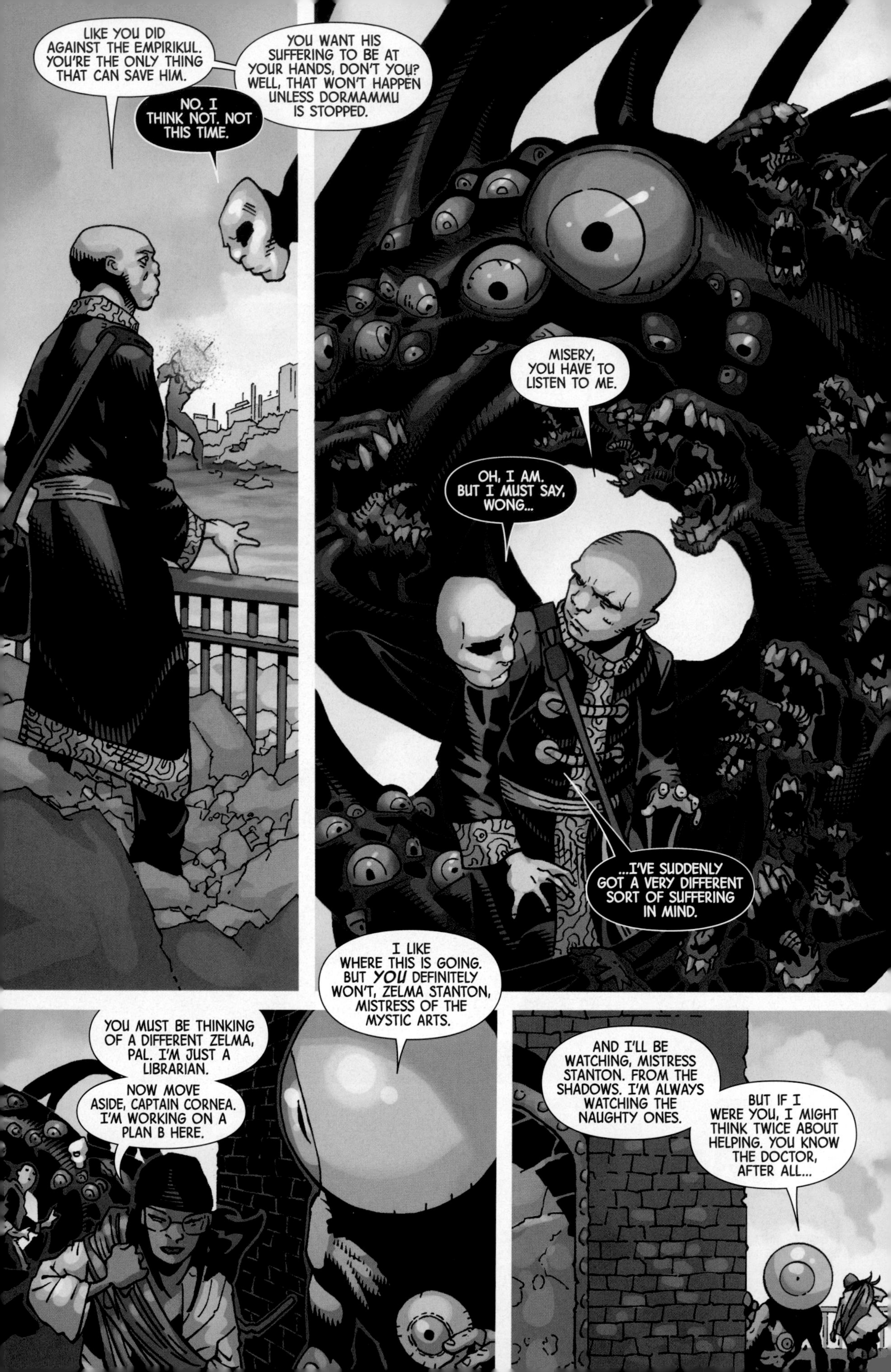
LIKE YOU DID AGAINST THE EMPIRIKUL. YOU'RE THE ONLY THING THAT CAN SAVE HIM.
YOU WANT HIS SUFFERING TO BE AT YOUR HANDS, DON'T YOU? WELL, THAT WON'T HAPPEN UNLESS DORMAMMU IS STOPPED.
NO. I THINK NOT. NOT THIS TIME.
MISERY, YOU HAVE TO LISTEN TO ME.
OH, I AM. BUT I MUST SAY, WONG...
...I'VE SUDDENLY GOT A VERY DIFFERENT SORT OF SUFFERING IN MIND.
I LIKE WHERE THIS IS GOING. BUT YOU DEFINITELY WON'T, ZELMA STANTON, MISTRESS OF THE MYSTIC ARTS.
YOU MUST BE THINKING OF A DIFFERENT ZELMA, PAL. I'M JUST A LIBRARIAN.
NOW MOVE ASIDE, CAPTAIN CORNEA. I'M WORKING ON A PLAN B HERE.
AND I'LL BE WATCHING, MISTRESS STANTON. FROM THE SHADOWS. I'M ALWAYS WATCHING THE NAUGHTY ONES.
BUT IF I WERE YOU, I MIGHT THINK TWICE ABOUT HELPING. YOU KNOW THE DOCTOR, AFTER ALL...

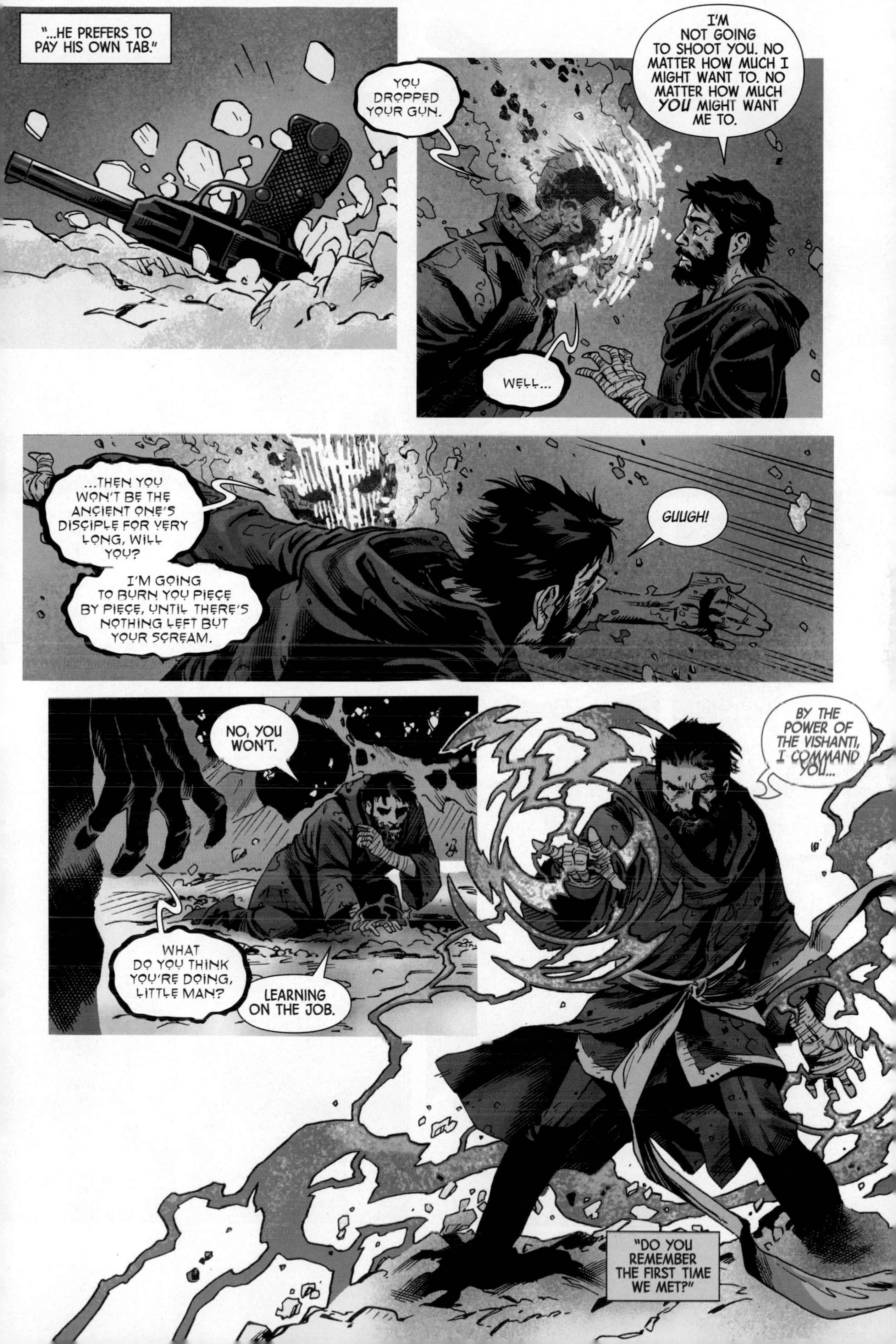
"...HE PREFERS TO PAY HIS OWN TAB."
YOU DROPPED YOUR GUN.
I'M NOT GOING TO SHOOT YOU. NO MATTER HOW MUCH I MIGHT WANT TO. NO MATTER HOW MUCH YOU MIGHT WANT ME TO.
WELL...
...THEN YOU WON'T BE THE ANCIENT ONE'S DISCIPLE FOR VERY LONG, WILL YOU?
I'M GOING TO BURN YOU PIECE BY PIECE, UNTIL THERE'S NOTHING LEFT BUT YOUR SCREAM.
GUUGH!
NO, YOU WON'T.
WHAT DO YOU THINK YOU'RE DOING, LITTLE MAN?
LEARNING ON THE JOB.
BY THE POWER OF THE VISHANTI, I COMMAND YOU...
"DO YOU REMEMBER THE FIRST TIME WE MET?"

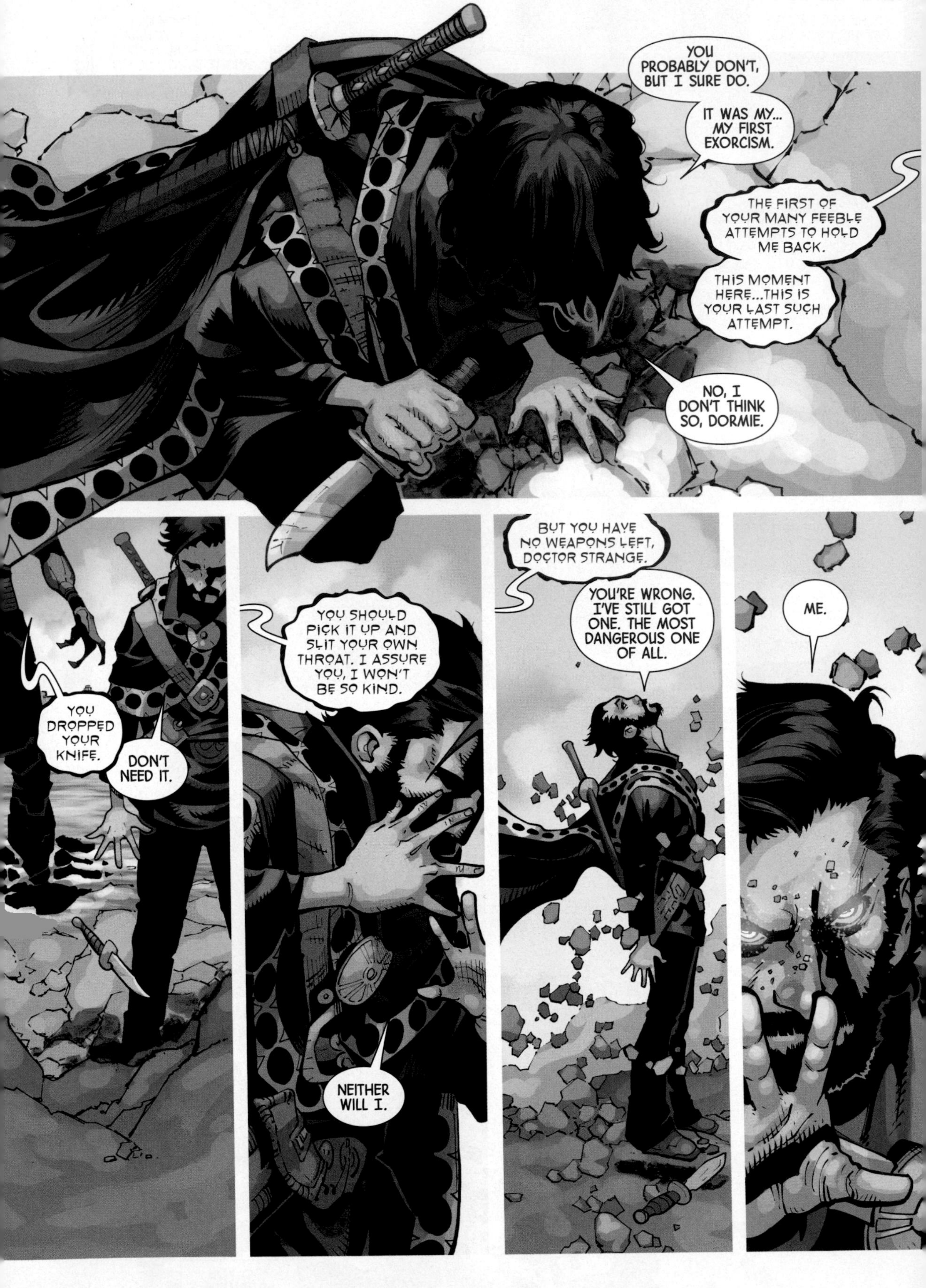
YOU PROBABLY DON'T, BUT I SURE DO.
IT WAS MY... MY FIRST EXORCISM.
THE FIRST OF YOUR MANY FEEBLE ATTEMPTS TO HOLD ME BACK.
THIS MOMENT HERE...THIS IS YOUR LAST SUCH ATTEMPT.
NO, I DON'T THINK SO, DORMIE.
YOU DROPPED YOUR KNIFE.
DON'T NEED IT.
YOU SHOULD PICK IT UP AND SLIT YOUR OWN THROAT. I ASSURE YOU, I WON'T BE SO KIND.
NEITHER WILL I.
BUT YOU HAVE NO WEAPONS LEFT, DOCTOR STRANGE.
YOU'RE WRONG. I'VE STILL GOT ONE. THE MOST DANGEROUS ONE OF ALL.
ME.

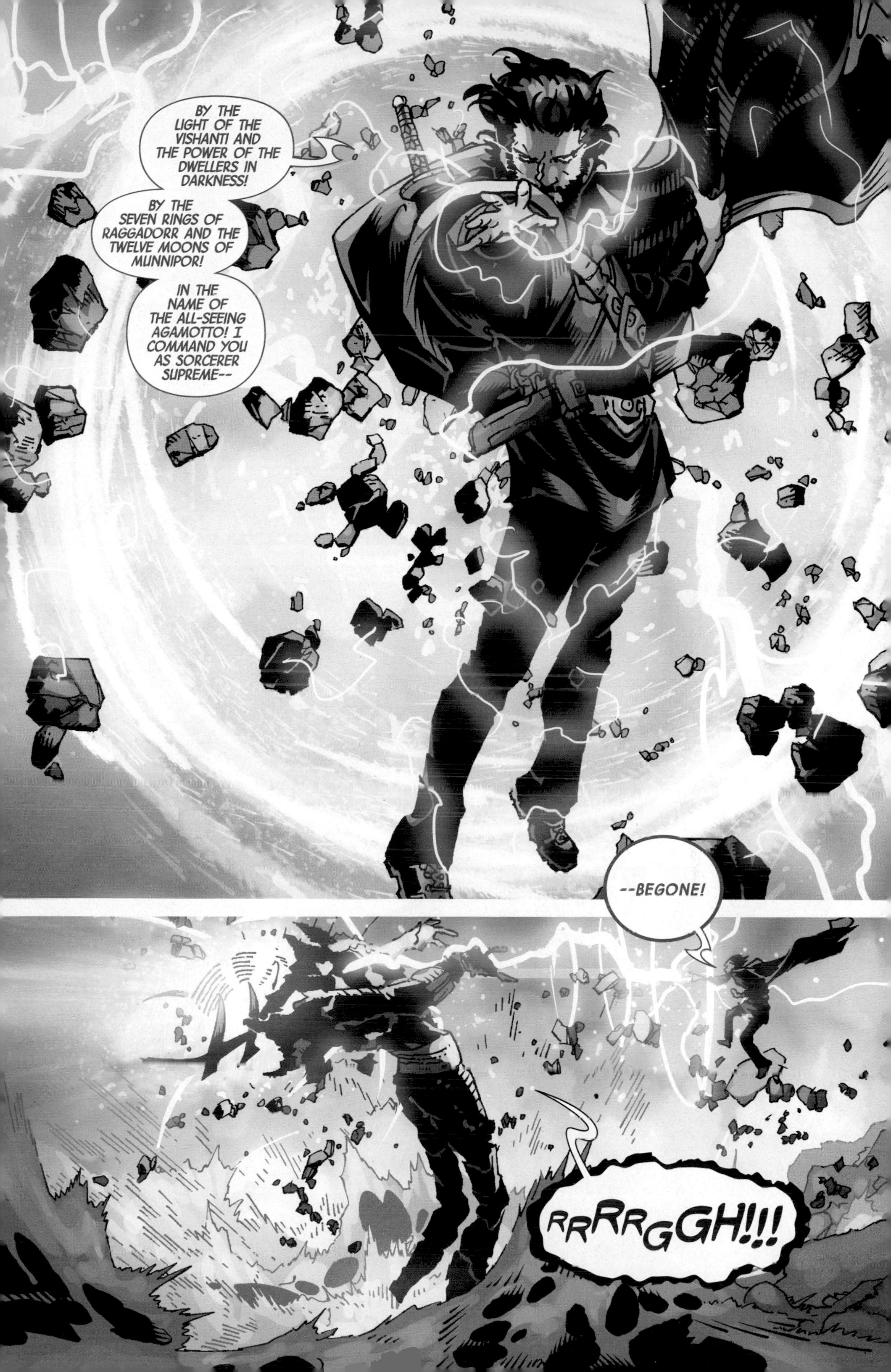
BY THE LIGHT OF THE VISHANTI AND THE POWER OF THE DWELLERS IN DARKNESS!
BY THE SEVEN RINGS OF RAGGADORR AND THE TWELVE MOONS OF MUNNIPOR!
IN THE NAME OF THE ALL-SEEING AGAMOTTO! I COMMAND YOU AS SORCERER SUPREME--
--BEGONE!
RRRRGGH!!!

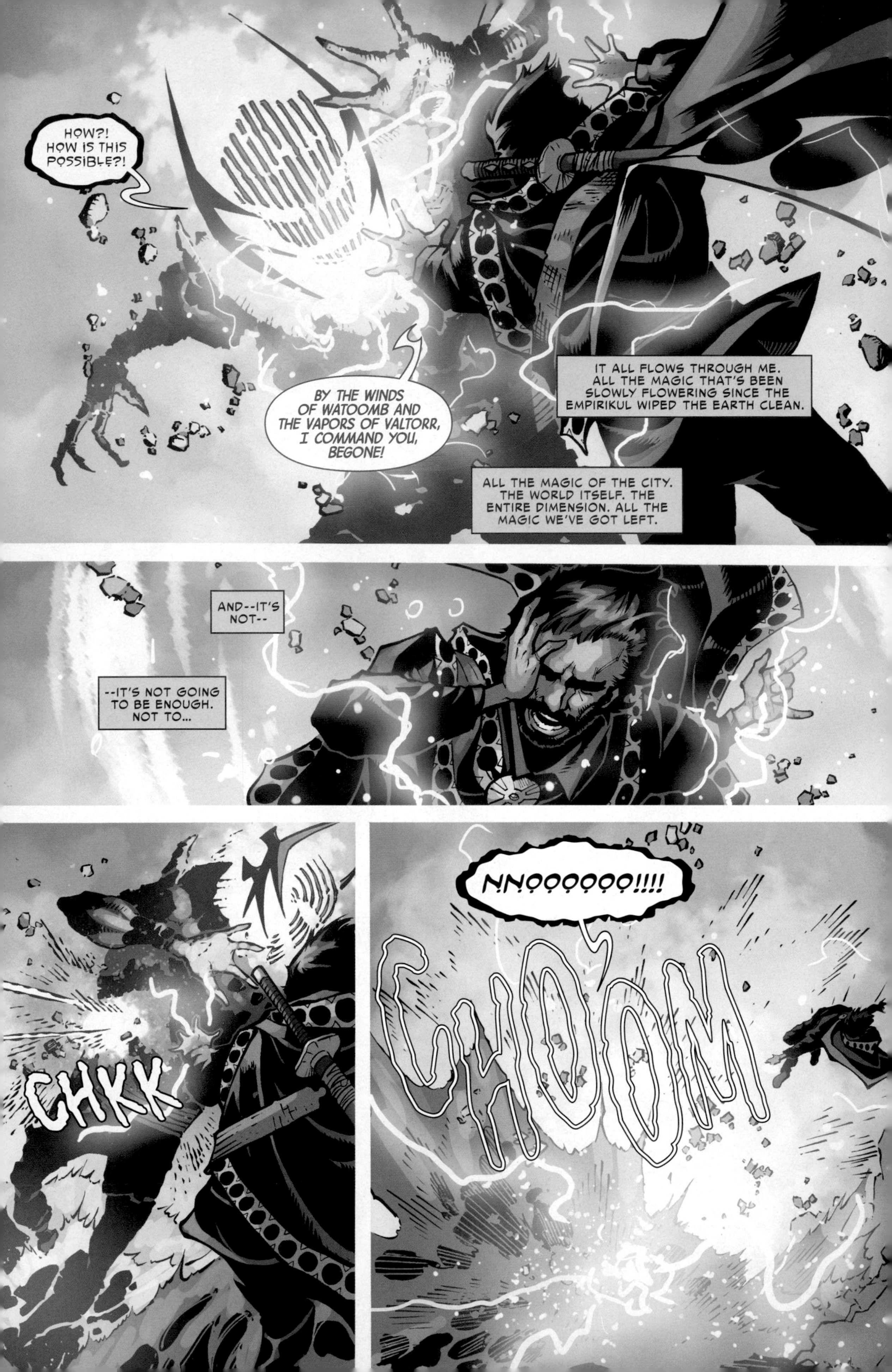
HOW?! HOW IS THIS POSSIBLE?!
BY THE WINDS OF WATOOMB AND THE VAPORS OF VALTORR, I COMMAND YOU, BEGONE!
IT ALL FLOWS THROUGH ME. ALL THE MAGIC THAT'S BEEN SLOWLY FLOWERING SINCE THE EMPIRIKUL WIPED THE EARTH CLEAN.
ALL THE MAGIC OF THE CITY. THE WORLD ITSELF. THE ENTIRE DIMENSION. ALL THE MAGIC WE'VE GOT LEFT.
AND--IT'S NOT--
--IT'S NOT GOING TO BE ENOUGH. NOT TO...
CHKK
NNOOOOOO!!!!
CHOOOM

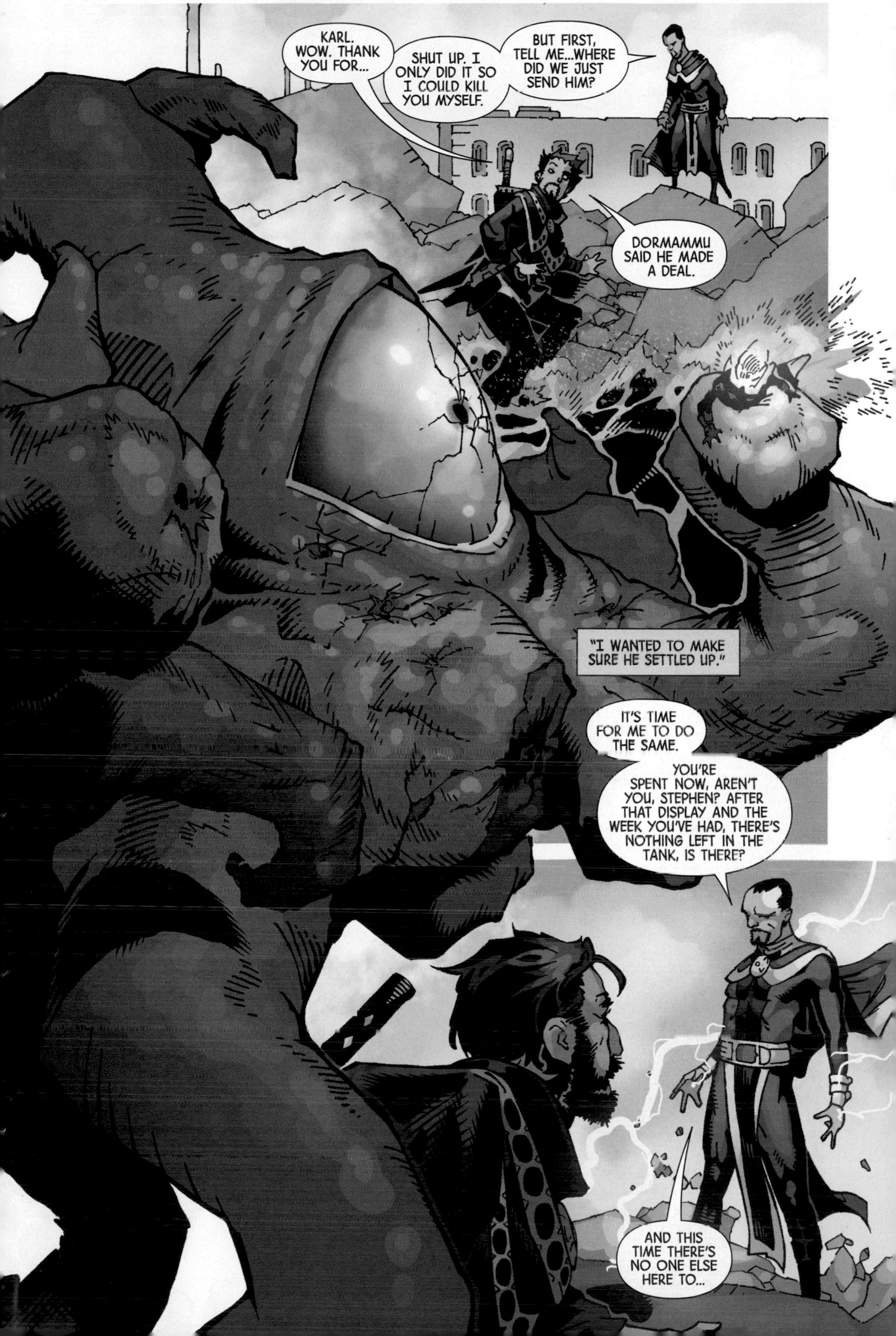
KARL. WOW. THANK YOU FOR...
SHUT UP. I ONLY DID IT SO I COULD KILL YOU MYSELF.
BUT FIRST, TELL ME...WHERE DID WE JUST SEND HIM?
DORMAMMU SAID HE MADE A DEAL.
"I WANTED TO MAKE SURE HE SETTLED UP."
IT'S TIME FOR ME TO DO THE SAME.
YOU'RE SPENT NOW, AREN'T YOU, STEPHEN? AFTER THAT DISPLAY AND THE WEEK YOU'VE HAD, THERE'S NOTHING LEFT IN THE TANK, IS THERE?
AND THIS TIME THERE'S NO ONE ELSE HERE TO...

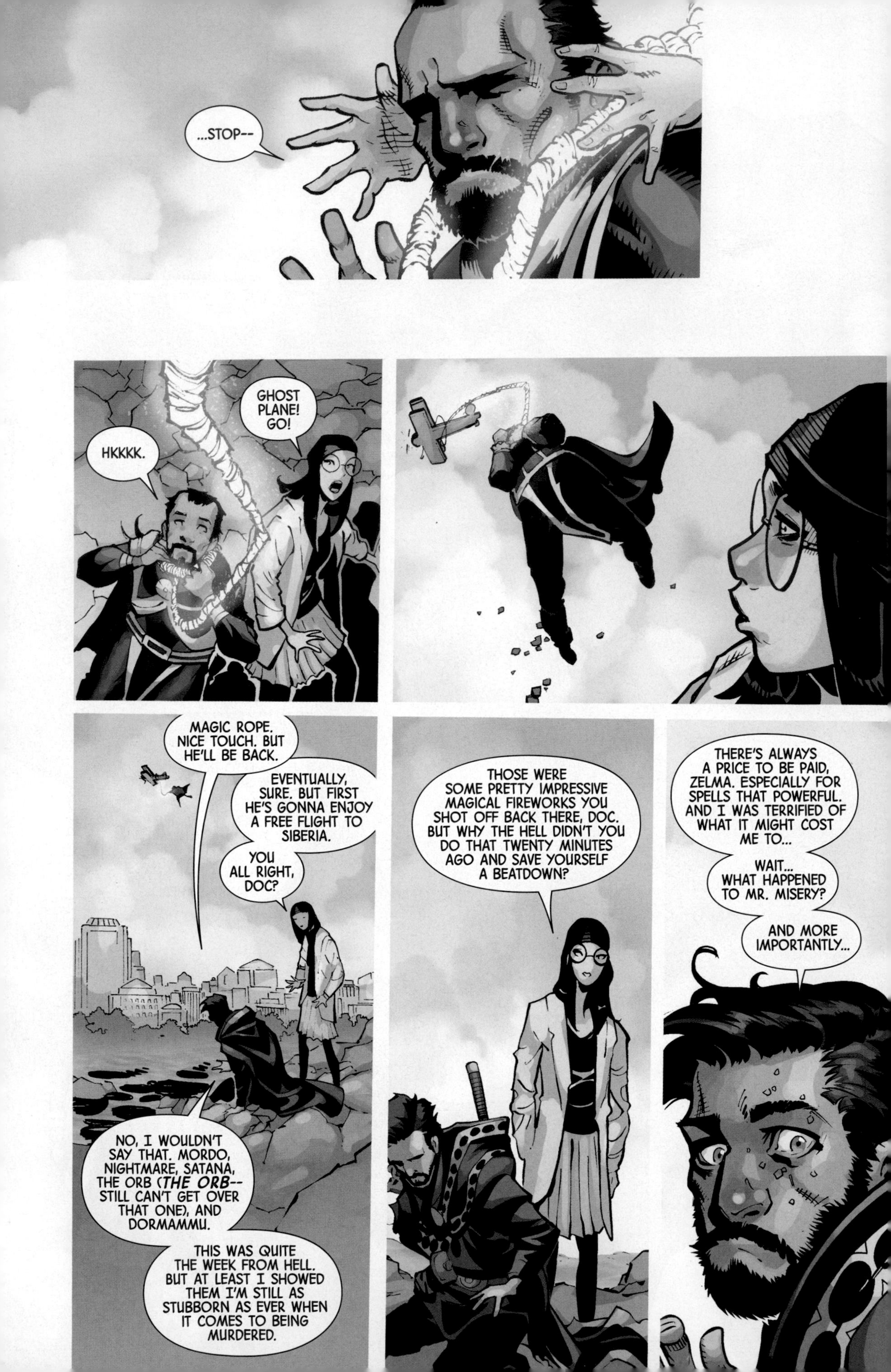
...STOP--
HKKKK.
GHOST PLANE! GO!
MAGIC ROPE. NICE TOUCH. BUT HE'LL BE BACK.
EVENTUALLY, SURE. BUT FIRST HE'S GONNA ENJOY A FREE FLIGHT TO SIBERIA.
YOU ALL RIGHT, DOC?
NO, I WOULDN'T SAY THAT. MORDO, NIGHTMARE, SATANA, THE ORB (*THE ORB*-- STILL CAN'T GET OVER THAT ONE), AND DORMAMMU.
THIS WAS QUITE THE WEEK FROM HELL. BUT AT LEAST I SHOWED THEM I'M STILL AS STUBBORN AS EVER WHEN IT COMES TO BEING MURDERED.
THOSE WERE SOME PRETTY IMPRESSIVE MAGICAL FIREWORKS YOU SHOT OFF BACK THERE, DOC. BUT WHY THE HELL DIDN'T YOU DO THAT TWENTY MINUTES AGO AND SAVE YOURSELF A BEATDOWN?
THERE'S ALWAYS A PRICE TO BE PAID, ZELMA. ESPECIALLY FOR SPELLS THAT POWERFUL. AND I WAS TERRIFIED OF WHAT IT MIGHT COST ME TO...
WAIT... WHAT HAPPENED TO MR. MISERY?
AND MORE IMPORTANTLY...

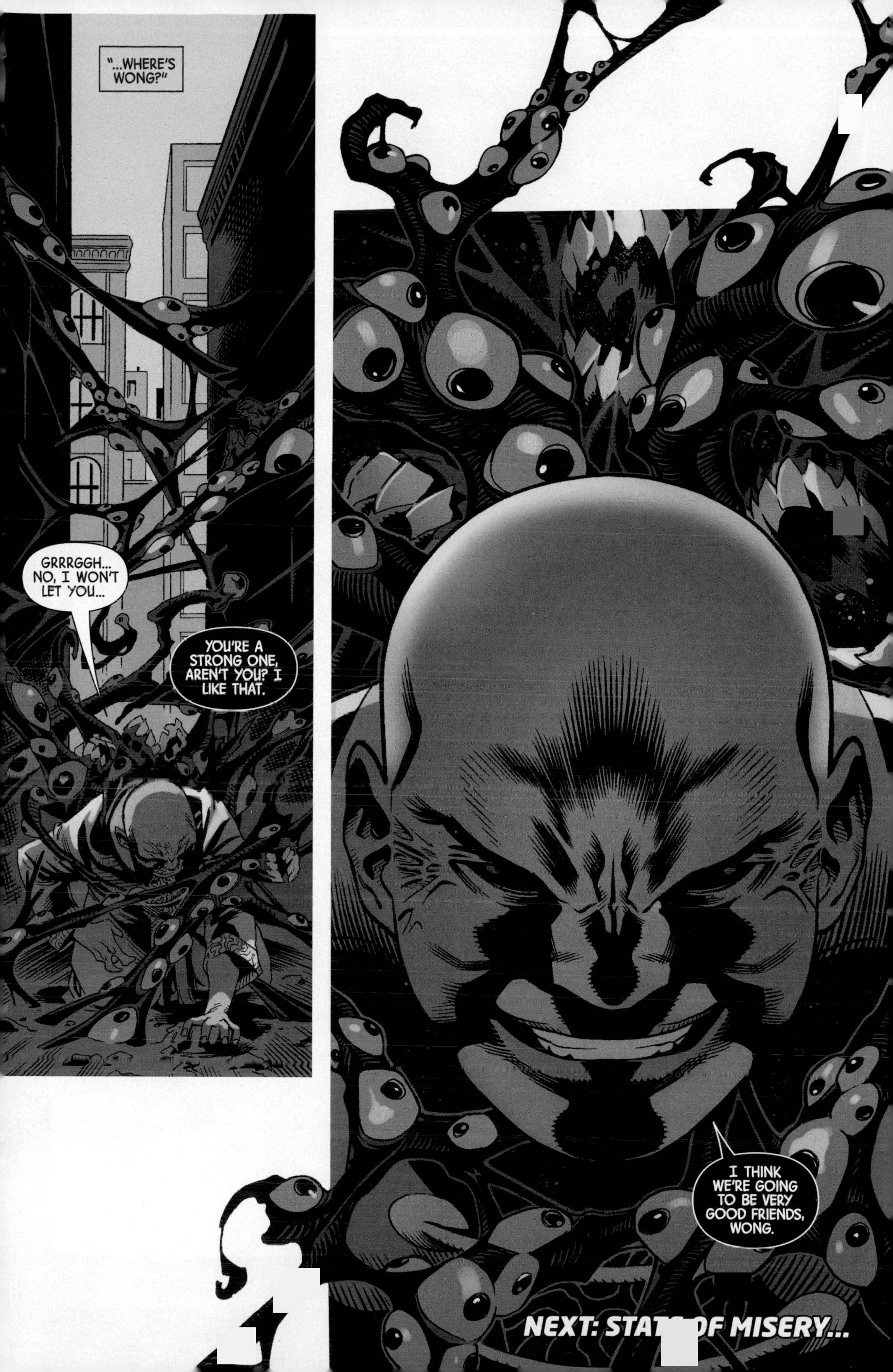
"...WHERE'S WONG?"
GRRRGGH... NO, I WON'T LET YOU...
YOU'RE A STRONG ONE, AREN'T YOU? I LIKE THAT.
I THINK WE'RE GOING TO BE VERY GOOD FRIENDS, WONG.
NEXT: STAT F MISERY...

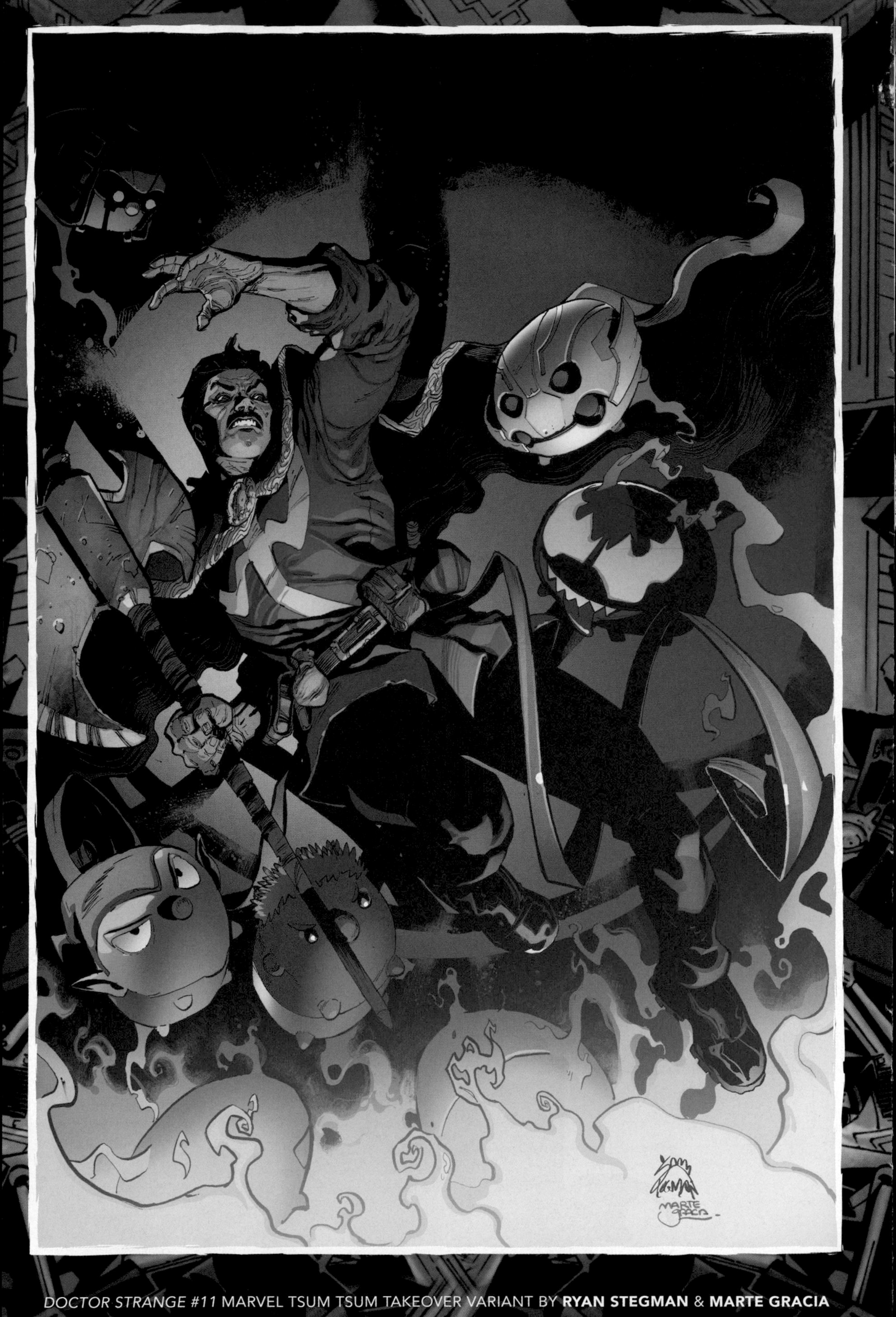

DOCTOR STRANGE #11 MARVEL TSUM TSUM TAKEOVER VARIANT BY **RYAN STEGMAN** & **MARTE GRACIA**

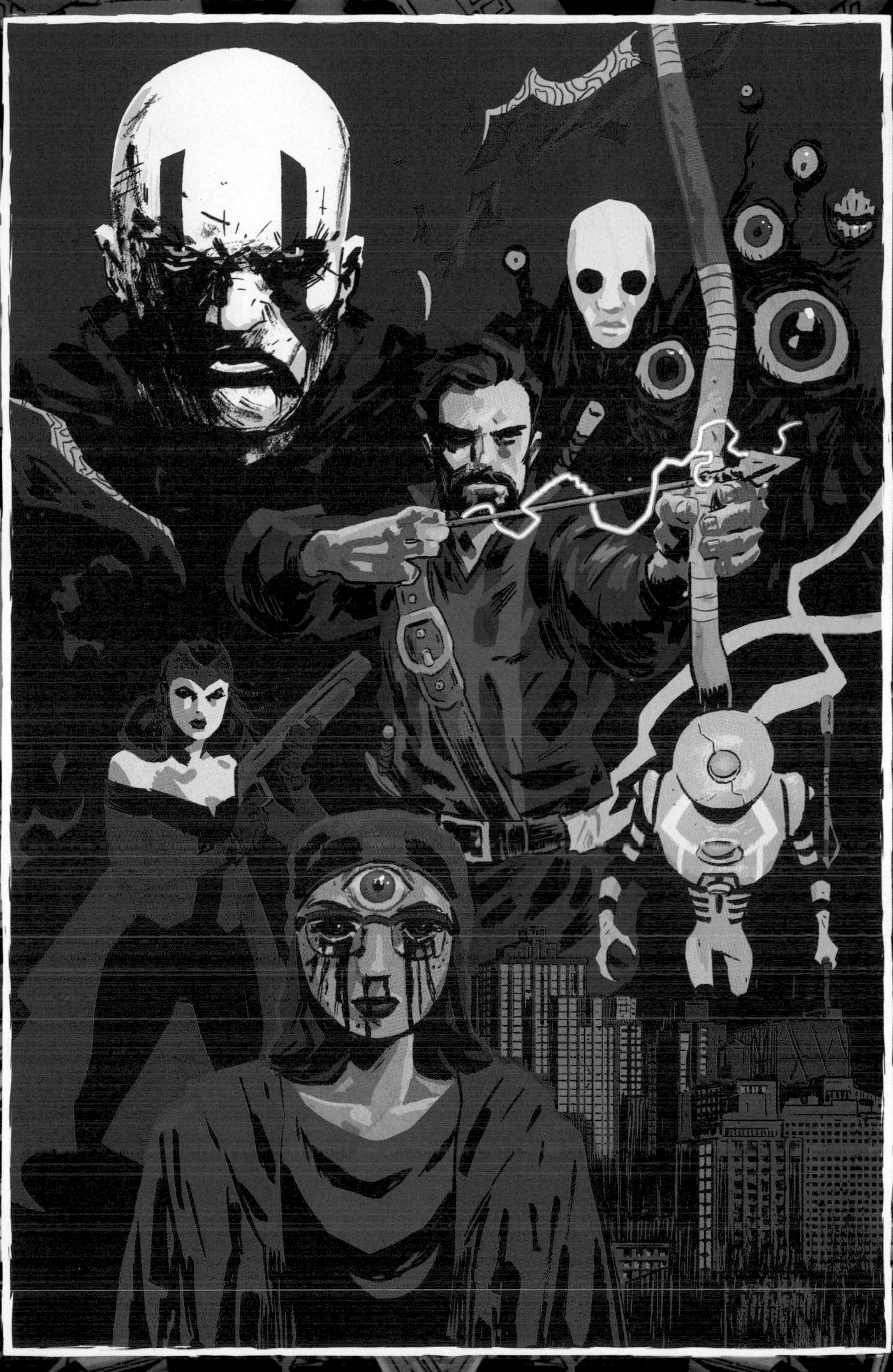

DOCTOR STRANGE #12 STORY THUS FAR VARIANT BY **MICHAEL WALSH**

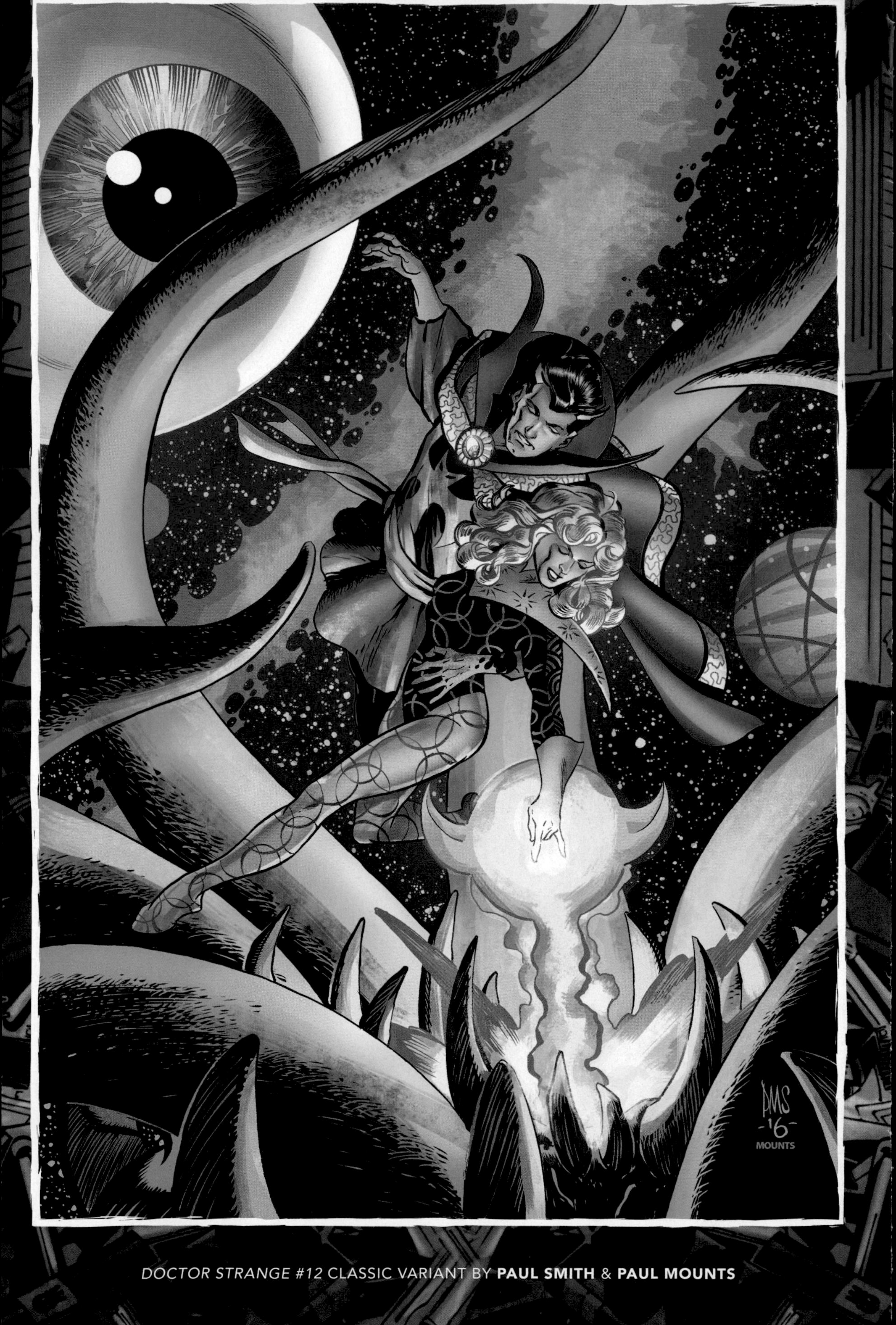
MOUNTS

DOCTOR STRANGE #12 CLASSIC VARIANT BY **PAUL SMITH** & **PAUL MOUNTS**

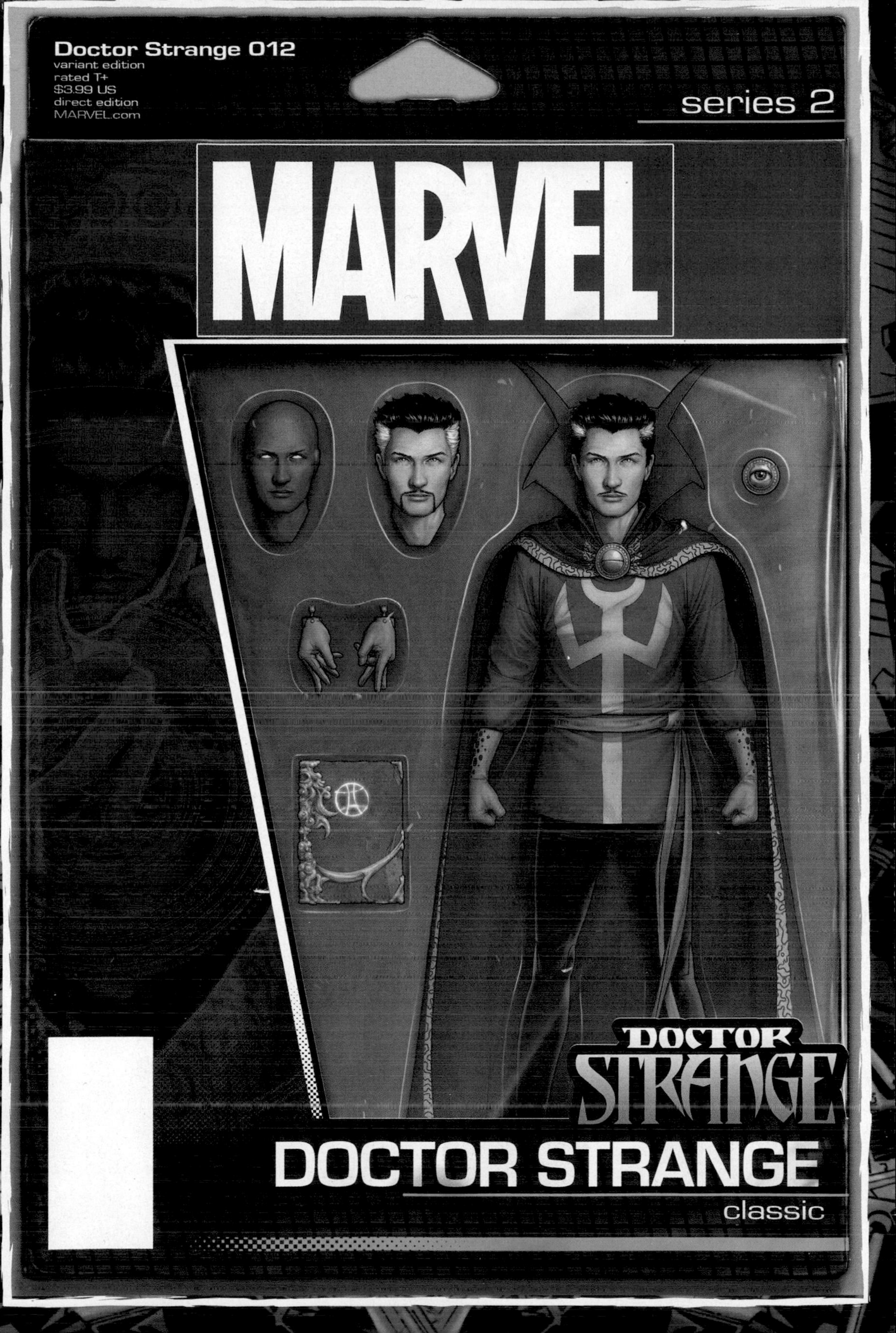
Doctor Strange 012
variant edition
rated T+
$3.99 US
direct edition
MARVEL.com
series 2
MARVEL
DOCTOR STRANGE
DOCTOR STRANGE
classic

DOCTOR STRANGE #12 ACTION FIGURE VARIANT BY **JOHN TYLER CHRISTOPHER**

Free Digital Copy

TO REDEEM YOUR CODE FOR A FREE DIGITAL COPY:

1. GO TO MARVEL.COM/REDEEM. OFFER EXPIRES ON 2/2/19.
2. FOLLOW THE ON-SCREEN INSTRUCTIONS TO REDEEM YOUR DIGITAL COPY.
3. LAUNCH THE MARVEL COMICS APP TO READ YOUR COMIC NOW.
4. YOUR DIGITAL COPY WILL BE FOUND UNDER THE 'MY COMICS' TAB.
5. READ AND ENJOY.

YOUR FREE DIGITAL COPY WILL BE AVAILABLE ON:
MARVEL COMICS APP FOR APPLE IOS® DEVICES
MARVEL COMICS APP FOR ANDROID™ DEVICES